ORCHIDS IN A JELLY JAR

May your life be filled with "orchids"
May Dixon

By

MAY BAILEY DIXON

ORCHIDS IN A JELLY JAR

Published June 8, 2008
PRINTED IN 2008

Printed in the United States of America
Digital Publishing of Florida, Inc. – www.digitaldata-corp.com

CONTENTS

PURPOSE

My purpose in writing this book is to relate the unexpected joy discovered in serving on the mission field in Peru for over 31 years. It is an effort to express that joy through anecdotes of life as we experienced it there. It is not only an attempt to show something of Peruvian life and customs, but to let people know that there is a very human and humorous side to missionaries. These little stories were written down and sent back in letters to the USA. Most of them went to my mother, and she saved them all. As I began this, my intention was to preserve these for our children, but as others expressed an interest, the idea of "Orchids" was born.

Our Remembrances Carefully
Held In Distinct Stories.

ACKNOWLEDGEMENTS

I wish to express my appreciation to all those who suffered through the reading, editing, and revision without ridiculing the work or the author, and to those who gave encouragement along the way. There are many of you and I love you all; thank you so much.

DEDICATION

I dedicate this effort to the memory of my Mother, Myrtice Bailey, who saved all of these letters, and to my husband, Rodolph, who would not let me rest until I compiled them into a book, and who did everything else to see that it got published. The cover design, editing, pictures, etc. are all his--so this is our book together.

MYRTICE JOHNSON BAILEY
June 15, 1905 – March 29, 2000

ORCHIDS IN A JELLY JAR is published to honor
MAY FRANCES BAILEY DIXON.

It is with profound gratitude that we, her family, wish to
acknowledge that *May, Mom, Grammy* lives before us each day
the love of Christ. We publish this book because she fills our lives
with joy!

God has given May a unique gift to see and feel the majesty in his
creations; and with deep spiritual qualities she consistently touches
the lives of her family and others through expressive illustrations
of that beauty. May's career of mission service in Peru provided
countless opportunities for successful communication of those
vibrant descriptions of her faith especially through the multiple use
of her talents and education in the field of music. She faithfully
accomplishes her role as wife, mother, grandmother, and above all
as a servant of God. With this publication we say, "thank you, and
we love you."

"MAY'S EIGHTEEN"

INTRODUCTION TO ORCHIDS

Jan. 1, 1968
Dear Mother,
*   What a way to start a New Year! Every New Year I say I am going to change my ways, but this is ridiculous!☺ We went to our first church service yesterday and I never understood a single word that was spoken. They introduced us and all the people smiled and waved, and I smiled until my jaws ached and "Buenos Dias-ed" everybody I saw. It makes you feel so dumb!*
*   A little boy came to our door with a bag and we thought he was selling something and we just said, "No!" and he scampered off. Later we saw him at another house and they were giving him bread, and we realized we had turned away a little hungry boy begging for food. When David finally understood what we had done, he was so upset that he hardly spoke to us for a week.*
*   The countryside is so beautiful here with gorgeous flowers and all, but there is so much poverty it is hard to describe. I know it would make you smile if you could see the centerpiece on our table. I have a dozen lavender orchids sitting there in a jelly jar.*

These are excerpts from the very first letter I wrote from outside the USA, and thus began a weekly correspondence that covered a span of over 30 years. My husband Rodolph, our 6-year-old David, our 2-year-old Merry, and I had just finished up 16 weeks of orientation at Ridgecrest Baptist Assembly in North Carolina. There were 98 of us recently appointed missionaries going through this intensive training, and I am not sure if there was ever an accurate head count of children!☺ Let's just say there were quite a few in evidence at any given moment of our stay and we adults were badly outnumbered. We were the very first extended orientation session for the Foreign Mission Board and there was a lot of speculation as to whether it was worth the effort and expense. Shortly after our arrival on the field, I remember one of our Peruvian missionaries making the comment that he didn't see much improvement in our group compared with those having only a short orientation. The reply I made to this observation was that there was just no telling how bad we might have been without it, though!

We became very close with many of our colleagues at those orientation sessions, and it was painful when we all left for different parts of the world. Some of these we have not seen again up to the day of this writing. If furloughs didn't happen to coincide we were never together again in the USA until retirement.

We left the USA in December, 1967, and arrived in Costa Rica for a year of studying Spanish in the language school located there. The above letter was written three days after our arrival. The plane trip down was the first of many white-knuckled flights for me and the first time I had ever traveled to a foreign country. I was awed and scared and excited and homesick and worried and proud and eager and--well, just about every emotion you can think of. Somehow I acquired the role as the main letter writer for our family, so I tried to convey these feelings to the family back in the USA by writing letters to describe the people, the places, and the events that we experienced. It seemed to me an impossible task to find the proper words to express or explain our feelings because much of the time we, ourselves, could not interpret how we felt--so I let the stories speak for themselves and for us.

My mother was known to save papers of all kinds for years and when she passed away in March of 2000, we slowly began the necessary task of going through those things. It was a pleasant surprise to find bundles of letters that we had written through the years relating things we had completely forgotten. It was like having a journal of our life on the mission field. Thus, we have a first-hand account of happenings near the date they occurred and not tempered with time and nostalgia. These letters are what I wish to share with you in an attempt to not only tell of Peruvian life and customs, but to show the human and humorous sides of missionary life.

These are excerpts, of course, accompanied by notes and commentary, but basically they are the original letters reproduced verbatim. There is no attempt to put them in chronological order for several reasons; the main one being that many of the letters had no date which makes it a practically impossible job. Many times I did not specify names of colleagues because I did not want to cause embarrassment for anyone nor exalt one over the other. These people are family, and while I have asked permission of some, I pray the rest will not disapprove if they recognize themselves or their happenings in this account. Our lives were so entwined that there is no way I could write of our "orchids" without including them and expressing our love and appreciation to them. Our missionary family makes up a major part of our "floral arrangement."

The first missionary, the apostle Paul, wrote in his second letter to the church at Corinth: "We have this treasure in jars of clay to show that this all-surpassing power is from God and not from us" (2 Corinthians 4:7). This has always been a comforting thought for those many times when I have felt so inadequate but also felt that it was something God wanted me to do. It always amazed me when I saw that beautiful things could result from even my blundering efforts. It's the way I feel about attempting to write of our experiences in Peru with those precious people who became our "hermanos" (brothers and sisters). I pray the Lord will take this and make something worthwhile of it so that you can see how lovely and loving they are. In my mind there are so many treasures, like those orchids, found in such mundane sites and circumstances--so many unlikely places and personalities.

When applying to what was then the Foreign Mission Board of the Southern Baptist Convention, we had to write our autobiographies. I began mine this way, *"Monday's child is fair of face, Tuesday's child is full of grace." This nursery rhyme has been a source of amusement for me as I've been told I was born on Tuesday, May 8, 1934 in Columbia, SC. I was always coordinated enough to play ball, climb trees, skate, and outrun any boy on our block, but when it came to feminine graces, my anatomy seemed to be incapable of capturing that which sets one apart as being dainty and delicate. As I began to think of writing my life history, however, the thought came to me that truly I am a child of grace. "For by grace we are saved." Through the grace of our Lord I experienced the salvation of my soul and it is through His grace that we acquire the abilities and skills we need for service to Him. At this moment I feel so incapable of being a missionary, but I also feel confident that the Lord will prepare me for anything that He would require of me if I will seek His direction and guidance.*

Recognizing our need for the Lord's guidance and actively seeking it have always been paramount in the thinking and daily living of our family. Even as Rodolph and I planned our wedding, we came upon the idea that instead of the traditional bride and groom figurines to adorn the top of our wedding cake we would have an open Bible with the words of Proverbs 3:6: "In all thy ways acknowledge Him and He will direct thy paths." We have depended on that promise ever since, especially during the many times of empty jelly jars with no orchids in sight yet! Sometimes it has even seemed hard to find jelly jars!

After finishing our year of language study in Costa Rica, we went on to Peru to begin our service there in December of 1968. We were assigned by the mission to the city of Trujillo where we were to teach in the seminary. Everyone arrives in Peru via the capital city of Lima. We spent our first three weeks there in the apartments provided by the mission for any personnel coming and going and even for vacation time. We had to do paper work and wait for our crates to clear customs before going on to Trujillo in January, 1969.

I did not find a letter relating the incident, but I'll never forget our first Christmas outside of the USA. We were excited and ready to get on to a place where we could settle down, get to work, and call "home." At the same time, we were scared, confused, anxious, and lonesome for family and North American traditions and customs. We found ourselves with these two little children who were confidently looking forward to the usual kind of holiday celebration and realized we had come into a completely unknown environment with only 6 days left before Christmas. To make matters worse, we were informed that we had to do our paper work with our legal representative in the government offices during this time before everything closed down for the holidays.

So here we were--no time, very little money, and no knowledge of the city. Someone took us to the Baptist bookstore where we bought a couple of books for each of them, and then somewhere we found a stuffed llama for Merry and a pogo stick for David. That, plus some candy, was their entire haul of Christmas bounty for that year. The other missionaries in Lima had put up in the apartments the most pitiful "Charlie Brown" Christmas tree I had ever seen! I was all ready to be pitiful myself until I saw the joy our kids had in that tree and those meager presents! They were just as happy as in former and later years with all kinds of spectacular secular preparations for this wonderful holy event. It was later, too, that I discovered our pitiful little tree was one of the best you could get in Peru at that time, and it was at some effort and expense that the other missionaries provided it for us. Fluffy evergreens are just a little hard to come by in the desert; most of the local people there have only seen them in pictures. This was just one of the many, many times that we have had important lessons taught to us by our children--and an inkling of the joy the Lord would provide in unexpected ways and places and unlikely circumstances.

It was also the beginning of the realization of what the mission family means. These people really became our sisters and brothers and became aunts and uncles to our children. We cherished that relationship all through our time there and even now in retirement. There is no one else who can quite understand like those who went through the same experiences and supported one another during times of crisis and joy.

This was before the time of e-mail and cell phones, and our sole contact with our home family was "snail mail," with the exception of a phone call for a very important occasion or a fellow missionary's ham radio contact. This is why we have Mother's letters which have become the most important source of the stories that we want to share. These stories are our "orchids," and from these I have picked the "bouquet" to offer you in the following pages. I pray this "jelly jar" in which they are contained will not detract too much from their God-given beauty.

COSTA RICA

These are more excerpts from that first letter written from Costa Rica:

Dear Mother,

We left New Orleans about the time we should have been arriving here in San Jose. Six hours of chasing Merry in the terminal while waiting for our plane to be repaired didn't improve my disposition much, and she kept saying she was hungry. We tried to wait because they kept reporting that we would be leaving any minute now, but finally we bought her a hotdog and I was putting ketchup on it when they announced our plane's departure. We had to throw it away and she yelled bloody murder! Then we could not find David anywhere--we were beginning to panic when we located him in the gift shop with a new friend he had made. We barely got on the plane in time! The take-offs and landings were breath-taking, and we had 5 of them before arriving in San Jose. We touched down in every Central American country between the USA and Costa Rica and all have landing strips nestled down among high mountain peaks that make it necessary to almost dive into them. Being my first plane trip I have nothing with which to compare it, but surely they won't all be like this or I shall try to find some other mode of travel (or just stay put wherever I am). Merry loved it; she thought all that diving and bumping around was done for her benefit.

Our house leaves a little bit to be desired; now don't get alarmed--it isn't unbearable--but it surely does make one aware of how much we take for granted back home. We have bars on the windows but no screens, everything is pretty moldy and damp, and the refrigerator is very small and rusty. We can't drink the water from the faucet (it must be boiled first) and fresh fruits and vegetables must be soaked in iodine before eating. Not being able

7

to talk to people gives you the strangest feeling--it makes you feel so helpless! You should have seen me trying to decipher labels on what groceries I had here. Tell Hampie I am so glad I brought the tea bags as they are a luxury here I understand--BUT--the climate is great and there are so many beautiful and interesting things to see. Poinsettias grow everywhere and some grow to the size of trees. There are brilliantly colored flowers in such profusion that it takes your breath, literally, because some are cloyingly fragrant. We are going to see a live volcano on Wednesday. No kidding, it is still active! Banana trees and coffee bushes are everywhere. They plant the coffee bushes and then plant banana trees to shade them.

I can't get the money straight to save my life! It is in colones and it takes 7.77 colones to make one dollar on the current exchange, and it takes 100 centimos to make a colon. A colon is about 12.5 cents American money and it is extremely confusing to someone like me. I guess it is a blessing not having a lot of money to count?☺

Please don't worry about us; the life here is really fascinating. Sat. night and Sun. morning I was ready to come home, but the longer I stay the more I like it. We have been here only a couple of days and I have already gotten used to some things which seemed impossible before. We are well, the other students take care of us, and we are happy--as much as one can be when one doesn't know what is going on!☺

Dear Mother,

Merry is fine now, but wouldn't you know that our child who is never sick came down with a temperature of 104 degrees. Here we are only a week in the country, don't speak the language, don't know a doctor and have a sick two year old. We called our appointed "big brother," who has only been here 3 months himself, and he took us to a Tico (Costa Rican) pediatrician named Dr. Ortiz. We managed to find his office and tried to talk to the receptionist. We could not understand her and she could not understand us. I was so upset and Merry was so sick. We finally got in to see the doctor and he looked at the card the receptionist handed him. I was all geared up for another war of words and just about in tears. He looked at me and asked, "What seems to be the trouble with your little girl, Mrs. Dixon?"---in perfect English. I could have kissed him! He is a good doctor and has studied in the USA and gave her the same medicine that we have used before with David. That was one hurdle behind us. We now know where to take our children when they get sick and for whom we should ask. As I said, Merry is all recovered now.

I am getting worried about myself because this house doesn't look all that bad now. It still scares me to ride those buses, though, and we usually have to ride back from school every day. It costs only about 3 cents apiece. You can hardly beat that for cheap transportation! Of course, you take your life in your hands every time you ride or even cross the street walking.

I can speak, read, and write Spanish better than I can hear it. The sounds still all run together. People seem to understand me now when I attempt to speak with them, but I don't understand what they tell me back.

In answer to your question--Of course, Merry remembers you, she prays for everybody by name, even at the table. (We often have very cold food.)

We went out to the airport to see off a couple who are returning to the USA because the lady is sick. It gave me a funny feeling to think she would be with her family there tonight. David wanted to know why we couldn't go too. He said he didn't want to come in the first place. Sometimes he really gets to us with his attitude and questions. We have laughed at him with his money. He thinks colones are play money and he always wants us to give him some real money. He is a tight wad, too; he has not spent any of it. He did put his tithe in church but he wasn't too happy about it. He wanted to buy his lunch today instead of carrying one like usual and I said, "Okay, but you will have to pay for it yourself." He was horrified at the thought! He wouldn't do it and said that his usual lunch would be okay. He said that he would have had enough money if his daddy hadn't made him put so much in church. So when Rodolph got home they had a little father-son talk. (Can't you just see them?) I heard Rodolph ask him, "Son, why do we give our money to the church?" David answered, "We give our money to Jesus so that when we go to heaven to be with Him it will be there waiting for us to use!" I didn't hear what was said after that--I had to leave the room!

We met a couple who have been in Peru and are here for a refresher course. They have been living in the jungle and travel up and down the rivers on a houseboat. He had a map of the river that he had drawn on a long strip of bandage! Some of the tales he told made our hair stand up on end! It makes us realize that many other missionaries will have it a lot worse than we will in terms of physical comforts.

We have yet another concern for the children playing without close supervision. There is an outbreak of rabies among the dogs that roam the streets here in San Jose and several people have been bitten. One is the husband of a lady in my class at school.

Dear Hampie,

Sure, just ask me anything you want to know about Costa Rica--and when I can find someone who can tell me in English, I will be glad to answer it. We are beginning to get around a little by ourselves, though; we took the children to the zoo here and while it wasn't much of a zoo, I have to admit they had an authentic looking jungle exhibit!

All the stores close from around 11:30 a.m. until 2:00 p.m. Different stores vary the hours but all close for siesta time. In fact, stores and everything else that deal with the public do just as they please and when they please. It is a standard joke here with the students that when someone tells you to meet them at a certain time, you ask them if it is North American time or Tico time. Tico (Costa Rican) time means it could be any time around what they tell you within a couple of hours after. (Not before--no one ever arrives early.)

It is not uncommon to see an ox cart right in the middle of that wild traffic in the heart of the city. These ox carts aren't what you would expect either; they are all painted up with bright colors and geometric designs and resemble a circus wagon more than a utilitarian vehicle to bring produce to market. You never know what you might see downtown; Rodolph said he saw a man cutting out a piece of canvas right in the middle of the main street yesterday. He said there were cars and buses zooming by on all sides and the man was kneeling there, calmly cutting away.

We are fortunate in that we have not yet had plumbing problems and don't have an unusual bug problem. Several of our group are fighting bedbugs and fleas and no water and stopped up plumbing, so we do have something good.

We went to a party last night for all the language school students and teachers and there were about 200 people there. This is a traditional thing they do to celebrate the newcomers getting through their first two weeks of what is called "Basic Dialogues." They kidded the first term students a lot. Someone had set to music all of those phrases we had been learning each day and they sang them to us. The performance was really clever and we had a lot of fun.

Dear Mother,

There was a procession going by while we were in church this morning and after it passed, we heard and felt things hitting our building. The people in this group were throwing rocks at us. The stoning continued until some of our men went outside and stopped them. It was a miracle some of the windows didn't get broken, but they escaped somehow. I now feel like a real live missionary!

I got tickled at Rodolph this morning when they called on him to pray. He did really well in his Spanish until he got to his final sentence and he said, "Ayudanos este dia--through Your grace and love--En el nombre de Jesus. Amen." I thought he had

11

just forgotten his Spanish and substituted English, but he said he was completely unaware of it. This is what is happening to us now. We don't know enough Spanish to really use it, but we have learned enough to confuse our English, and sometimes we can't think of either one. We get what we call "Spanglish"--half and half. The church thought he was wonderful for trying in Spanish, though, and I was proud he tried, too. I couldn't have!

We heard a good one about trying to learn another language. It seems a fellow was called on to pray in Spanish after just 2 months of studying it in class. He said when he prayed that God spoke to him immediately. When questioned about what God said, he told them that God said, "Huh?" I can relate to that!☺

NOTE: I find that one of the problems I am having in writing this book is that this computer won't accept my Spanish spelling of common English words. I see that little wavy red line under my word that indicates my error, but it looks perfectly right to me until I look it up in an English dictionary. Even then, I doubt what I am seeing. Spanish is a whole lot easier because you spell it like it sounds. The grammar, though, is another matter altogether!

Dear Mother,

You asked about getting wet?--Well, when it rains here it just starts all at once and pours down like out of a bucket and if you don't have an umbrella, you are drowned in a matter of seconds. Even if you do have all the rain equipment, you still usually get a little wet anyway! It is not cold, though, and you just have to change clothes if you can, and if not, you just have to dry off. I haven't bought any shoes since I have been here, but I surely am going to have to shop for some soon. The rain quickly ruins them and you rarely have a dry pair to put on. Somehow all of us have managed to stay well, and we know to whom we give thanks for that!

Everything seemed so strange to us at first, but it is funny how many of the things they do here now seem to make more sense than some of the ways things are done back in the USA. I am not sure if this is good or bad?

You had better believe that what happens in the USA affects life everywhere and especially in missionary work. Many of the Tico people feel like if what they hear about our kind of life back there is what we have to offer from a "Christian" country, they are better off like they are. The things we would like for them to know about our life there are rarely in the news that reaches here.

We had a horrible thing occur Monday morning. Right out in front of our house an eleven year old boy was killed, and Maria was cleaning our windows at the time and saw it happen! He was washing the bus over at the service station on the corner and was leaning out of the door of the bus to reach the windshield. The driver was new and was practicing his driving and backing the bus up into the station. He lost control and came across the street and ran up on the curb. He ran the bus right between a utility pole and a guide wire and crushed the little boy between the bus and the pole. The pole is right at the corner of our house. When we got home, Maria was in such a state that I sent her to bed. I did the dishes and other household chores, and I think that upset her even more. She is really something!

Did I tell you about the beautiful fruit salad she makes? She cuts a pineapple in half longwise, stem and all, and then hollows it out. She then fills each half with all kinds of fresh fruit including the diced pineapple and then covers it over with whipped cream and puts colored marshmallows on top. It is delicious as well as beautiful. If I could just learn this pesky language, I feel like Maria and I could be friends. She has already told me about her family and I have told her about mine--but of course, it is quite possible with my brand of Spanish that she thinks I have a dozen brothers and sisters.

We had another crisis when we got in from Wednesday night prayer meeting. Maria was all upset; she said David had come running in to get her from the kitchen and told her that Merry had put a snap up her nose. She said David was just in a panic and crying for us. She said she looked in Merry's nose and throat and couldn't see anything and tried to get her to blow her nose. Well, they were asleep when we got in, and we couldn't get anything out of David; we just couldn't get him awake enough to make sense. Merry got awake but you can't take what she says for sure, and her nose did look a little swollen to us, so we got the flashlight and looked and looked. Finally I saw the edge of a double gripper snap way up in her nose. It was one of those big ones that she had on her sleepers. When she would cry or move too much we couldn't see it. We couldn't get it out because she wouldn't let us. (It was too far to reach except maybe with tweezers, and she wouldn't let us try that.) We were afraid we would push it completely out of reach if we tried to hold her down. We became sort of worried; so Rodolph went to call the doctor to ask if it had to come out that night or if we could wait until the next day. We didn't want to be silly, but we also didn't want it to get lodged way up in the nasal passages somewhere that would cause a dangerous condition. While he went to call the doctor, I tried to get her to breathe through her mouth and blow out through her nose so she wouldn't sniff it further up. She tried this and began to laugh and make a game out of it. I got some pepper and blew this in her face and she sneezed one time really big and blew a couple more times, and it came down where I could get it! We were so relieved. There is never a dull moment with Merry!

David is having a good time here now because he has made friends with some Tico children in the next block. They treat him like royalty. He has been playing soccer with them, and yesterday I looked out and they were playing on two of those skate board things like he had in the States. After watching them awhile, I realized David had one all to himself, and all the other children were sharing the second one. He loves playing with them. (Who wouldn't?) They speak no English and he speaks practically no Spanish but they all seem to have a really good time. They are so cute and I try to talk to them, but it takes a lot of effort for me to understand them because they talk so fast. I asked them if they liked to play with David and if it was okay with their mothers for him to play with them. They all said their mothers liked for them to play with David because he didn't use "palabras malas" (bad words) like some of the other children in the neighborhood did. I assured them they would have no trouble along this line with David (in Spanish anyway)! I feel I could also assure them he would be acceptable in any language; he is a good kid. He seems to be doing well in his studies, also, because he is not in second grade yet and can read almost as well as I can. I fully expect him to pass me in Spanish very soon. (Merry already has!☺)

I was on the bus yesterday and I saw a sight that unnerved me. A little boy about David's size was digging through a garbage can behind one of the stores. He was dirty and ragged and digging for all he was worth! You hear about that kind of thing but it shakes you up to actually see it. I saw something else on the way to school Friday morning that shook me up too. I had to step over a tarantula! It was dead, but intact, hairy legs and all, and was at least 4 inches across. I think I would die of heart failure if one of those things got near me alive! I didn't like it too much dead, for that matter!

Dear Mother,

I made my first trip to the beauty salon--it was quite an experience! Rodolph is still laughing at me and I am going to pop him! I had to wash my hair here at home and go to the "salon" with it wet. They dried it, put some gook on it, and cut it, then they rolled it and dried it again. After that they teased it and combed it and put more gook on it and then dried it again! I am pooped and I look like a monkey! My hair feels like a poor grade of broom straw. At least it is cut now and I can work with it, and all it cost me for everything, including the tip, was $2.

Dear Mother,

We went to church with the missionary here and he said he was supposed to preach. After they finished like they usually do, they dismissed the congregation and left him sitting there. We got so tickled! Lo and behold this is the custom for this church! All this time we thought they weren't having preaching service in the morning because they don't have a preacher, and their normal schedule is to have Sunday School with an assembly and devotional before and after, and then go home. They do have an evening service. I think David has had his prayers answered; he has always wanted to go to a church that didn't have preaching after Sunday School!☺

We invited the young people to our house for their meeting last Saturday and had a good gathering. We had 15 who showed up, and they nearly ate me out of house and home! The first ones in line emptied the plates and bowls and I had to get more for those who had not been served yet. They just grabbed everything in sight, and those who were last in line would have been out of luck if I hadn't kept some back in the kitchen. I had a BIG bowl of hard candy that I had to fill up 3 times before all 15 got served. They would have eaten more, but I didn't give them more. The first ones ate the 30 little cakes I had put out, but I, thankfully, had some more for the last ones. I also had sandwiches and banana bread and drinks, and they finished up everything. I now know why people are served a plate here with their food already on it and not invited to help themselves.

We always seem to have some excitement at church, or going to and from there. As we left yesterday, two bulls got loose from somewhere and began to run in the streets. It happened just as church let out and all the people were in the street. Some young boys were chasing them and got them mad and one of them began charging at the people. If it hadn't been so dangerous it would have been funny, because they were jumping into windows, over walls, under cars--just like in the cartoons! We were in the car and could see everything from a safe place. Merry kept yelling for the "mules" to come back! One of the boys had a bull by the tail and he was running and jumping and being dragged behind him for quite a distance. They were huge, fierce looking animals with tremendous horns--and were really mad! I guess they were finally rounded up, because we didn't see them or the people running any more.

Dear Mother,

These religious processions are really something! I don't know quite what to make of them. They have re-enacted all kinds of scenes from the death of Christ. They have parades in which real live people are dressed for the part, but they also use statues, and sometimes it is hard to tell which is which. All the people are so solemn and have their heads covered, and the bands play funeral dirges. They had a glass coffin with a statue (I think) of Christ inside, and someone dressed as Mary, all in black, was following it. It was so morbid and sort of eerie. I didn't have to tell Merry and David to be quiet, I think their hair was standing on end as it was! On Good Friday the whole city closes down; there is no bus or taxi service and everyone stays indoors. They actually throw stones at cars that don't observe this ritual. On Easter Sunday it is all over; there is practically no celebration of the Resurrection of Christ! This is strange and upsetting to us! The portrayal of the death of Christ constitutes the biggest procession of the year and hundreds of people take part in each one, in every community, all over town. Having a role in the parade is considered a huge honor for the participant.

Rodolph bought a little rocker from another student who is leaving and Merry loves it. She rocks her "babies" all day long and has a fit if David even looks at it. We heard him singing "Rock-a-Bye, Baby" the other day and wondered how in the world he was managing to sit in it long enough to sing a whole chorus. When we looked, we saw him sitting there with Merry in his lap. She is almost bigger than he is and they looked so funny. David is getting bigger now and filling out some. He looks like just a bad boy now, instead of a bad little boy!☺

Dear Mother,

   Your granddaughter has the ability to make us laugh at the most unexpected times. I told Merry that it was time for her nap and we were going to "siesta" now. She asked in all innocence, "Mommy, who is Esther? Are we going to 'see Esther' now? Is she coming here?" We almost lost nap time that day.

Dear Mother,

   I am an inventor. I just may get this thing patented. We had to give talks in class the other day and it was the kind of thing that would have lent itself well to using a flannel graph like we did back in the USA. I thought about what I could do, and I discovered that Merry's old cloth diapers that are worn and soft work just as well as flannel. Also, if you put glue on the backs of cut outs and let it dry they will stick nicely to it. So I lined a folded piece of cardboard with a diaper on each side and I have what is probably the first and only "diaper graph" around. It works great and I am the envy of all the students!☺ Some of the other substitutes we have found are just as amazing, and it has sort of become a game to see who can find a new one and share it with the other missionaries.

   As I have told you, apples are not grown here and if you ever see one, it is imported (probably from Chile) and has a price that no one I know would pay. For that reason, I am sure, apple pie has all at once become everyone's favorite and there is an expressed longing for the taste of one whenever we have a gathering. Someone came up with the discovery that green mangos have the same taste as apples in a pie. I doubted it until I tried it and found this to be true. Due to the fact that mangos are everywhere and dirt cheap, we have been enjoying "apple" pie a lot lately.

Dear Mother,

   We got back home at 2 a.m. from our trip with the resident

18

missionary here, and we couldn't get Maria to come to the door. She had come home late from her weekend out, assumed we were all in bed, locked the door, and bolted it from the inside. She went on to bed out in her quarters in back, and obviously is a sound sleeper, because no matter how much we called and banged, she didn't come. When we questioned her the next day, she said she didn't even hear us. We finally managed to squeeze David through the bars on the window to his room, and he got in and went to the door and opened it for us. We were relieved to get in, but wondered if it would be that easy for someone else to do the same. Those bars aren't as safe as they look. The trip was supposed to be only a morning visit to a church in a town not too far distant, but while there, the missionary was invited to preach in another church farther away for their evening service. When you don't have your own transportation, you are at the mercy of those who do. I would never have taken the children for such a long hard day, but I guess that is what missionary kids have to get used to. It didn't bother Merry a whole lot, she just slept whenever and wherever she wanted to. The rest of us were pretty well wiped out. It was a valuable experience to see how the churches outside of the city function, and also to see some of the countryside.

Merry is such a character--the other day we bowed our heads at the table for the blessing and reached out to hold hands like we normally do. Just as we joined hands and got quiet, but before anyone could say a word, she roared out with, "Ring Around the Rosy!" It was so unexpected and so funny we all just about died laughing. What are we going to do with her? Both Merry and David were dancing around to the music on the radio and acting silly, and Maria told them they couldn't be good missionary children because missionaries don't dance. It would have been funny except I am pretty sure she was serious. The attitude of many evangelicals in the Hispanic community is that the sins of stealing, telling a lie, or even having children out of wedlock, would not be nearly so bad as dancing. It is an interesting concept.

We knew that Costa Rica has no army, but it came as a

huge surprise to learn that their policemen cannot wear guns. They can only write a ticket when they see something amiss. They are instructed to take the license plates off of a car that has violated some traffic law, so they wear a pouch for their screwdriver in place of a gun. I wonder what we will find in Peru?

BEGINNINGS AND EARLY YEARS

Dec., 1968

Dear Mother,

Here we are in Peru! I have to report that our beginnings here have been a little more exciting than I imagined! Our first misadventure came about upon entering the airport in Lima. The officials announced that because of the widespread "Hong Kong" flu epidemic, every single person getting off the plane was to have his temperature taken, and anyone with fever would be turned away to prevent disease being brought into the country. There we sat with thermometers in our mouths, and when they checked them, wouldn't you know that David had a slight temperature! They said they thought it was just a little cold but we would have to leave the address where we were staying in Lima so they could check on us if necessary. We only had a post office box number and, of course, they wouldn't accept that, so I asked if I could step outside and get one of the missionaries (who were all outside the glass looking in at us and wondering what was going on). They allowed me to do this, and the rest of the family stayed there with Rodolph while he did the necessary paper work. I found a veteran missionary who came back with me.

Now Peru has just gone through a bloody coup and a tough military dictatorship is in power. There were guards everywhere with machine guns, tanks in the street, and a real feeling of unrest and concern for the future. I was following this kind benefactor back through the airport when we came to a sort of check point which a soldier was guarding with a machine gun. The missionary said a few words to him and passed on through. I started after him rather tentatively and the guard waved the gun and said, "Sigue no mas, Senora." I ran that through my one year of Spanish training and it literally translated as "Follow no more, Madam." So I skidded to a complete stop and planted myself right there in front of him. He continued to wave the gun and repeat that phrase, and I

21

continued to stay glued to the spot. My missionary friend finally looked around and saw I wasn't behind him and came back to get me. When I told him what had happened, he got a good laugh out of it. And so begins my life in Peru! I guess I will not soon forget that this is an idiom (uniquely Peruvian) where that phrase "no mas" used like that, means a very polite "go right ahead." The poor guard was telling me to please feel free to go right on in, and I was not budging an inch. I guess it will take me awhile to live this one down (along with many more in the past and many more yet to come).

Dear Mother,

Well, a year ago we arrived in Costa Rica, and this December 30th here we are in Peru (which is pretty unusual by stateside standards, too). We went down to the beach just a short distance away, and the scenery was incredibly beautiful! We stood on the crest of gigantic cliffs that dropped off into the sea, and we could see fellows on surf boards riding huge waves all the way in to a beach that looked like it was covered with pebbles. The great cliffs and mountains are nothing but rock and sand; there is no vegetation anywhere, except where there is some type of irrigation.

The people in Lima are more European looking than in Costa Rica, or maybe I should say, more North American looking. The Indians from the mountains stand out from the city people and seem to retain some customs that are really different. You usually see them selling something or begging on the street, and most are dressed in the typical outfits of their villages way up in the Andes. The women have the babies and toddlers tied to their backs. Both mother and child seem satisfied with this arrangement.

Dear Mother,

Our speaker today said we should treat people on the mission field like you would a moving train--In trying to board it, you run along side awhile to judge its speed before stepping on.

We should do the same in approaching people. Move along side with them rather than a direct approach or walking right into the train. He said we must earn the right to be heard. I was pretty impressed with him; he says things I believe. Now if I can just do it---

Dear Mother,

I got the sweetest letter from Hampie the other day. You know how hard it was for us to leave her, especially knowing how sick she is. I prayed she would understand. I also felt I couldn't pray for her and expect God to answer my prayers if I said no to what we felt He was asking us to do. She said she missed us and was proud of who we are, what we are, and where we are. She said that as much as she would like it, she would not have us be her next door neighbors if God wanted us in Peru. I have to admit, that letter brought a tear or two.

Dear Mother,

I had a most unusual birthday cake this year. We were in meetings up north and were staying with a missionary family in that town. We had breakfast at their house, but ate our other meals where we could in between sessions. Our hostess was very gracious and when she heard that it was my birthday, she served us pancakes for breakfast that morning, and my plate had a stack of pancakes with candles stuck in it! It was a cake, it had candles, they sang--so it was a legitimate party. We make do with what we have. I loved it!

June 2, 1970
Dear Mother,

I hope you can read this, I am writing it by candlelight. We have had no electricity since the earthquake Sun. afternoon, but we do have a trickle of water and I am grateful for that. We are really having a time here, but not as bad as the poor people just south of us where the epicenter hit who have had their cities completely leveled. Much of Trujillo is destroyed and much more will fall soon with all these aftershocks that are almost as strong as the original quake. Some are quite long and strong for our upset nerves and we are all jumpy! The big quake came Sun. afternoon just after we had sat down in the living room. I had Spencer in my arms and Merry was cutting paper on the floor at Rodolph's feet. David was out playing with his friends. We grabbed up the kids and stood in the doorway, but then as we began to realize how bad it was, we managed to get to the center of the park across the street. It seemed to last forever! (We were told later that it was 5 min. at the epicenter and 3 min. and 45 seconds in Trujillo.) Things were falling in the house, the car was purely dancing around, and the ground was weaving as well as vibrating so that we could hardly stand up. Poor David ran home from several blocks away and was scared and out of breath, but you can imagine how glad we were to see each other! We really didn't get too frightened until we saw the damage elsewhere in town. In our house things were tossed about and broken, but that is nothing compared to the poor people who are homeless now.

Our Baptist Bookstore caved in and our church building is destroyed. We are afraid it will continue to fall and cause more damage or injury, so Rodolph hopes he can get the seminary students or someone to help him take it down first. We have all been sleeping in the living room on the sofa bed or in our sleeping bags, fully clothed, so we can leave in a hurry if we need to. The food supply has been cut off from Lima, but if we can just find formula for the baby, I feel we will be able to manage all right. Rodolph has been out helping people move into safe places to live like Central Church which lost only a few windows. Most of the people are living in the streets with the few possessions they could salvage from the destruction. We are told this is the worst earthquake in the history of South America because the death count is between 65,000 and 85,000. The mudslides in the mountains account for most of the deaths. There are some really sad tales coming from up there.

One of the saddest stories that I heard reported came from one of our Peruvian pastors who went way up into the Andes Mountains to the village of Huaraz which was the nearest to the epicenter and was almost totally destroyed. He went to help with relief work, and there he found a pastor and his family that he knew. They told him that their little girl died in the earthquake. She was trapped under a fallen wall and they could not get her out. She was crying and calling for her mother who knelt down beside her and managed to reach her hand. Her mother said to her, "Just try to go to sleep now, and when you wake up, you will be with Jesus." Her mother stayed there beside her and held her hand until she breathed her last breath. That big old   pastor stood there sobbing as he related this, and you can be assured that there was not a dry eye among those listening.

Another very touching thing came out in our paper about the orphanage in Huaraz. It was completely destroyed and many lives were lost there. Search and rescue workers who were digging through the rubble came upon the bodies of a nun and several children. As they uncovered them as carefully as they could, they discovered that the nun still had her arms around as many children as she could reach, trying to shelter them with her own body.

One funny thing happened, too. Well, after it was over it was funny, but at the time it was pretty scary. The same evening of the big quake I was talking on the phone to a friend. The electricity had gone out immediately, but for some reason we had phone service for a few hours. Rodolph had gone out to help where he could and I was at home with the three children. We had candles on the table and I told David that if we had another aftershock strong enough, we might have to leave the house again and while I got the baby, he was to blow out the candles and help me with Merry. Well, sure enough, while I was talking a really strong one came and the first thing David did was to blow out the candles. He did exactly what I told him to do, but the problem was that I couldn't find the baby. I had put him on the sofa across the room and without electricity anywhere--it was pitch black! By the time I had felt my way across the room and got to him, the worst of the aftershock had passed. We revised our strategy after that.

NOTE: I have remarked many times since those days of no regular electricity for nearly seven months, that I fail to see the romance in a candle-lit dinner or candle-lit anything else for that matter! The lights came back on with some regularity on December 15, just in time for Christmas. It was a wonderful present!

Dear Mother and all,

Well, I can't remember what I wrote you and what not! I do know that I have written about the earthquake, but even at the time I wrote you I didn't know all that it had done even here in Trujillo. Somehow we were spared great numbers of deaths right here in the city (about a dozen reported) but I don't see how! Many places caved in completely, but just about the whole center of town is being torn down because it is falling down or is on the verge of doing so. Other areas are declared unsafe even though they don't show it. There are big DANGER signs written everywhere, and you can't park your car anywhere without feeling like it may be buried under falling rubble before you get back to it. Everyone walks in the middle of the streets to go to the few stores that are open. We are cut off from Lima right now for products, so things are getting scarce. People are speculating on products and buying up in quantities, so it is getting hard to find many things like we feel we need.

We are wondering when it will all end or just what will come of it. We have not had electricity since the earthquake, and the candles at night are really getting on my nerves, especially when Rodolph is out! The tremors have about stopped now, I think. I haven't really felt a hard one for about two days now and that helps to settle the nerves, too. Also, as if we didn't have enough to drive everyone crazy, someone spread the alarm that another "terremoto" (earthquake) was to hit at one o'clock in the morning, and the people panicked and ran into the streets and screamed and prayed to the Virgin Mary. These are the times when I feel like a "real live missionary."

I couldn't believe it when the post office opened up and there was a letter written by you on Monday waiting there! It cheered me up more than I can tell you! One of the big tremors hit Wed. night and Rodolph couldn't wake me up until it was just about over. That upset me terribly! I hate to think that I could get so tired, that maybe sometimes when he wasn't here, I could sleep through one and not get the children out! To hear from you and know that you are praying for all of us--really means a lot. Please tell everyone to continue to do so; there are so many here who have lost everything! Not only in other places but here in Trujillo, too.

The church we attend had to be torn down (Rodolph helped them do it) so we don't have a building for worship right now. We are meeting in the open space where it used to be. The piano has a piece of clear plastic draped over it that I lift it up off the keyboard to play for the service. The rest of the few pieces of furniture there are covered with red checked oil cloth or other bright colored waterproof material (gathered from heaven knows where and donated) to help protect it from the mist that comes in from the sea. The unfavorable condition of being out in the elements has not shortened the services, though; we still have a couple of hours at least in preaching service after Sunday School is over. (Since Rodolph has to sit through these, too, I hope it will have the effect of helping him to have mercy and shorten his sermons, also.☺)

School hasn't started back for anyone here as there are hardly any classrooms safe enough to use. In fact, I don't think I have heard of a single school that escaped damage. Just think what it would have been like if this had happened on a school day! I don't like to think of what it would have been at the kindergarten where Merry goes with 250 children and 6 teachers! Actually, this may be the saving of Trujillo, because these terrible old buildings will have to be replaced and progress can now begin on safe and modern ones. I believe in preserving history, but not to the extent of endangering lives. There are some towns and two big cities that

27

are 100% destroyed. Not a building left standing! The death toll right now is estimated between 50,000 and 100,000. The spirit of the people is wonderful, though; it is surprising in the face of their panic and the Latin nature. They are really pitching in and working, and there has been little or no looting.

We are all being very careful with water and have had our typhoid booster, etc., but I really think, with the exception of our electricity, that things will soon get back to some semblance of normality. (Whatever that is!☺) There is talk of no electricity for 6 to 9 months because our power plant is in the area wiped out up in the mountains. However, don't let all this scare you, we are perfectly safe here and just have inconveniences of food shortages and roads being out. The Methodist missionary was visiting in a nearby town and said some products were already arriving there, so things are looking up.

Dear Mother,

Well, I guess we will get the hang of some of these customs after a time here. I hope so anyway! We got our first invitation to a meal with a Peruvian family that is not from our church. This is a neighbor who has been really friendly. She said she was having a few of her family and friends over for dinner and would like for us to come. We had been told that one should never be on time for a Peruvian dinner invitation. It is considered polite to arrive later than the indicated hour, so we got to her house about an hour after what she had told us. I just knew everyone was already there and we would make a grand entrance, and I was worried about it.

Well, we were cheated out of a grand entrance because the hostess was not even dressed when we arrived. We were let into the house by the maid and waited and waited for the hostess to come down and greet us. After she got there and we chatted for what seemed forever, the first guests began arriving. We were invited for 7 p.m., we got there after 8 p.m., and the guests started arriving sometime after 9 p.m. Finally, the crowd had assembled and they started with cocktails. The alcoholic drink posed a dilemma for Baptist missionaries, but they were gracious and gave us ginger ale. We finally got to the dinner table after 10 p.m. It was a long and complicated meal served in courses, but we did right by it except for the beverage. They served wine, and once again we got our soft drink. I think we had coke that time. The interesting thing is that this time, a good many of the other guests drank a soft drink also. (You don't dare drink water because you have to be sure it is boiled and don't dare ask if it is or not.) The hostess was very solicitous and we enjoyed the hospitality.

Then after dinner, coffee was served. Well, you know that suited Rodolph just fine, but you also know that I just can't get it down to save my life--and they came to serve me first! When I refused the coffee, the hostess exclaimed, "Doesn't your religion let you drink anything?" I was so embarrassed, but Rodolph made up for my lack in the amount he drank. They gave me tea. It was past midnight by this time, and I was surely ready when we could politely make a departure.

I guess this is the way you learn customs, and I have to admit they were more than gracious and understanding in the light of the many violations of Peruvian etiquette we made that night. I am sure we gave them a chuckle or two for future conversations.

Dear Hampie,

When I arrived at choir practice this week, I was told that the pastor was seeing about a little boy who had come to the church with all his official documents in his hand. He also had a small bundle of his belongings. He said that his mother had sent him there to ask if someone would adopt him because she just didn't have the means to care for him any longer. He was ready to go home with anyone who would take him. I think they said he was about 7 or 8 years old; I didn't see him. I have to find out what happened. I am always afraid that I misunderstand things because of the language, but apparently the mother was abandoning him and thought the church would be a good place to send him. Does that affect you like it does me? Knowing you, I expect you would be here on the next plane to get him, if you could. I guess this rule our mission board has about our not adopting national children is valid, because we would all have a house full! Also, there are so many governmental regulations that it is an expensive and time consuming process which rarely turns out with the desired success.

There is a famous evangelist coming for our "Campaign of the Americas," and his musician is also pretty well known in Latin circles. He has a lot of recordings, etc. I have been asked to play for all the meetings, and some of them are in the civic coliseum as they are expecting to have quite a gathering. I am a little nervous; I think I can handle the music, but I am not sure about the Spanish.

Our church is celebrating its 5th anniversary and Rodolph volunteered us to carry 100 ham sandwiches. (I was not there.) Now you know I don't ever mind doing my part, but ham is a luxury here and we don't buy it for our house. Also, I wasn't too thrilled about making all that mayonnaise! I ought to insist that he make it; isn't that just like husbands?!☺

Well, we went to the big celebration for which our pastor's wife had made a huge cake. It was not only beautiful but good. I was asked to cut it for them, and it nearly broke my heart to pass out pieces to everybody with those little ragged kids begging for more! After they had gotten their slice, they came back up to me and said, "Senora, regaleme una mas." (Give me one more.)--with their little hands out, and their little eyes so big! I just couldn't eat the cake thinking about how much they wanted it. The pastor's wife apparently saw this, because after it was all over she handed us a big chunk that she had saved because we didn't get any during the social time. Rodolph said it really got to him, too. Both instances were touching.

(NOTE: As I am copying this letter after 30 years of experience later, my thought was, "What little con artists!"☺ See how much we have changed?)

Rodolph worked all day with the people out there helping them to put in lights and clean up. While he was doing this, a seminary student came up to him and said that was the first time he had seen a missionary with a broom in his hand and he was going to write it up for the paper. (We assume he was kidding.) Rodolph told him he might not be able to speak so well, but he surely could sweep--so maybe he has made more of a witness sweeping than preaching so far! Apparently the people here would like a little action to back up the words of love that are spoken.

I really do think they are beginning to accept us now at church, and that is a big thing, because everybody here considers us filthy rich (and we ARE in comparison to them). Our pastor makes more than any of his members, and his salary for one month is exactly what we make in one week! How about that?

Rodolph was so upset last night because he was playing with one of the little boys and when he caught the boy in the back of his shirt, the whole shirt came to pieces in his hand. They patch their clothes until you can't tell what was the original material. He said the little boy was embarrassed and, of course, so was Rodolph. We have plans to buy him a new shirt, but I expect when the other boys see him with a new shirt they will all try to get Rodolph to tear theirs, too!

We have a new puppy. She is just a little mutt, but the children love her to death. She is cute and we are glad to have her, but she is still really little and misses her mother and cries at night. One night David and his buddy took her to bed with them to get her to stop crying. Needless to say, I didn't know about that until the next day. Last night at 3 a.m. Rodolph was up heating milk for her, and I have to admit I have done the same thing. I never thought of something like this as being part of a missionary's duties, and I am pretty sure the picture the average church member has of missionaries doesn't include the man of the house running around in his shorts, heating milk for the dog, in the middle of the night.

Dear Mother,

Did Hampie tell you what Dani said? I thought it was priceless. She wrote us that she was so touched by the plight of the

31

little boy who came to church with his papers so someone could adopt him. She asked Dani if she would like to have a little Indian brother. She said her response was immediate and emphatic. Dani said, "No, I don't want an Indian brother--I want an Indian sister." Hampie went on to say that she thought we could learn a lot from our children if we would take time to listen.

Dear Mother,

I had my first experience playing the pump organ at church yesterday. Remember the little army surplus field organ that folds out from a carrying case that we brought back in our crate? Well I discovered that when I sat down to play it in an old cane bottomed chair which sags in the middle, it was all I could do to keep both my hands and feet going and keep my dress down at the same time! I was so low in the chair I was afraid my knees would hit me in the chin and I had to reach around them to touch the keyboard! Well, picture this dilemma in your mind, then imagine how I felt when a big ole hound dog came right up to me and licked me on my leg! All I could think of was how this would look to a congregation back home.

Dear Mother,

We saw the prettiest little baby girl at church yesterday, and when we admired her, the mother tried to give her to us saying that we could give her a better life than she could. That broke our hearts!

Dear Friends,

Thank you for the money you sent for the needs here; also I want to let you know how it was used. I bought pillow cases and sheets (one set) for a lady in our church who has had a stroke and is paralyzed on one side. She is very old and a faithful church member, but her daughter with whom she lives now is not taking care of her very well. The last time I visited her, the bed was just filthy and covered with food spots, etc. and, of course, flies (and I suspect other insects). She is living in a one room shack out behind the adobe house of her daughter. It has a bed and a bench in it. There is a dirt floor and not even a picture on the wall. She can't move from there unless someone picks her up, and so I thought that since she spends so much time in the bed that maybe sheets would help to cheer her up as much as anything. Actually, we have to buy the material and make the sheets as we can't buy ready-made ones in the stores here.

Also, I gave about $10 to one of our finest young girls. Her family is very poor but they try so hard to live a good, clean, decent life. They are trying to send this daughter to school and the matriculation is more than they can manage at times. I heard by the grapevine that they couldn't make it at all this year and that she was going to have to drop out; she is 15 years old and a beautiful girl. She will make a wonderful Christian leader. They live in two rooms with an outside kitchen area. They only have a table-top kerosene stove for cooking, and somehow they manage to make cakes to sell on this. There are 4 boys, this girl, and their parents who sleep in one room, and the other room is a living room; yet they are always neatly dressed and clean. I feel like they deserve all we can do for them because they try so hard, even though you could say their need is not as great as some others. The $10 should be enough for her tuition I think.

(NOTE: This young lady went on to finish nurses' training at the top of her class in Lima at one of the most prestigious hospitals there.)

The other case was brought to my attention by our pastor's wife. We have a lady who lives alone with her little 9 year old son and has no income. She, too, is a wonderful Christian and very faithful to the church. She lives in the poorest area of Trujillo called "Florencia de Mora" or "Flowering Blackberry." This is really like a joke because it is pure desert sand and rock with no vegetation whatsoever. The wind has blown the shifting sand up the side of the mountain and this has formed a new area of unclaimed land. Since this land is free, many people have come and built houses of adobe, mud and straw. There are no lights, water, or sewage, and it is a day-to-day existence at best. Our pastor's wife told me that this particular lady was having such a hard time that she had been sending her little boy to our Bible Institute each day to beg scraps from the garbage. We are making plans to have something available for her at the Institute each week for as long as the rest of the money holds out. I can't give it to them in a lump sum because they do not understand how to save something for later needs. It is a pitiful situation. I can't describe it to you because you would have nothing like it there in the USA to which I could compare it and make you understand. I know I didn't until I saw it with my own eyes.

Thank you again for the relief from suffering and the pleasure you have brought into these lives. Thank you, also, for the lift it gives to our spirits, personally, to know that you really care what happens here at what must seem like the ends of the earth to you--so far removed from your daily life.

Dear Mother,

They still talk of that great day when you had the honor of "throwing in the first stone" (Peruvian expression for "laying the cornerstone"). That really was a wonderful honor for all of us. Rodolph and all the men of the church have really been working so hard ever since then, as I have reported to you all along. The anxiously awaited day finally arrived and we had the dedication this past Sunday. I am enclosing an account that you can share with the church since they might like to know that the money they sent us was put to good use.

We had a ribbon across the door and the pastor cut it and everybody entered, reciting the verse from Psalms while they walked--"I was glad when they said unto me, let us go into the house of the Lord." Then we had a program of dedication during which he expressed his appreciation especially to "our brothers in the USA who have sacrificed so much to help us have this beautiful building." He said that he knew we have all worked together to build it, but that you people there have given so much to help us that he is sure you have done without clothes and food and other things you needed to send us so much. He said, while looking around him, that this church is a dream come true. And at that, he broke down and cried like a baby and couldn't go on for several minutes. I wish I could translate just what he said, but English is just not as expressive as Spanish at times, and it was really impressive and touching. The building is very simple. It has unpainted brick walls, cement floor and the roof is the ceiling, but it is by far, the most beautiful and elegant building in the community--all the rest are of adobe, mud and straw. During the service they presented us with a plaque that expressed their appreciation for our help, and at that, Rodolph and the pastor both cried. (Rodolph is getting to be a real Latin.)

The church was packed and people were standing outside, and afterwards we had a reception. We served hard buns with a little sliver of chicken or something similar to lunch meat inside and also had cookies (courtesy of the missionaries because most of our church people don't have ovens, just kerosene burners on which to cook). We had chicha morada to drink, which is made from boiling this purple corn they have here. You would have to taste it to believe it. We always have that or cinnamon tea. I bought some little plastic cups and donated them this time, because usually we serve out of the 30 we have and then fill them up again without washing and serve 30 more and continue until all are served! They are usually really thoughtful of us missionaries and try to serve us first because they know we are sort of funny about things like that, even though we always try not to show it.

The program was to begin at 3 p.m. and we finally got started about 4 p.m., and then we continued until after 6 p.m. This was an extra program after our regular services in the morning which lasted nearly 3 hours. Then we began our evening services at 7 p.m. and we got home about 10:30 p.m. after taking some members home. I was so tired that I thought I just couldn't make the last service, but we did, and we had the happy experience of seeing David make public his decision to accept Christ as his Savior! So we feel like yesterday was an especially wonderful day in every respect!

Dear Mother,
We have a watchman on our street now since the latest visit by a thief. We don't have an over abundance of confidence in him, though, because two nights after he started working, someone stole our doorbell off the wall right where he is supposed to be standing. They tell me he is 70 years old, and one of the maids said she saw him drunk at least one night for sure and suspected it on other nights. He has a gun but says he only has one bullet (sound like Barney Fife?) and he wants us to buy him a dozen. I think maybe we will just look for someone else as soon as we can! I think I am more afraid of him than the possibility of a thief coming in.

Dear Mother,
    Remember us telling you about our night watchman? Well, the other night we heard a commotion in the street and someone came running for Rodolph to take the guard to the hospital as he had been shot. Rodolph did just that while we waited impatiently for the story of how our watchman had defended all of our lives against these vicious criminals who wanted to do us harm. As he returned and related the story, it seems that our brave defender had leaned against the wall and somehow managed to accidentally fire his weapon and shoot himself in the leg. (I guess he is out of ammunition now, because we didn't buy him any more bullets!)

Dear Mother,
    I was devastated to learn that the milk I have been buying and pasteurizing each day has probably been watered down, and whereas the process we use for the milk would normally make it safe, it is not strong enough to kill the germs that are in that added

water. So I decided to buy my milk straight from the dairy. We have been going each day out there and I take MY bucket and give it to them. It is a smelly place and we fight flies and dirt, but we see them milk the cows and pour it straight from their bucket into ours and bring it directly to us, so I have felt good that we are getting milk that is pure. One of the older missionaries mentioned yesterday that we still couldn't be sure, because we didn't see if they had put water in their bucket BEFORE they went to milk the cow. I don't think I will ever get the hang of living here and staying one jump ahead of those who are out to trick the public. I am getting a little more worldly wise each day, though.

We also discovered that many of the eggs you buy in the market are really old and none of them are refrigerated. So we found an egg farm and we went to buy our eggs fresh from them. I really think we got good eggs, but we learned another lesson there. One does NOT carry the 100 eggs one has just bought in one basket in one's lap-- especially if one is traveling over very bumpy roads in the desert. I have heard many speak of an error that they had made as having "egg on the face," well, this WAS an error and I am sure there was egg on my face because it was everywhere else! After that we purchased a plastic leak proof container in which to carry them and put it on the floor of the car. We still broke some of them, but it was not nearly such a clean-up job.

Dear Mother,

One of the things Rodolph got for his birthday was a surprise party from the church members. About 20 of them came over about 9:30 p.m. Saturday night and brought him a beautiful cake that the pastor's wife had made. She had told me about it, so I had cokes for all of them. They sang, recited poems, and ate until really late, but Rodolph was so surprised and appreciated it so much. The next day when he returned home he was carrying a live hen that one of the members had given him. It was from a very poor family that we take home after church every Sunday and they wanted to do something for him, and he was so pleased. He killed it and Cleo cleaned it, and I cooked it, but it was as tough as leather! Merry and David nearly died when he told them he was going to kill it and eat it. Merry cried and said that she wanted to keep it for a pet and she wasn't about to eat a bite of it. (Actually, none of us ate too much of it for differing reasons.)

Dear Mother,

When you have a chance to talk to folks at church, tell them about appreciating what they have and not to worry continually about getting more. I don't know what I will be like when I get back to the USA, but I know that I will never be the same because of seeing the conditions of fellow human beings like they have to live here!

All of these new and different things that we see, make me wish that I could show them to you and talk about them with all of you. I always think, "Hampie would surely love to see this."--or I wonder how you would react to something.

Merry is having a ball here; it doesn't matter to her how dirty her friends are when they come to Sunday School. She loves them all and kisses them and eats their food if I don't watch her. (I don't mean I don't want her eating Peruvian food, I just don't want her eating her share and theirs, too, especially when they have so little.)

David has all the friends he can handle and plenty of places and space to play. We have to drag both of them inside to eat and sleep. It is such a relief to see them happy. God is good.

Some of the men here (we ladies are smarter) got the idea to write the slogan of the Campaign of the Americas on one of the mountains nearby. The settlement at the base of the mountain is "La Esperanza" (The Hope). The slogan is "Cristo, La Unica Esperanza" (Christ the Only Hope). The mountain has sand blown up on it at its base, but other than that it is bare, solid rock. The work was really dangerous and it took them all day long just to write, "CRI." They carried lime up that mountain all day in the broiling sun, and had to cling to the side of cliffs on ropes in places. What nuts! Now that they have started, they feel like they have to complete it, so they are going back this Saturday. He is picking up some of the men at 4:30 a.m. I can't imagine how long it will take them to finish; it is quite an undertaking, but also will be quite impressive if they can pull this off. We can see those three letters from our house and we are on the other side of town. Those four words would be the message we long to bring to these people who seem to have so little hope.

NOTE: They did manage to chalk that message in big bold letters that stood out against the stark cliffs of that mountain for months and months. The winds blowing the sand up across it, finally erased it, but hopefully not before it made an impression in the minds and hearts of all who saw it.

OUR PEOPLE AND CUSTOMS

Dear Mother,

I told you how hard it is to get accustomed to the countryside around here with nothing but sand dunes and bare rock mountains; well, there is another thing I have noticed lately that I thought was just a natural geological formation at first. I realized that there were too many of them so very similar that they had to be man-made. I began looking more closely at them and discovered they were made of adobe bricks which were covered over with sand in most cases. Upon inquiring more, I found out that these are called "huacas" which are burial mounds.

I was told most of them are empty because grave robbers are continually digging everywhere in the countryside to find something they can sell. There are tons and tons of valuable pottery and gold and silver items that have been taken out and sold, and untold treasures of historical worth destroyed and just scattered about by these ruthless vandals. The government is trying to crack down on them, but it is impossible to have the manpower to patrol the countryside in these isolated spots all through the desert and mountains. Sometimes we ride by places where the desert floor has been riddled with holes by robbers who were looking for an underground burial site. It is very common to see pottery shards with designs, fragments of woven material, and human bones scattered carelessly about in these places. Just about every time a big building is under construction around here, a newspaper article comes out indicating the type of artifacts that were discovered in the excavation, and many times they have found mummies and human skeletons intact. It doesn't have to be a huge construction, either, sometimes a person just digs in his own property and his shovel brings up something of great historical value.

We have people coming to our gate quite often with a bag slung over their shoulder and wanting to sell us something they have "found" that is a "rare treasure," but they will sell it cheap because they need the money right now. Some of their wares are blatant fakes, but some are selling genuine archaeological finds. Selling historical artifacts is illegal, so both types of these venders are crooks and we steer clear of them. Every once in a while someone will find pottery or an art object while plowing on his farm and bring it to town to see if it is worth something, but the unscrupulous ones outnumber them by far. This place is an archaeologist's and geologist's paradise. It is mind-boggling!

We went out to visit the "Temple to the Sun" and the "Temple to the Moon." It was fascinating to see these great structures of adobe rising up off the desert floor hundreds of feet into the air. One was built into the side of the mountain and was a sort of huge square. Parts of it were covered by the sand blown up onto its sides and top. The other was enormous and had the shape of what could have been something like the pictures I have seen of the Sphinx in Egypt. It didn't have a head, but it had steep sides that looked like they may have come to a point before they were eroded so badly. It did not have equal sides like a true pyramid; it was elongated and the front end was taller than the other sides. It was gigantic! It took quite an effort to climb it and we had an incredible view of the countryside from the top. We could see the ocean way off in the distance. There were little bits of pottery everywhere and we sifted through the debris looking for souvenirs. When the wind picked up we could not stand the blowing sand, it was like having your skin scraped away, and the dust and grit got into your eyes and nose and mouth. We made a hasty retreat to the car but reveled in yet another unique experience.

These "huacas" are not only scattered all over the countryside, they are located right in the middle of cities, too. We have seen several in Lima and one is only a half block from our mission apartments. Sometimes they are fenced in and for a fee you can tour the parts that have been excavated, but more times than not, they are just there and no one seems to pay them much attention.

(NOTE: It is a strange sight to see something of that

antiquity located only a few doors down from where there is now a pizza parlor and a block away from McDonald's and a major super market.)

Some of our friends offered to go with us to see another of the biggest tourist attractions of Trujillo. It is between the main part of town and the airport, so it was a very short trip. I was amazed at the vastness of the place. It is advertised as the largest mud city in the world and I believe it. There are remnants of the walls of enormous buildings made entirely of adobe that had covered the countryside in that area. Because of the dryness of our desert, the walls are preserved in an incredibly good condition. The roofs have long been gone and even some of the walls have melted a little in rains from those long ago "El Nino" years, but some of the walls have designs like fish and pelicans that are so distinct one would feel they were put there only a few years ago instead of a thousand. "Chan Chan," as it is called, was home to several civilizations down through the centuries.

We have gone through it several times and each time we have had a guide, we have gotten a different tale as to what function the buildings served, so we are not quite sure of the historical value of what we have heard. "National Geographic" and other very reputable publications are always sending representatives here to dig up more information (pardon the pun) and there are differing accounts with each new report of findings. Some of "Chan Chan" has been restored but much of it is just as it was a thousand years ago, and to stand there and think that those very same walls existed that long ago gives one a real sense of awe. There is no denying that it is a fascinating place and worthy of all the time spent on deciphering the secrets it yields up.

Dear Mother,

Weddings in Peru are something! They may not have as much money spent on them as in the USA, but they are every bit as celebrated and enjoyed by the families involved and the friends invited. We have been invited many times to be the "padrinos" (godparents) as I have told you, but we have now discovered why. We have a black car and it seems that this is the preferred mode of transportation for the bride to arrive at the church. If you are the one who is giving the bride away, you can hardly refuse to go fetch her at the proper time, so we now know why Rodolph has that role so often. (I guess I thought we were just that popular!☺)

I have been asked more times lately to just play the piano and I don't know if that is because I am such a good pianist, or because even they think I look a little silly coming in with the groom and being at least a head taller than he! Rodolph and I, both, always try to get the couple to have their own parents in the role of "padrinos," which is the tradition of the mother of the groom walking in with him and the father of the bride walking in with her, but sometimes in the absence of one or the other we fill in. Then, too, some of the parents just don't want to do it and I guess it doesn't matter if the missionaries want to or not, it just seems to be expected of us.

(NOTE: After every furlough I took back a dress suitable to wear to weddings and that one dress served for the following four year term.)

Of course, playing the piano for a wedding here is another story. I think my record is 1 hour 45 minutes of prelude before the bride even arrived at church, and this was not beginning at the announced hour of the ceremony. I never start playing for at least a half hour after they have said it will start. I carry a big stack of my music books and usually get in a pretty good practice session before the wedding party arrives. The only times I am spared this is when the wedding is held somewhere that a piano is not available. The music then is usually a guitar or a tape player with the volume turned up to the highest pitch. If possible, it is then amplified through a sound system that raises the volume to decibels that split the eardrums and vibrate the walls. Like I have said before, it seems here that "loud" is synonymous with "good." If I leave here with my hearing intact, it will be a miracle!

The decorations are quite lavish, too; when flowers and ribbons are affordable, they are everywhere. If not, there is white toilet tissue strung and draped and made into bows and hanging from every possible site that will support it. The groomsmen usually look very handsome in whatever they have been ordered to wear, but the bridesmaids and even the flower girls are hardly recognizable with so many frills, lace, ribbons, bows, sequins, pearls, curls, and gobs of cosmetic make-up! Several times I have wondered if I were attending the wrong wedding because I could not recognize the bride at all. I could usually count on the presence of the groom to confirm that I had arrived at the proper place because even though he was uncommonly elegant and usually ill at ease in a rented suit and fresh slicked-back haircut, there is only so much one can do to dress up the male counterpart of a matrimony, and who cares anyway? Everybody is looking at the bride.☺ It is quite a gala occasion for even the most humble who bother to have a real ceremony.

The refreshments are another interesting thing. It is quite a feat to juggle a flexible plastic plate filled with rice and stewed goat that has a lot of juice made red with peppers. One must also juggle a flexible plastic glass of purple corn drink, and yet arrive home without a stain on that special dress that has to last a whole 4-year term. There is usually a cake of varying types and sizes with every inch of it decorated. There are colored lights placed on some as well as real flowers, dolls, and other trinkets--some of which are really not too appropriate for weddings. The one that "took the cake," though, was the night they took the cake! There, sitting in its place of honor, was a huge "torta" that filled up the entire table. It was decorated beautifully and looked like it would be delicious and enough for everyone to have a chunk. They never cut it and finally the people began to sing for them to slice the cake, and someone came in and took it away. We wondered why and found out that the "cake" was made of cardboard and iced to look like a real one and it, too, was rented like the clothes and decorations. Each time I attend a wedding here I wonder what new surprise is in store for us.

Dear Mother,

Here is an article someone gave us out of the paper; it gives a good account of what life is like here and what we are up against in trying to get our couples in the church to get legally married. I think I told you about the time when Rodolph and I were the witnesses for a mass wedding of 60 couples out at our church? We had to sign papers in duplicate for each of them.

Here is the article from Lima, Peru--"Basilio Mendoza, 59, and Leoncia Ipana, 74, finally got married after 30 years of living together, 4 children, and 30 grandchildren. The couple, who said they never knew how old each other was until their wedding day, were united Sunday in a mass ceremony along with 200 other couples. The ceremony was the largest so far in a Peruvian government program to legalize common law marriages in Lima's slums. One of the younger brides in the same ceremony barely made it through the wedding because of labor pains. As soon as the ceremony ended she was rushed to a nearby clinic to have her second child."

I don't think I need to comment on this.

Dear Mother,

I think my work as music promoter for this area is going to be a little harder than I anticipated. Our missionary colleague told us her hilarious version of the solo they had in her church yesterday. It was performed by a little man who stood there and beat on a homemade drum for quite a while and then announced that it was something he had always wanted to do. She reported that the rest of the congregation seemed to be quite appreciative of his efforts. She has also had us in stitches describing the frequent rendition of a favorite duet by a couple of their ladies. It is entitled "Look Out Samson Delilah's Gonna Get You."

Dear Mother,

We heard comments that there was an interesting difference

between Christians and non-believers in their reactions to the earthquake. Our pastor's wife said that during the earthquake she looked up into the heavens thinking it was the end of time and the Lord was coming to get her. One of her neighbors said he looked at those cracks in the earth and thought the devil was coming to get him. I think Rodolph has a good sermon illustration in that.

Dear Mother,

We were the "padrinos" in yet another wedding and I wonder how it would compare to the last wedding you attended there in the States? We went out to Shiran and then on to Poroto, the town across the river that would compare to a county seat back home, I guess. Anyway, we went to the mayor's office where we were the witnesses for this little old couple who had decided to make it legal. They had 8 children and numerous grandchildren who were all there too. After the legalities, we all went back to their house and had a wedding lunch. They live in a dirt floor adobe house and we had a place of honor inside at the table. There were people everywhere and I much preferred outside in the open air, but this was their plan, so we did what was expected of us. The table was a rustic construction of unpainted planks and there were two benches on either side. I removed a cat from my place and sat down. There were other cats, dogs, and even a llama named "Juan" that roamed about freely.

We ate the traditional meal of goat (except this was made of sheep because it is cheaper), rice, and yuca, and it was okay. I ate an acceptable amount and was congratulating myself for doing so well. Then they came out with a huge bowl of the worst looking stuff I have ever seen and informed us this was the traditional wedding dish of "patazca." It was a stew of fuzzy looking gray meat and corn kernels floating in some kind of liquid. Those were the only two things I could identify and was scared to look more closely. We were informed that the meat was the sheep's stomach that was boiled with the other ingredients. I got helpful at that moment and served everyone else and managed to go unnoticed as not having had a helping.

There was a huge glass jar of 5 gallons or more of fruit juice on the end of our table. It had whole pieces of various kinds of fruits in it complete with their rinds and seeds, and looked extremely dirty and unappetizing. The worst thing about the drink, though, was that there was only one glass for all of us. Actually, there was one glass and one little plastic cup, and they would fill one of them and let someone drink and then fill it again for another. There was a lady with her little girl about 3 years old across the table from us and she kept asking for more fruit juice for the child. She finally apologized for her daughter drinking so much but explained that she had a fever and really needed liquids. I thought I should be helpful again and began to ladle the drink for everyone.

I wished I had never removed the cat from my place when I saw that Rodolph was feeding it. I wondered why he had suddenly become such a cat lover. We had both looked for the dogs, but they were having too good a time outside, I guess. We have discovered that these hungry dogs can put away a lot of food in record time if you can just slip it to them under the table. We both have become experts in this and usually check out the dogs before a meal of this kind. The party was still going on when we left and I would like to report that we survived and didn't even have a stomach problem as a wedding souvenir.

Dear Mother,

When you get your copy of the mission magazine be sure you look up the article about us, it will give you a laugh. The photographer doing the piece was really impressed with the procession he saw on the road to the airport. Every 5 years the patron saint of the fishing village is brought into the city to "visit" and then returned after a week's stay. To accompany this statue into Trujillo and then back to the church where it normally stays, they have elaborate parades that have hundreds of participants. There are doves that are let loose at intervals, marching bands, and many school children in different roles and costumes. Typical dances of all kind are performed, but one of the most impressive is done by the devil dancers. They wear bright clothes and headdresses with horns, and they have bells on their legs that jangle when they cavort about in what are rather grotesque antics that are considered the authentic movements of the devil, I suppose. The photographers took rolls of film of them alone. They were very intrigued with these characters. We were, too, because even though we had heard of them throughout the years, this was the first time we had actually seen the procession.

We introduced our visitors to as much of the work here as possible and to as many of our people as we could. We had no idea what type of article they would write, but it was a surprise to see the title that came out---"The Dixons of Peru-They Minister Where Devils Dance." I had to read it to make sure it was about us; I was glad to see they had included some of our pastors and other people in it. It gave us a chuckle to think of the impression the title must give when we saw those "devils" for the very first time along with the photographers. It WAS rather disconcerting, though, to see devils dancing along the same highway you travel to catch a jet plane out at the airport. It does something to your mind.

Dear Mother,

I don't know how many more weddings I can attend here and survive both physically and emotionally. I began playing for the 7 o'clock wedding at 7:30, and at 8:15 everybody began marching in, everybody that is, except the bride. I played for another 20 minutes while we ALL waited for the bride to arrive-- the groom, attendants, flower girls, and ring bearer, as well as the congregation. I played the wedding march complete with trumpets so many times I lost count, and then I resorted to hymns and anything else I could think of. Then the lights went out and I played by a candle and finally someone brought a lantern. The bride came and we got them married, but each wedding brings its new problems and adventures.

Oh yes, I meant to tell you. Remember the seminary students we are helping, but are making them work a little? I think it might be to our advantage to just give them the money and ask them to stay away. They have made so many mistakes in cutting down the wrong shrubbery and breaking things that we decided to just let them wash the car each week. They came and we gave them a bucket and detergent and the water hose and put them to work. They did a great job! They washed the car with the detergent and hosed it down very diligently both on the outside and on the INSIDE! We came out to take Amy to school and everything was soaking wet. We had to let it dry for days before we could use it, and even then when she put the seat belt across her it made a black mark on her clothes. I despair when I think of the future leaders of Peru. I guess I ought to just try to think of those boys' satisfaction in doing a really thorough job for us.

Rodolph and I have picked up a code word to say to each other which helps to console us after episodes like this. We don't remember which of the tire companies there in the States had the slogan "It's Time to Retire," but we refer to that phrase by saying, "Goodrich," and it reminds us that if things get to us too badly, it just might be that we are arriving at that age. It gives us a chuckle and no one else knows what we are talking about.

Dear Mother,

We were walking in the park this morning and saw a man stealing the fence posts. We stopped him and made him put them back. He told us he was getting them so they could cook their meals. I felt like telling him he could have them.

At the WMU meeting at the church this afternoon, we ladies played soccer. Yes, you read right. All of us old and over-weight ladies got out there on the church playing ground and ran around like children. Most of them were in dresses, but some of us had the advantage of long pants. There was a lot of breathless giggling and a steadily increasing number of shocked onlookers, but it was a unique experience that I am sure will be the topic of conversation for a long time to come, both by participants and spectators. And before you ask--no, I did not plan this, but I think maybe some of my unorthodox ideas are beginning to rub off on some of these ladies, here. They have finally learned they can be Christians and still laugh and enjoy themselves in wholesome and silly activities for recreation and relaxation.

NOTE: This was definitely an orchid to see them instigate something off-the-wall, yet healthy and free that would help them forget those hard lives that most of them have to endure, even for just a short time.

Dear Mother,

Amy and I were at church this afternoon and a lady was there with a baby carriage and said she needed a place to spend the night. We both wanted to bring her home with us, but the pastor wouldn't let us. The reason he gave us was that there are so many terrorists' tricks to get into homes now, that he felt like this might be one of them. He thought she was suspicious, and while he provided a place for her at church, he didn't think any of us should take her into our home. We had to trust him because he has a softer heart than any of us and always takes in strays, but he also has a pretty good intuition. Then, too, he usually has updated information about what is going on from his family, who are in the police department and military. Even so, we felt bad about leaving her there. I guess it is a good thing that we didn't see the baby.

We began a Bible study at our house and were so surprised at the number of our own neighbors who showed up to take part. Most of these are well-to-do residents who can afford to buy what they need, but very few of them have ever owned a Bible. We were thrilled to give them their very first personal Bible and most of them seemed thrilled to receive it. We had 19 present for this first meeting; one of them is the lady I walk with in the morning. What joy!

We had quite a bit of excitement at the beginning of the meeting, though; Rodolph went outside to let someone in at our gate and heard one of our neighbors scream. He ran to help her and scared off two men who were trying to steal her car as she was putting it into her yard. I asked him what he would have done if they had pulled a gun on him like they did her and he said he didn't stop to think, he just did it. My husband, the hero, I am proud of him!

Dear Mother,

I walked by the court house downtown and there was an old white haired lady asleep on the steps going up to the main entrance. Apparently she had been trying to sell little pastries because she still had the tray of cakes balanced precariously on her lap. She looked so tired and vulnerable that my heart went out to her. Just a few minutes later, a man walked by with a huge hog tied to the end of a rope and he sauntered along as if they were going for an afternoon stroll. There is no end to the sights one can see in the central part of Trujillo every single day.

Gladys's sister asked us to take her to our Medical Center down at Central Church to see if the dentist there could help her. Her brother advertises himself as a dentist because he has had a 6 months course of some kind and has borrowed some "tools" from a friend. He spends at least 6 months out of the year in the high mountains traveling around and "curing" people with a toothache. The rest of the time he does the same thing in Trujillo, but doesn't have as many patients here as up in the Andes. He not only has a practice here and there, he also has a family both here and there. He has two wives and children by both, and his sisters express concern for him because he has to work so hard to support two families! Can you believe that? Anyway, he tried to fix his sister's tooth, and she arrived at our house with her jaw all swollen up, infected, and in terrible pain. We took her to our dentist down at the church and the folks there took care of her.

We get so angry when we see ones like this unscrupulous renegade taking advantage of poor folks who don't know any better than to trust him. Stuff like this happens all the time all over the country, and this is one reason why our clinic has been so successful and popular. It is known that our doctors take a personal interest in their patients and ask only a small fee to help defray costs. There is no charge at all if the person cannot afford to pay. The clinic has been a blessing to many, both those receiving medical help and also those of our congregation who have found a place of service there.

That reminds me, we got a letter from Spencer saying he had gotten the prescribed braces put on his teeth and he gave a very descriptive report of what they felt like. He said, "My front teeth feel like they all want to occupy the same spot. I guess it is kind of like standing in a Peruvian bus." We got a real chuckle out of that because we have all had that experience of being on one of those buses where they try to put in more than it can hold. I still can't believe that group from Greenville did this for him, and I still don't know who they all are to thank them properly. We are grateful and humbled by it all, and I pray God will bless them as they have blessed us.

Oh yes, I was very upset for a couple of days because my clothes dryer stopped working when I had a lot of things to get ready for camp. Of course this kind of thing always happens when Rodolph is out of town, and I didn't know what to do. We always dry all we can outside on the clothesline, but we only have so much line space and it takes a long time for things to get dry that way in this misty weather we have been having. I finally broke down and asked a fellow missionary if he would just look at it and see what might have to be done. He was very kind and came right over. As he walked in the door of the laundry room, he exclaimed, "You have a rat in there! I can smell him." I told him we had never seen a rat out there and he said we were about to see one now. Sure enough, he opened the part behind the motor and there was a rat that had electrocuted itself by touching the wrong thing at the wrong time. I didn't understand what had happened or how it had happened and didn't want to know. I was just grateful for my missionary colleague that would come, know what to do, and do it even though it wasn't a pleasant job. (He accused Rodolph of leaving town to not have to attend to this.☺) This is what I mean by our missionary family.

Dear Mother,

　　We saw quite a sight on the way to church this Wednesday evening. You remember the little grassy median area on that main street out in front of the church? Well, as we arrived for services, we saw several cows tied to each tree all the way down the block. I thought I was seeing things. I could not believe they were letting the animals graze right there in the center of town, but then stranger things than that have happened. As we parked and began to ask about them, we were told that a terrible wreck had happened between a bus and a cattle truck. The truck had overturned and the poor animals were trapped--some were dangling and about to choke because they had been tied in. Witnesses to the accident ran to help and as they freed them they realized they had to do something with them to keep them from straying, so they tied them to the trees. They were still there because the owners hadn't come back from the hospital yet to claim them. It made an interesting scene and quite an unusual entrance to our church's main door. All during the service, we could hear the cows mooing and bellowing their distress at the situation.

Dear Mother,

　　We are always getting unusual and sometimes really strange requests for help, both financial and otherwise. The other day the young couple who let us use their home to start the church in Shiran asked for a loan to help them buy a cow that could provide milk for that community. It is hard to say no to someone like that, so we managed to scrape up enough to enable them to buy it. Imagine our surprise this Sunday morning when they arrived at our house with another request. They had bought the cow, but had no way to take it to their home out near the camp, and they wanted Rodolph to take it in his truck. I could almost see him

54

flinch as he thought about dirtying up his brand new prized possession that he had acquired only a couple of days ago, but he agreed and did it. The task made him late for church, but he felt like he had done a good deed.

NOTE: After this couple's grape crop came in, they came to our house with the "first fruits" and wanted us to have it as thanks for helping them. They also wanted to give us a tithe of their earnings and, of course, we told them to give it to the Lord, through the church.

The other request we had this week was to help the wife of one of our pastors to buy some teeth. She had some type of ailment that caused her to lose all of her teeth and she has not been able to chew or even talk well for such a long time. We were all worried about her, but to her credit, she has not missed much of the activities required of a pastor's wife even though she has suffered much pain and much embarrassment. We helped her all we could, too.

NOTE: After getting her new teeth, she came to see us, thanked us, and gave us the brightest smile you could imagine. That was payment enough.

Dear Mother,

One of our missionaries came in with a funny story of the latest wedding at which he officiated. He said he had the couple standing there in front of him reading them the vows, and he heard a baby crying somewhere in the congregation and felt a little commotion going on, but didn't think much about it because those sounds are always present in any meeting here. He said he looked down at his book to read another bit, and then looked up to see the bride calmly breast-feeding her baby. It is such a common thing here that I am sure no one but the missionary thought it was unusual, but he said he thought he may have just performed a one-of-a-kind wedding ceremony. He said he only sputtered a little and missed a few words, but went on as if it were the most normal thing in the world. We all got a chuckle out of hearing him tell it.

Oh yes, I meant to tell you before now about those "wonderful" birds that were given to us and have been such a headache to take care of. We had two of them, and finally, one of them died. Now while I didn't exactly delight in its death, I have to admit I wasn't too sad and had ideas of returning the one left to its owner. When I tried that approach, I found it was definitely the wrong thing to do. They not only wouldn't take it back, they gave us two more to keep it company so it wouldn't be lonely! The kids were delighted, of course. Sometimes I feel like I take several steps forward and many more backward.

We were invited this week to a meal and told we were having "cabrillo burgers" (goat burgers) since there was no beef available, due to the rationing all over the country. We found out it was a joke to cover up the fact that we were eating beef during a time when it is illegal to serve it. (The law applies to public places and not private homes, of course.) I was sort of disappointed; it may have been a new dish to vary our menu.

Dear Mother,

I never have my camera when I need it, but if I could take it with me at all times, I could have some priceless pictures of things that are transported on bicycles, motorcycles, trucks, and even very small cars. The things they cram into and onto a car would surely make "Ripley's Believe it or Not." I saw three people on a motorcycle carrying two double mattresses, I have seen 110 lb bags of rice and sugar being taken on a bicycle, and there are always huge market baskets balanced in front and back of several riders on both of these vehicles, as well as animals of all sorts that are live or otherwise.

One of the funniest of all we saw in Lima, coming in from the airport. There were two painters wearing caps alike and covered with paint; they had paint buckets over the handlebars of their bicycles and brushes in their pockets. This was nothing of which to comment, but they had a ladder that was at least 40 ft. long slung over their shoulders. The one in front was trying to maneuver around the corner in such a manner that the other painter following him could also round the corner without losing his hold on the ladder or falling off his bike. Their ladder needed a hinge in the middle because they finally had to stop and walk it around and remount the bicycles on the other side. They stopped traffic both ways while they did this, and although there were horns blowing on all sides, they went on their way completely unruffled it seemed. It was something like out of an old black and white silent movie comedy (except for the horns).

On our way to camp we are always seeing what looks like an enormous bush that is moving along the road. Upon closer inspection you can finally determine that there is a little burro under there that is completely covered with alfalfa or other types of hay, which is being transported from its growing place to its eating place. They only leave a small spot for its eyes so it can see where it is going.

The trucks and buses going up into the mountains (and also returning) are filled with incredible things crammed inside, perched on top, and hanging from the sides. There are bundles, boxes, bags, stalks of bananas, animals of all kinds, baskets of fruits and vegetables, pots and pans, and wares of all kinds to sell. They bring things down from the mountain to sell and take back up the things they buy with the money they earn. We have followed trucks and buses along the road and marveled at how so many people and animals could balance themselves on top and not fall off on the dangerous curves of those one lane roads, and also not get asphyxiated by the dense clouds of dust thrown up by every turn of the wheels, both their own wheels and those of everyone else passing. It all amazed me at first, but now it takes a really outlandish thing to get my attention. Actually, there are still enough of those around to make any day outstanding if one looks for it. Like I said, though, I only seem to see it when I don't have my camera for proof.

Dear Mother,

Amy and Pam (another MK) made cookies in my kitchen (using my stove and my ingredients) to earn money so they could produce a yearbook at school. It was a noble cause and I was glad to help, but I thought they were pushing it a little when they tried to sell the cookies to me, too!☺

We gave Luchito, Gladys' little brother, 15 soles. He bought an ice cream with 3 soles and spent 12 soles to buy 12 little chicks to take back up into the mountains and raise. He is a tiny thing and looks and acts like a little old man. He is so cute and we all love him and we feel so sorry for him now that he has lost his mother. We wonder what will happen to him up there in the mountains in such isolated conditions.

We were taking David those avocados that our caretaker had raised especially for him. They were huge, nearly the size of small watermelons. As we entered the airport security, they have a new x-ray screening machine through which we had to pass, and they stopped me to ask what that was in my luggage. They showed me and I had to laugh. On the screen it looked like a stereotyped cartoon picture of two bombs, complete with fuses where the stems were. I was afraid they would cause a problem, but the lady just laughed and said the security guards had a bet as to what they were. As it turned out, they were not afraid of bombs, but of someone taking out pottery from the tombs. They didn't even make me open it up to show them.

It surely has hurt to have to let our helper go after 7 years of having her here in the house with us. I thought we had really been able to reach her, but this boy friend she has recently acquired must be a really terrible person. We have lost so much money and so many personal things. Some things were valuable and some were of just sentimental value, and the loss of these hurt much more because they can't be replaced. So we finally had to face the fact that she was stealing us blind and we had to fire her. She denied it, but we had proof. I guess we should have called the police, but we just couldn't do that. We did make her leave right away, though. It has been especially hard on the kids; they loved her and don't understand how she could do a thing like this. I don't either. She even stole from the children and from some of our guests.

Dear Mother,

We had a father and son who came for baptism, and as you know, everyone is asked to give his testimony in front of the whole church body before the actual ordinance begins. Well, the father was rather long winded and the son, who is a young teenager, spoke right after his dad. He said, "Well, I was a sinner, but not as big a one as my dad, here." That was a bright moment in the service for a lot of us.

Dear Mother,

It seems the funniest things happen at the most solemn moments in a service. We were attending a baptism yesterday and during the pause between candidates entering and leaving the pool, a little girl asked her mother in a very loud voice, "Mommy, has he bathed you yet?"

Dear Mother,

We were downtown and saw an unusual sight. I guess it would be unusual for you back in the States, but nothing is unusual for us here now. Right in the middle of the sidewalk on one of the main streets, someone had spilled bright yellow paint. There was a whole pool of it, and there were bright yellow footprints in all sizes leading off in all directions. A little shoe shine boy was sitting there using his finger as a paint brush and giving his little stool a fresh coat of free paint. He finished the legs and then turned the seat upside down in it to coat it all at once. He seemed quite pleased with his good fortune because he flashed us a great big smile as we passed by, being very careful where we stepped.

Dear Mother,

Have we told you about Porfirio? He is one of Julio's projects. He is not a very young man, but has to have much care like a child because his brain has just been "fried" due to drinking so much alcohol over the years. He has taken a liking to Julio and the church and attends regularly. He seems to be harmless as to doing physical violence, but he can surely disrupt a worship service. He talks out loud and expresses his pleasure or displeasure in very descriptive terms, or just adds his own comments at will. Merry sang one morning and he sighed loudly and carried on about how pretty she is. One guy, who does not sing all that well, had a solo the other day, and when he finished Porfirio said in a falsetto voice that could be heard all over the church, "Ah, just like a little bird." That brought down the house because the man has such a coarse voice that the only bird he could bring to mind would be a buzzard or something equally as tuneful. The young people delight in him and wait to hear what else he might say to send them into gales of laughter. Every time he sees me he grabs my hand and kisses it and says, "I have so much respect." Then he bows and kisses it again. It is funny, but it gets a little old, too, and some people are getting a little tired of his capers. Julio, however, is adamant in trying to help him. That is what I mean about his being inclusive. He wants everyone to come to know the Lord regardless of who or what he is. You have to admire Julio even when you are aggravated with him.

Dear Mother,

Remember my telling you about Porfirio? Well, he did us all a big favor this week. For years now we have been fighting the battle with Julio over not serving the "hard stuff" for communion.

The very first time we had communion after Julio arrived I drank what I thought was the grape juice, and I am sure my eyes rolled around and my hair stood on end. It was my first taste of liquor. It had to be liquor and not wine (probably the Peruvian version of Stateside moonshine) because it was the nastiest stuff I have ever put into my mouth. I asked others, more knowledgeable than I, and they seemed to think the same. We questioned Julio and he said he was trying to be Biblical and using what the scriptures said. We told him the Bible also says they had unleavened bread and we had sweet rolls that were broken up, but that didn't count with him. It got so bad that when you entered the church on the day that we had communion, it smelled like a brewery. We finally decided to just not drink that awful stuff and would just leave ours in the cup. We noticed that many others were doing the same thing. This went on for a long, long time, but Julio would not give in.

Well, one day Porfirio's family came to Julio and told him that he was having a hard time keeping to his vow to not drink any more and the main reason was that when he came to church on those Sundays that we had communion, the smell of the "wine" set him off on a drinking spree again. Finally we had grounds to serve plain grape juice and Julio agreed because he didn't want to be a stumbling block for anyone. So now we have sweet rolls and grape juice and while that may not be "Biblical," either, I am sure we could have Inca Kola and cookies and that would be effective if it were done in the right spirit. We can get so caught up in the rituals and petty stuff that we can lose the real significance and, therefore, the blessing.

Dear Mother,
The men came back from the mountains with yet another funny story to share. They were having a communion service at the little church there that had a young lay pastor. He was not too experienced and was a little flustered with so many visitors and gringo missionaries. For one thing, they had only enough cups to serve about a third of the people there. They served the first third, and he spoke words fairly well suited to the occasion about doing this in the memory of Christ. They then served another third of the people, and he shortened his words considerably and seemed to stumble a little and struggle for something to say. By the time they

61

served the last third of the people he just lost it, raised his cup, and said, "Salud!"--which is "Your Health" or the equivalent of "Cheers" to the drinking population. It was really hard for our men to keep the somber reverence the service demands after that. Just picture this happening in our church back in the States.

Dear Mother,

We had a funny thing happen this week. The Baptist Convention for the whole country was held at our church and for the first time we had delegates from a little church newly organized over in the jungle. They not only were very uninformed as to the way of carrying on the business of a group like this, but they arrived in clothes most inappropriate for mixed company, and even though it is summer they were nearly freezing. There was some rapid scurrying around to find them something with which to cover themselves. They were also discouraged from hawking their wares of souvenir blow guns, beaded bracelets, necklaces, and feather headdresses to the delegates during the sessions. It was all done in innocence and the delegates were kind and patient with them. Their testimony was something that caught the attention of everyone; you could have heard a pin drop while they spoke. Some didn't speak Spanish very well and our national missionary interpreted for them in places. It was a sweet time to have them with us, and it brought home to many the plight of others and the missionary work that we all need to be doing.

(NOTE: I'll bet they could have brought some real orchids, but they surely qualified as one themselves.)

Dear Mother,

A seminary student came to see us last week and begged Rodolph to go up to the mountains and bring her mother back to the hospital. Rodolph asked Max to go with him and they set off with the student. They found the mother really sick but were able to get her in the car and started back. They got about half way down the mountain and the lady started to scream that she was dying and wanted to go back up the mountain and die in her own home. She appeared to be extremely ill, but the student said to not listen and to take her on to the hospital; that was her only chance. They didn't know exactly what they should do, but since it was two hours to Trujillo and two hours back up to where she lived and harder to go up than down, they came on. Thankfully, it was the right decision because the lady did get some good help at the hospital and is recovering now. Missionaries have to make some tough decisions at times and do some earnest praying in situations like that.

NOTE: This incident was the beginning of a new church. Upon her return to her home she let her house be used as a meeting place, and a group was formed that eventually became a strong church in that little village.

Dear Mother,

One of the stranger things we have encountered here as a Peruvian custom comes from the mountains and is practiced here during the time of "Carnaval" or what would correspond to Mardi Gras in the States. It is the "Palo Cilulo." In small villages the whole town participates, but in the city it is done by neighborhoods. The person in charge has to find a tree, which is not easy to come by here in the desert. Every now and then a live tree can be located nearby, but usually they have to bring one down from the mountains. Up there they can use a living one and not have to plant it in the community for the celebration. In town they dig a hole and set it up in a central location and they decorate it with all kinds of things. It depends on the person in charge. We have seen bottles of liquor, plastic dish pans, buckets, toys, food, cups, plates, toothbrushes, deodorant--anything that occurs to the imagination and is available and can be tied to a tree limb. These are not like our Christmas trees; these are not evergreen, but shade trees 20 to 30 ft. tall with sturdy spreading limbs on which they can tie these heavy things. Well, when the big day arrives, which is usually one of the last Sundays in Feb., all the people dance around the tree and everyone takes a chop at it with the hatchet (or axe) that is provided. They keep on going like this until the tree finally falls over and everyone runs to claim the gifts. The person whose blow caused the tree to topple is in charge of the fiesta for the next year. Many of the folks, especially in the mountains, wear colorful dress and it is very picturesque, but I don't exactly understand it. I don't guess I have to.

Another custom for the whole month of Feb. is throwing water. Anyone and everyone are targets and there are no exceptions. Water filled balloons are thrown on the streets at young and old and by young and old. Water is thrown into the windows of passing buses, taxis, private cars and trucks. It is a common sight to see someone nicely dressed and nicely soaked, and no one seems to think it is anything but what is to be expected in February. Some of the kids have gotten really mean and put other things into the balloons or buckets like shoe polish and paint and even worse, and this is condemned, but I find the whole custom hard to accept.

We were down town this past week and Rodolph was doused by a grown lady who threw a full bucket of water on him (dirty water at that). He was wearing his Sunday clothes and thankfully had taken off his coat, but his good pants were dry-cleanable only. (You notice I used past tense.) All the kids love this time, but it is the bane of people who have to leave home to go to work through all of this. I saw a group of people on a truck and they had several big barrels filled with water and were throwing it by the bucketful on everyone they passed. I guess if you live where water is scarce, it is a perverse sort of celebration to waste it!

Dear Mother,

Rodolph and one of our pastors went up to the mountains to hold a series of meetings in the town that is known as the "Capital of Carnival." They forgot that it was February and how every day of the entire month is celebrated big time there. They arrived and were parking the car when someone jerked the door open and put grease all over the pastor's face before he could react. Rodolph had his door locked and was saved. Apparently this is a common occurrence, and it is certainly a warning to not plan a visit to this place in February. It is bad enough here in Trujillo. We get wet on the trip to camp every week, going and coming, if we forget and leave our windows down. You are expected to take it in good humor, but it is hard sometimes. We always warn the kids that while it is okay to play with the ones who want to play, they are not to wet others who don't, and they are certainly not to harass innocent passersby.

Dear Mother,

Rodolph got back from the mountains yesterday and had quite some stories to tell. If I didn't know him so well, I would think he was making them up. This past week he was in a little village and they had nothing to eat but potato soup for the entire time. He said they had it for 3 meals a day and it was not the kind we are used to. They called it soup, but it was only potatoes boiled in water and served lukewarm with the liquid in which it was boiled. It was not only the best they had, it was ALL they had. On the day he left he saw a man walking in with a load of corn that he was bringing to trade for some potatoes, so he suspected the menu for the next week would be more varied--potatoes, corn, or potatoes and corn. Rodolph said he hated to eat the soup, not only because he was awfully tired of it, but he was also afraid he was taking food away from someone else who needed it more than he did. When I lament the fact that we don't have peanut butter, cereal, and many accustomed conveniences, etc. and I look around me at all we do have and see how some others have to live, I am startled that I could be that insensitive and indifferent.

Dear Mother,

I thought maybe we were through with those processions when we left Costa Rica, but this October we found out differently. The whole month of October is dedicated to "The Lord of the Miracles" and there are parades all over the city and in every part of Peru during this time. It got its start when there was an earthquake in Lima, I think, years ago. There were some people kneeling at a statue of what is called "The Dark Skinned Christ" when the quake struck, and all the walls came down in its vicinity except this particular one. A divine miracle was declared, and every October since then replicas of this statue are paraded through the streets, and all the people wear purple. The men wear purple ties or arm bands and the ladies wear purple sack-like dresses with a white cord at the waist. Some of them wear these dresses all month. It is considered to be a very sacred time by the devoted.

Rodolph tried to take a picture of the procession downtown in Trujillo and he climbed up on a wall to get a good shot. Some city official made him get down because he was higher than the statue and this is not permitted. It is puzzling to us to see such devotion during special times like this and the fervor with which they defend it, because we have not been able to see the evidence that they have a real knowledge of what they believe or why they believe it. Even worse is the failure to show in their daily lives that they are personally affected by their professed religious faith. It is something they are born with and they plan to leave this life with it intact, but apparently it doesn't have to interfere with anything in between except for a few fiesta days scattered here and there. There are some really good folks who are truly devoted and could certainly teach us all some things about sacrifice, but these, sadly, are not in the majority.

Dear Mother,

I know that if you are sharing the tales we send you about what goes on here, they must think I am making a lot of it up or you are misinterpreting it. I promise you I would not put anything into writing but the truth. (Now don't hold me down to not stretching a verbal tale or two!☺) The reason I say this, is that we still have things happen that make us say, "Where else but in Peru!" and everybody here understands what we mean.

For instance, we were traveling to Lima on the plane and were told after we had boarded and were buckled into our seats that this flight would go to the city north of us to refuel. (Lima is south.) We didn't understand that because there is a fueling station in our airport. There was nothing we could do about it, though, unless we chose to find a parachute and bail out, because we were in the air by the time the announcement was finished. We did land in Chiclayo and waited and waited and waited. They finally announced that the fuel tank there was locked up and the man who normally attended it had gone home for the night and he had the only key. They informed us that they had sent someone in a taxi to look for him and as soon as he arrived and they could fill the plane with the necessary fuel, we could be on our way. This took forever and many people were getting anxious because they had international flights to catch that night. When the plane revved up once again, they announced that since we were so late and there was room on the plane, they were going further on up north to a city near the Ecuadorian border and pick up the passengers there. After we were in that city for what seemed an interminable wait, the pilot began his next announcement and I held my breath, because if we went any further north, we would be out of the country! We finally headed south on what was now over a 2 hour trip to Lima. (It is 40 min. from Trujillo.) We arrived in Lima about 3 a.m. when we should have arrived in the early evening, allowing for some expected delays. Many passengers were stranded in the Lima airport. We were so grateful for the mission apartments when we finally got there. (I'm not so sure the housekeeper, who had to get up and let us in at that hour, was quite as happy as we were, though.)

Another thing that I am still thinking about is our prayer meeting the other day with a group of ladies from our church. One very faithful lady said she had a prayer request and she shared it with us. Mine wasn't the only head that snapped up when she told us, so I knew it wasn't my lack of Spanish that made me hear such an astonishing plea. She asked us all to pray with her that her lover would leave his wife and be faithful to her alone. She elaborated, while we were all stunned into silence, that he had promised and promised her to leave his wife and his family but just kept going back to them. She wanted us to pray that God would help him keep his word to her. I am not really sure what all was said right after that, but I can assure you the forthcoming prayer was not exactly as she requested. I admit that I did ask someone after it was all over if I had heard right and she confirmed that I did.

Then the other thing that got our attention was the new believer who was ready for baptism and refused to use the baptistery at the church. He said he might consider it if he could be first, but he really wanted to be baptized in a flowing stream. When questioned further about this curious statement, he explained that when his sins were washed away he really wanted them gone, and what's more, he was not about to step down into a pool which was filled with the sins that had been washed off of the others before him. Like I said before, "Where else but in Peru?"

Dear Mother,

Happy Mother's Day! I wish I could be there to spend it with you, or you could be here to spend it with me--just be together someway. If I didn't know you understand why we are here and support us in it, I don't think I could get through days like this.

There is another reason I wish I could be with my own mother on days like this. Although the men are very macho in this Latin culture it is really a matriarchal society; the women are who hold the family together and who are revered. Mother's Day is right up there with Christmas in importance and I guess some of it comes from the Catholic worship of Mary as the mother of Jesus. Anyway, there are always programs that sometimes last for hours with all the children saying poems with dramatic hand waving and little songs presented with kisses, etc. Many times we have a drama that is always about the sacrifices the mother makes for the good of her family. Usually they give out little bookmarks or other favors that the children have made and present them to each mother with a hug. Not only do the children and young people have to kiss and hug each mother, but the men do, too, and even all the mothers greet each other. "Feliz Dia de las Madres" (Happy Mothers' Day) is repeated each time. When you attend a church that has over 300 in attendance and everyone there has hugged and kissed you at least once, it begins to get a little old. I told Rodolph that my cheek felt sort of slimy after all those wet kisses. Our ladies love it, though, and look forward to it each year as do all the children and other church members--except me. I feel like the "Grinch" of Mother's Day. It is made worse because my birthday always falls so near the day if not right on it (as you very well know). If they don't think of it at the moment and give me two kisses, one for each day, they come back and greet me again. (Thankfully, we are not like Paraguay where they kiss you on both cheeks in greeting!☺)

Dear Mother,

We are still laughing about this trip. Rodolph and a pastor went up into the high Andes to be at a small church there. They arrived in the evening and Brother Juan, the lay pastor of the little group there, was to be their host. He lived right there at the church in very small quarters. He said he had a bed they could use because his wife was away visiting relatives. Rodolph assured him that he had brought his sleeping bag and was planning to use that. Rodolph pulled in 10 chairs from the church, put the seat parts together, and put his sleeping bag on them for a passable bed. The man said that was fine and the pastor could sleep with him in the one bed they had. This is no problem for Peruvians; they can put quite a few people in one bed and think nothing of it.

Well, they all managed to get to sleep and Rodolph was awakened about 3 a.m. with the pastor shaking him. When he could make out what he was saying, he realized the pastor was asking for the keys to the car. He wanted to go out there to sleep. When Rodolph asked him what was the problem, he said the lady of the house had just returned and got into bed with the two of them.   He decided it was time for him to find other accommodations. How we have teased him about this! The tales they tell about those mountain trips make us wonder if they are making them up, and then I realize it would be hard to make up some of those stories.

Dear Mother,

When Gladys' mother died all her family came down from the mountains and we got to meet them. I can't tell you how many they are, but the one who impressed us the most is her littlest brother, Luchito. He is only 6 years old and looks like a miniature of a little old mountain man with his big straw hat and adult-looking clothes. He has a round face, jet black unruly hair, and the almost slanted eyes of an Oriental, but has the red chapped cheeks of a high altitude mountain child. He is painfully shy but I made friends with him, and to help out the family I invited him to stay here with us during much of the preparations for the funeral. He seemed to like that idea and he and I got along really well. He asked to come and stay with us, and his family could not believe he would want to. I let him play with some old toys of our kids that I keep in a basket to help amuse visitors' children that invariably accompany their parents, but he was content to just be here it seemed.

When the time came for them to return to the mountains, I bought him a little truck in a box as a going away gift. He didn't respond much and I thought maybe he didn't like it, but they tell me it is his prize possession and he still keeps it in the box and won't let anyone touch it. I can still see that little round face with the shy smile and wonder what kind of life is in store for him.

Dear Mother,

Do you remember my telling you of my friend, Luchito? He is Gladys' little brother and stayed with us during the time of her mother's funeral. Well, he sent me a live turkey (a white one) down from the mountains for our Christmas. Gladys said he had raised it himself and wanted the Senora to have it. I was so humbled to think that little boy would want to do something like that for me! He is 8 years old now. Gladys has a picture of him and he looks just like he did to me. She says he is little for his age, even for a Peruvian. My only concern is what do I do with a live turkey? It is a long time until Christmas and it is too skinny to kill now. I will do what Amy says I do with everything else--send it out to camp.

Dear Mother,

Remember that white turkey that Luchito gave me? Well, I sent it out to camp to be included in the flock of the caretaker until Christmas. Guess what happened? Someone came in and stole one turkey--you guessed it--mine! It was the only white one, but the thief could have stolen any one of the dozen or more in the flock. I hate it, not because I am anxious to have turkey to eat, but because Luchito gave it to me. I hope we are still big buddies.

Dear Mother,

Do you remember the hard-working little lady who always helps us out at camp in the kitchen? Well, when we asked if she could help us this year, we were told she was too ill to do it. Upon further inquiry we discovered that their family is just about to starve to death. This economic crisis brought on by so much political upheaval has really taken its toll on many who were doing fairly well before. Her family is one of these, and they finally arrived at the point of not having enough food to keep them all going. We were told that this dear lady had been giving all her food to her grandchildren, and she, herself, was just not eating.

We decided that we could appeal to her to come out to camp by reminding her that there she would not be taking food off the table at home and would get her food free here and could take home leftovers on the weekend.

She came and, whereas before she had been a dynamo, she was like a zombie now! She could barely move and her eyes were completely lackluster with no expression whatsoever. Before she always had a smile, a pleasant greeting, and would hurry to do the necessary things in the kitchen or wherever something was needed. We were so worried about her, and each of us did what we could to make her life a little easier. We all tried to get her to eat and let her rest when she would. We noticed a little difference in her by the end of the week. The next week we seemed to see a little more life, and by the end of camp she had completely revived and was her old self with sparkling eyes and sweet nature. We were so grateful for her recovery. We truly believe when we found her she was near the end of her strength, and those 6 weeks at camp helped to save her life.

(NOTE: A special orchid in the bouquet)

Dear Mother,

I have a good philosophy of life passed on to us from our pastor's little girl in the hospital. Her nurse told us that she wanted to eat her fried chicken before her soup and was told the soup should be eaten first. Her reply was, "But what if there is an earthquake before I get to the chicken?" I think that will preach-- don't wait for the best part--do it first!

Dear Mother,

We have had crazy weather lately. Last night we attended an anniversary celebration for a church and it was cold and windy and actually rained. (A Trujillo rain-a foggy mist from the sea) We were outside and their cake almost melted. The only reason it didn't was that it was too hard!☺

Dear Mother,

When we got back to Peru after that first furlough, I mentioned that at functions in the USA when asked to put on typical dress, I represented Peru in a mountain Indian costume. The ladies at church nearly had a fit and wanted me to have an outfit like they use in the fiestas here in Trujillo. The mother of Merry's friend offered to make it for me. I supplied the money for the material and she did everything else. It is a beautiful thing and done in excellent taste with exquisite work. It had to be hard work, too, because the skirt has 16 yards of material in it and is so heavy that I can hardly stand up when I put it on. The pleats are so deep that the skirt is wide enough to hold up both sides of it at once (up above your head) and the front and back stay straight down in place. My dress is aqua, Merry's is yellow, and Amy has a pink one. The fellows all have ponchos and big straw hats so now we can really be a "spectacle!" (Not that we aren't anyway!☺)

We are having a two week school for our mountain people here at Central Church. They are coming from all over and will sleep and eat at the church and learn how to better serve in the little churches and annexes way back up in the hills. I am to teach the music courses. It should be interesting; I may learn more than I teach.

Dear Mother,

The WMU ladies came for the usual Mothers' Day party; it seems to have become a tradition now. Even though there was a bus strike, 45 of them showed up. I used every chair and stool and all my plates, etc. Joy and Amy had some good games for them and I had a gift for each lady so we could play the "White Elephant" game. Some of the gifts were nice and some were not; some were used and some were new. At first they wouldn't take anyone else's gift (I don't know if they were just being polite or just wanted to open a new gift), and then Maria took one away from another lady and the fun began. One lady lost a good gift and when she opened the 2nd one, she put it into her purse and said, "No one gets this one!"--and no one did! Right at the last another lady tried to take a gift away and this lady put it down inside her dress at the neckline and said, "NO!" I laughed, thinking she was joking, but we found out soon that she wasn't. It was a riot! Some of them brought me the typical birthday gifts (hand-made items, as well as china swans, and red plastic roses). The WMU gave me a set of wooden spoons, so I had a birthday party, too, even though I hadn't planned it that way. It was a good day, but I am just as glad that I don't have to do it again this week!

Oh yes, a cute thing happened at the meeting. A lady, who is really tiny like Mrs. Davalos, had her little girl with her, who was about 3 years old. The little girl looked at me and then looked at her mother and asked, "Why is she (me) a big Mami and you are a little Mami?" Her mother told her that if she would eat her vegetables she would grow big like me. What a role model I am!

Dear Family,

Our roses have been spectacular recently. I am looking at our orange rose bush and it has 9 buds and two full blown blossoms on it and the fragrance is wonderful. The poinsettias are really showing off, also; we have two big trees and two small ones in the back and one with double blossoms in front. The flame trees are beginning to bloom, too. All of these, plus good weather, really help to lift one's spirit.

It looks like I will have quite a birthday celebration this year--the WMU is planning a "surprise" party for me. Several have told me to be sure and be there today for something special. Also, my Sunday School class informed me they are going to give me a luncheon at MY house on my birthday. I appreciate their love and recognize the sweetness in their plans, but I would much prefer skipping this kind of thing. They get such joy out of doing it, though, that I can't deny them that just because it makes me uncomfortable.

Dear Mother,

At times it seems one takes a step forward and then a couple backward. The other day Julio had a good talk on being reverent during the worship service and especially during the more solemn ordinances like baptism. He directed this rather pointedly toward our young people who have had the bad habit of finding something to laugh about in every service and can become quite distracting at times. We thought Julio had really made some progress and all of us were more aware of the real meaning of worship. Well this past Sunday we had baptism again and things were going much better. There was no snickering among the young people as we had heard in times past.

One of the young men, who is bright enough I guess, but who is just a little different and sort of stands out in a crowd, was to be baptized this morning. All the candidates came down to be immersed in the baptismal waters in their white robes and a solemn look of piety. This young man was no exception, he descended into the water in his long white robe and his hands folded like a monk, but wearing the brightest yellow plastic swim goggles I have ever seen! I, myself, had to gasp a little and I thought we would have to get oxygen for some of the young people who were suffocating with laughter. He had not done this for comic effect; he was worried about his eyes and this was his solution to the problem. I can't imagine what the reaction to this would have been without the preceding talks on reverence from Julio. For one of the very rare times in his lifetime, I think even Julio was without words.

Dear Mother,

Every once in a while I have a brilliant idea. I have been helping the ladies out at church learn how to cook economical, nourishing dishes and desserts that don't need an oven. I taught some sewing techniques until I learned they knew much more about that than I do. They do gorgeous knitting and crocheted pieces. I have tried to capitalize on this and also find other craft things that they could make and use in the house or sell. These are hard to find because they have to be made from things in nature or very inexpensive materials. They don't have the throw-away things we have in the USA like egg cartons, etc.; even jars are hard to come by. I have seen them carry their cooking oil home in a plastic bag from the market. (I have seen them lose it when it got punctured, too.) I invited a nurse in to talk to them about health, and I have tried to do very practical things to help them improve their quality of life.

I was at a loss as to what I could do next, when this brilliant idea came to me--I would ask THEM what they would like to have! With all the poverty there and the great need on all sides, their answer stunned me. They wanted to learn how to arrange flowers. Remember now, most of these ladies live in a straw shack or adobe hut, and it just never occurred to me that this would be an option. There are very few flowers in this area; most of it is just sand that blows dust over everything. Neither electricity nor water reach here yet, but we keep hoping the city will soon be able to meet the needs out here. Every once in awhile we have paid for a truck load of water to come and fill up our baptistery so our people can come with buckets and dip out what they need instead of buying it from the truck that periodically goes by.

Well, anyway, I got busy and found that the daughter of the Methodist missionaries here had recently taken a class of flower arranging from a local florist. I invited her to come and show us some of what she had learned. Up to this point when we had flowers in church, they were a handful someone had bought in the market and crammed (just as they got them) into the first available container, or they were garish plastic flowers, and even some crocheted ones. I wondered if this could ever be a practical thing for our ladies. (I still didn't get the message.)

Mary (the MK) came and she brought a simple, cheap container and began to show them what she had learned. She made the most beautiful arrangement you have ever seen from 3 calla lilies she had picked growing wild at the edge of the watering canal a few blocks away. She put a couple of big leaves behind them and cut them with scissors to the shape she wanted. It was a creation that anyone would have been proud to show off anywhere. She talked to them as she worked about how one didn't have to have a lot of things to make something beautiful, and then she let them try to make one with more materials that she had brought with her. They were thrilled and when they thanked Mary, they said they had always wanted to know how to do this so they could put something nice in the church each Sunday. Thankfully, flowers are cheap in the market and I hope to see that they have some to carry on this project if it gets to where they can't do it themselves.

NOTE: To this day when you go into this particular church, the flowers are usually made into an arrangement and not just crammed into whatever is available. I wish they grew orchids in the desert for these ladies, but they, themselves, have been lovely "orchids" for me.

Dear Mother,

I was in the central market today and met Marta who had been in the classes of crafts that I taught out at church. One of the sessions was about making necklaces out of different materials like seeds, triangles cut from paper, macaroni, etc. Marta was standing there with both arms extended and hanging from each arm was about 30 or more necklaces that she had made and was offering to the shoppers passing by. She gave me a big smile, showing a major portion of her gold teeth (a status symbol here), and said business was booming! I didn't know whether to be appalled, tickled, or really proud of her.

Marta gave me a gift the other day. We had learned to make latch-hook rugs with left over yarn. Well, Marta made me one that almost defies description. It is about 15 inches wide and about 20 inches long, and made of the most vivid psychedelic colors you could imagine. The background is bright orange, and most of the lettering is a royal blue, but it has a few letters in brilliant red and green (where apparently she gave out of blue yarn). She scattered in yellow and pink as border trimming and finished it off with a fringe. It reads in Spanish, "A remembrance for May." I looked at it for a lengthy space of time trying to think of proper words to respond to such a labor of love, and finally told her how much I appreciated it. I then asked what it was. She looked at me as if she couldn't believe I didn't know and said, "Why Hermana May, it is to protect your knees, so you won't get calluses on them when you pray." What a lesson Marta taught me!

NOTE: Marta's prayer rug has become a standard item to take with me on speaking trips, not only to remind me of the importance of prayer in my own life, but to nudge others a little about theirs, too.

PERSONALITIES

Dear Mother,

Let me tell you about the new pastor we have at Central Church, he is a real fireball! He arrived in town and went immediately down to the Governor's office and then on to see the mayor and informed them both that he was here to "tell the people of Trujillo about Jesus." They have two children and one is only two months older than Spencer, so we have a lot in common. His wife's name is Maria and she is of German descent and has light hair and fair complexion, so she, too, stands out in the crowd. They seem really dedicated and we are so happy to have them.

Julio was born over in the Peruvian jungle. As a young man he studied to be a Catholic priest, but he gave that up and went to Lima to "seek his fortune" like many of the youth here. He became an alcoholic and went from bad to worse. He was in a bar one evening and heard a radio program put on by one of our Baptist groups and went to the address that was given. He found a group of young people there who invited him to join them and also to go to a retreat that they were having at a camp out at a beach nearby. He went, accepted the Lord, felt called to the ministry, and traveled to Argentina to study at the seminary there. We did not have a seminary in Peru at that time. In Argentina he met and married Maria, and he served as a pastor there for several years. He was invited here to speak in the Campaign of the Americas, and during this time Rodolph spoke to him about the possibility of returning to his native land to become our pastor. They have given up much to do this. They had a good pastorate there and Maria is leaving all her family, so it had to be a hard decision. Like I said, we have a lot in common.

They are here, and they are already working under a lot of stress. Their living space is certainly less than adequate, but they have not complained. The conditions after the earthquake leave people unable to help them like they would have normally. Julio has hit the ground running and it looks like he has no intention of stopping. He has already made himself, and what he stands for, known around the area. He really seems to be the man for whom we have prayed and for whom we will continue to pray. I believe he will really make a difference in this place.

Dear Family,

Central Church continues to grow and Julio is still one of the main reasons that it does. His sermons are still original and most of the time hold your attention (and if not his sermon, the fact that he is likely to call on you when you least expect it). One of his illustrations recently gave us a few chuckles; he went into great detail to describe the fire fighting equipment of the USA, complete with accompanying dramatization. He said they put on suits that the fire can't penetrate and they also have special gloves and helmets. (This, too, is with detailed description.) Then they get into a little elevator that shoots them up and up to the place where people are screaming for help, in terror for their lives! (He gets very melodramatic at this part!) They are way up in a hotel room 40 stories high and the flames are leaping all around, and when the firemen get there the people say, "My, what a nice suit that is, why don't the flames burn it up? What is it made of? What kind of elevator is that? How can it come so high?" He then drove home his point by saying you don't need to have all your questions answered before getting saved. Get saved first and then take time to get the questions answered. It is a pretty good commentary on the state of many of our theological quandaries going around today, I guess. He is just so funny doing this. Everybody laughs at him, but you remember it.

Dear Family,

Rodolph says the work at the camp is progressing and I take him at his word, but it is hard for me to see it as he does. Julio continues to be a source of joy and frustration in equal proportions at times. Sun. night we went to the house of a family of whom the father (90 years old) had died. One son is a loyal member of our church and the other is not only a non-participant, but very antagonistic. On one occasion, he threw Julio out of his house and tried to hit him. Well, the body was lying in state in this brother's house and we had to go there to speak to the family members who belong to our church. We felt a little uncomfortable going there, but Julio not only got permission for a service but during the service told all the family gathered around, "Those of us who believe in the Lord will see your father in Heaven because he is there and we will go there, too---but the rest of you had better tell him 'adios' right now because this is the last time you will ever see him!" Like I say, he keeps us caught between frustration and laughter, but everyone has to give him credit for being spiritually courageous.

Dear Mother,

You remember that expensive material we brought back for Julio to have a suit made? Well, we gave it to him and paid the tailor to make it for him as a birthday present. He informed us that he thought it was a little too conservative, but the underside is somewhat brighter, so they decided to make it that way. He has had his suit made wrong side outwards, but it is his to do with as he pleases, and this is typically Julio. What a character!

Dear Mother,

I think I will start a journal just to keep a record of Julio's illustrations and comments. He is a riot most of the time, but he can also be very profound with stories that get right to the point of what he wants the people to understand. Some things he has lifted right out of books and some he has heard others say, and he never gives credit, but he is probably more effective than the original by the way he adapts it to himself and the situation. At a funeral the other day he said, "Death is like the eggshell after the bird has flown."

Since he is from the jungle he tells one about the missionaries and the monkeys there. He said the missionaries were traveling in the jungle and had to spend the night. The jungle is hot in the day but cool at night, so they built a fire to cook and to warm themselves. They sat around the fire and backed up to it to warm that part of their anatomy (this was complete with a dramatization more like antics than acting). The monkeys were in the trees round about watching. (He then gives a history of monkey life, how they like to mimic what they see, etc.) The missionaries left and the monkeys came down out of the trees to do what they had seen the humans do. They put sticks in a pile, they backed up to it to warm, and they acted like they were cooking. There was just one problem; there was no fire, no flames, and there was no warmth. They were just playacting and pretending; it was not real. He then got down to business and told us that many churches were like that nowadays. He said there is no real spirit, no warmth, and the members are just playing "church" and it is not a real experience.

It was a great illustration, it was funny, it had a great point, and it was one we all remembered. That is the weakness of Julio's stories; because we remember, there is almost an audible groan when he tells them over and over. It has gotten to the place that we can repeat them with him almost verbatim, and as good as they are, they can only survive so many times of repetition.

Julio started off his sermon yesterday with, "Why do people call you Christian? Is it because they don't know you?" In the course of this sermon he told about a couple who gave a gift in memory of their son who had died and another couple who gave a gift for their son who is alive. This was done in gratitude for what they have, which is all the more reason to give. He is very good in the application of his sermons to everyday life here. He was talking to the youth about peer pressure and their daily life style, and he said that you don't go down into the well to get a friend out who has fallen into that pit. You pull him out from above. One of the young people asked him what to do if that friend were unconscious and he replied immediately, "You could go get him out, but you don't have to stay there."

Julio has given us some great illustrations to use in our talks back home; one is about missions. He demonstrates this with an alforja, which is sort of like a saddle bag, but is put over the shoulder to carry things. It is made of woven material with two pockets, one on each end. When you put on a poncho it is hard to use a back pack, and so the men carry whatever they need in these two pouches, one hanging in front and the other in back. Julio says if you get this thing unbalanced, it will fall off, and so it is with us and life, and the church and missions. We have to balance something for us with something for others, or it fails.

I not only plan to use Julio's stories, but I plan to use him as an example when I have an opportunity to speak back home. He is certainly preaching a sermon with his missionary heart, enthusiasm, courage, untiring work, vision, and inclusive concern. We are so fortunate to have him working here with us in the area. We can always count on his help in any situation or emergency, and he is always a source of amusement and conversation even when it gets him and us in trouble. He is such a dreamer that he is rarely practical, but he gets things done. Much of what he does is fairly unorthodox, but when you see the success he has, it is hard to condemn him.

Central Church has standing room only and the highest attendance we have had was over 500 one Sunday! (When he came we had 32 active members.) He is instrumental in the planting of other churches all around, too; his efforts have not been just in Central. He is truly amazing and puts us all to shame with his dedication and unselfish devotion. We can call on him for anything and he has never turned us down.

Dear Mother,

Guess what? Julio has a car! We don't know whether to just be glad for him or to be scared. I can't even imagine all he can get into now with "wheels." He has needed transportation, of course, and Rodolph is probably happier than Julio because he won't have to chauffeur him around now. He had been trying to get a car for a long time and was finally able to obtain it through some help from outside the country. In typical "Julio style," he has already announced that it is the Lord's car and he will use it as such.

NOTE: Through the years, Julio's car has been a source of blessing, laughter, trouble, and disbelief. It has been stolen so many times that we have lost count. At one time he put a chain on the steering wheel with a padlock to help thwart theft. Not long after that we received a call from Julio to ask Rodolph if we had a hacksaw that he could borrow because he had lost his car keys. We wondered how he was going to start his car with a hacksaw until we realized he needed something to cut the chain. It was stripped during one robbery and he refurbished it as best he could-- he had an old sofa in the back to replace that seat for a long period of time. He was generous to a fault in offering rides and even offered to lend the car to one of our volunteers if he needed transportation. Many times when Rodolph was away in our car he would insist on giving our family a lift home after church, and I have prayed all the way out to our house each and every time he did! I never said much to the children about it but I think they felt the same, because I noticed on those occasions when we didn't have our car they would run to find a taxi for us as soon as the service ended, not even stopping to talk with their friends.

Dear Mother,

You know what a dreamer Julio is, well, he has always wanted our church to start a medical clinic, and bless my soul if he hasn't done just that. To our way of thinking it was an impossible feat, but he has carried it off! Since the church has built them a parsonage, he has convinced everyone that the quarters where they lived there at the church could be used to better advantage as a clinic than as Sunday School rooms. He has managed to secure volunteer doctors to attend the patients and is trying to collect equipment now. It is on the way.

NOTE: The clinic has grown through the years and is now a recognized and accredited asset to and for the community. It has an operating room and 6 beds and other equipment that churches in the USA have helped us to acquire and put to use. We have had volunteer teams and individuals from the USA who came to aid our doctors and patients. We now have doctors and nurses from Central Church who have finished their studies and are helping full time and part time. Julio's dream has come true.

Dear Mother,

Yesterday at business meeting down at the church we had a young man who is known to be affiliated with the communist party here. He comes off and on to the church and tries to cause problems when he is here. He kept on interrupting and trying to cause confusion in the meeting and Julio finally told him that we didn't need what he was doing. He went on to say that everyone knew him as being a communist and we didn't want that in our church and he asked some of the men to escort him out. I was astounded that he could be so bold and wondered if we would have repercussions from this. After the young man was ushered out, the meeting went on as if this was the normal way of things. It is amazing to see how Julio can denounce something like that, but in the same meeting give an impassioned plea to help the drug addicts he had met. He wanted the church to help this group of unfortunate souls. He proposed letting them sleep in the church and eat there to try to help them. There was a lot of opposition to this idea, but he managed to get enough support to give it a try.

NOTE: This was one of Julio's failures. He opened the doors of the church to any and all drug addicts and we were overrun with a crowd of really unruly men who wrecked the church property. It eventually became a den of thieves and a hideout for crooks. We had to get police help to finally get them all out. Julio was still lamenting their fate even when he knew they had to go.

Dear Mother,

   You'll never guess what we found when we got back here; Julio has a TV program! Now this is not just any kind of TV program--it is unique--it is very ecumenical. While we were on furlough, Julio managed somehow to convince the TV station here to let him have a program about who the Baptists are. After an airing or two, he got a call from a Catholic priest who challenged him on some of his statements. Now remember Julio had studied for the priesthood as a young man, so he not only invited the priest to bring on all the questions he might have, but invited him to do so on the air. As the program progressed with the two of them participating, the priest realized he was coming out a rather poor second, and so he suggested that they speak of what they had in common and invite phone calls from viewers. They did this for awhile and they discovered they had a lot in common. The priest professed to be a born again believer, and it went from there.

   The TV station finally said they could not give more free time and it would have to be paid for if they wanted to continue. No one else in this world could have come up with the solution that Julio did. He got a business man in town that he knew well to sponsor them, and so we returned to find our Baptist pastor with a Catholic priest on a TV program that was paid for by a Jewish business man! You just can't get much more ecumenical than that. After the program finally finished we had exchange programs with the priest, and he preached in our church with nuns attending. Julio preached in the Catholic church, and our seminary choir was invited to sing. It is a new day.

Dear Mother,

   If you run across anyone who doesn't believe the Lord takes a hand in our daily life, tell them this---Rodolph was on his way to the seminary to teach his class and there are any number of routes he could have taken, but he was traveling by the church where Julio's family lives. As he passed by he saw Julio running out front with his little girl in his arms and trying to flag down a car. Rodolph stopped and took them to the hospital. "Olguita," their smallest child, was having convulsions and seemed to not be breathing. They managed to get her to a doctor in time to get the proper attention. They seem to think there is some kind of lesion on her brain that is causing this and we are getting her to Lima for the specialized care that she can receive there. Please remember them all; this is devastating for them. They are a close family but have no other relatives here. Maria's are all in Argentina, so we, as fellow Christians, have to be the family on which they can rely. The missionaries are all rallying around to help where they can.

Dear Mother,

We had seminary graduation last night and something really sweet and sort of comical occurred. We have had the first national missionary in our area trying to get his seminary degree by taking the extension courses offered. He has been studying for a number of years and hitches a ride into town when he can to update his curriculum, and also to talk with Rodolph about the progress of our work up there in the mountains. He is a very humble young man who lives way back up in the Andes and has traveled all through those rugged peaks by foot or on horseback. Where there are roads he has the option of hitching a ride if he can, or use whatever other transportation that might be available. We understand he still has to walk a lot. In spite of the hardship this has to be on him, he has managed to start 23 churches in just a few years time! We are so proud of him.

(NOTE: In later years this first missionary was given a motorcycle to help him in his travels and our second missionary was offered one, also. This second one declined the offer of a motorcycle, but respectfully requested a mule; because in his words, "Only a mule could get to the places I have to go." The convention bought him a mule which changed the policies of the transportation committee somewhat---like reimbursement for gasoline, etc.☺)

Our seminary rector, in an effort to instill a little dignity in the ceremony, decreed that all the graduating students would wear a tie and coat for the services. There was not as much grumbling as I thought, because many of them did not own a dress suit or even a sport coat. They were all over town borrowing from family and friends and returned with some interesting combinations of colors and fits, but everyone was finally outfitted in the proper dress code and proud of it. I have to admit they really did look nice, even though some hands were invisible due to overly long sleeves and some coats didn't button due to an over-sized middle in an under-sized jacket. They were ready to graduate in style!

Then here comes our missionary who had just finished up his last courses and was ready to join the group of graduates. This poor man had one possession of apparel of which he felt inordinately proud, and that was a pair of white sneakers that someone had given him for his long walks in the hills. (Most of the inhabitants up there wear those rubber tire sandals that I told you about.) These were the nicest thing he had to wear and he came to the service wearing his mountain clothes and those shoes. Now, while it was no problem at all to him, the other students felt he must be dressed like they were, and you have never seen such scrambling around to find something suitable. (another pun ☺!) When they all went up on the platform to receive their diplomas, they looked so elegant and dignified and proud. Our missionary was right there among them with a much too big coat and shirt, much too short pants, and bright white tennis shoes. The students had taken care of him the best they could, but he refused to put on other shoes. He sort of stood out in the crowd, but then he does stand out in a crowd for the wonderful work he has done and the humble spirit in which it has been done. These are times when I realize how much love the Lord has given me for these our people here, and I am so proud to be a part of it.

Dear Mother,

We met one of our young pastors who worried me by what I considered a rather bitter and cynical attitude for one who is so young and even of more concern, to be in the ministry. I asked someone about him and heard the sad story of his life. He was married to a very beautiful and charming young lady and they both were in the seminary together. They had two little daughters and were a very sweet and loving family with so much talent and potential. The smallest one had to have a simple surgery there in Lima, and through an error of the attending physician, she was given too much anesthesia and died. This was a very heavy burden for a young couple trying to prepare themselves for the Lord's work, but there was more to come.

The young man had been asked to preach a revival in another town and went ahead of time to be in on the preparations for it, and the wife and other little girl were to come on later. They traveled by bus to meet him, and on the way the bus had a terrible wreck and both the mother and child were killed. So here was a young man trying to follow what he thought was the will of the Lord in training and preparing himself at some great sacrifice to preach, and having his entire family wiped out like this in a short space of time. What could one expect of him? I am astonished that he is still able to function and serve as a pastor, much less have a pleasing personality.

NOTE: I am glad to report that some years later, this young man found another beautiful and talented young lady a few years his junior. She is a fine Christian from a faithful Christian family. When she graduated from the university, they got married and soon had two daughters, both of whom are also very talented and beautiful. They came to Trujillo where he began to teach in the seminary and then eventually became the rector of it.

I think all Peruvian men want a son and this one talked a lot about having one. He even said he would shave off his mustache if his next child would be a boy. The baby was born and was a boy, but lived only one day. This was more sadness than I thought one person should have to bear. I am happy to report, though, that soon after that they did have that boy that he wanted so badly, and he is a fine handsome one, of whom they are so very proud. His dad was so happy when this son made his profession of faith out at the camp with our group one summer.

This family has been a great addition to the work in Peru. I give tribute to one who did not give up his faith even during some very dark days when I am sure he might have been tempted to do so. It was another lesson to me in how wrong I can be when I jump to a conclusion and criticize and even judge, without knowing all the facts.

Dear Mother,

The typical mountain dress (which many still use here in town) always gets my attention. The men's outfit is sort of nondescript, with whatever kind of pants and shirt hidden under a big poncho. The ladies always wear big, full skirts and blouses and usually have their babies tied to their backs. What they both always wear is a huge hat and rubber tire sandals called "yankis." The shoes are made from a piece of old car tire cut to the size of the foot and the inner tube from the tire is used to make straps that hold it on. One of the missionaries down south said that after a meeting in his house, his living room floor looked like motorcycle races had been held there.

NOTE: It was a delight to visit with this missionary couple; they could always make you laugh. I remember one meeting of our mission when the matter under discussion was changing the name of the "Institute" to "Seminary," and the participants were getting a little emotional over it. As feelings began to flare, this missionary offered the suggestion that we call it a "Semitute." Several of us doubled over with laughter, and it helped to defuse what could have become an explosive issue. They could see the humor in any situation, and it helped us all to remember that the ability to take ourselves lightly would be a great defense for those many tough times ahead that we would undoubtedly encounter.

This family had their share of suffering too. The father was diagnosed with a brain tumor in Peru and went to the USA where the diagnosis was confirmed and plans made to operate as soon as possible. The surgery was postponed for a few days until the doctor could return from a trip.

We were home on furlough during that time and kept up with them. I was speaking around the state in WMU meetings and I asked everyone to please pray for this missionary to come through the surgery and have a good prognosis after that. The day of the surgery arrived and we called that evening to ask the wife how he was. She replied, "Why he is just fine." We thought that was wonderful and told her so, but then we asked about what all the surgeons had to do and what they had found. She said, "They found nothing, they didn't operate, and there is no sign of the tumor now!" We hardly knew how to respond. During the few days they had to wait on the doctor to return, the tumor had disappeared. There was no medical explanation; it was just gone! The diagnosis originated in Peru, but he had to go through all the examinations over again here in the states. They arrived at the same diagnosis after a whole battery of the latest tests available in Atlanta. We were flabbergasted!

What I would like to know is--why was I? Why would I, a missionary colleague, ask people to pray for a successful operation and never once ask them to ask God to just heal him? The Bible verse that speaks of, "Ye of little faith," has taken on a new meaning for me.

Dear Mother,

There is a young seminary student who comes to our house quite often and we enjoy having him. He is quite debonair, a handsome young man with black curly hair and a flashing smile. He is "Mr. Personality" in the flesh and the kids really like him. He takes up time with them and plays the guitar and so, of course, David thinks he is great. He also plays a Peruvian flute and is quite good at it. I love having him in my music programs. Sometimes he comes to visit on a borrowed motorcycle and this is the icing on the cake. The girls in the churches think he is wonderful and they all vie for his attention. I don't flatter myself as to the reason he visits us so often--he loves to eat. All the students know that there is usually something they can find to eat here and are welcome. (So far, they have been good about it and have not worn out their welcome.)

His name is Javico, and he told us that he had been on drugs and was living in a compound in Ecuador in the most awful of circumstances. Like the prodigal son, he decided to return to his home in Lima where his family was rather prominent. He was walking the streets there one evening when he came upon a group of young people playing their guitars and singing on the corner near one of our churches. He approached and questioned them about what they were doing. They befriended him and invited him to go to the church with them. He became a Christian and felt the call to preach and came to our seminary. Javico is a curious mixture of sophistication, simplicity, sincerity, seriousness, fun, friendliness, and love of his fellow man and God.

To show you what he is like, David told us this story that he heard about him. He was walking down the street playing his flute when a beggar stopped him and asked for a hand-out. Javico said he didn't have any money, but he could tell him of something that was better than money and proceeded to witness to him. The man said that was easy for him to talk about God's love because he had good clothes and all. The beggar pointed to Javico's new Adidas and said, "Just look at those fancy shoes." Javico immediately took off his tennis shoes, gave them to the man, and walked back to the seminary barefooted, playing his flute all the way.

Dear Mother,

How do you like the little crocheted baby bibs I sent? Aren't they exquisite? I got Mrs. Davalos to make them for me and I always know I can count on her to do the most beautiful work. I am so glad when I can give her something to do for pay because they really do need the money. She will do anything in the world to help us in any way with or without pay. She and her family are amazing and are ones we rely on for so many things in our work here.

Mrs. Davalos was abandoned by an alcoholic husband years ago leaving her with 7 children to raise by herself. She has been faithful to our Lord and the church through all the years that we have known her. She, herself, is talented, but those 7 kids are really blessed with so many gifts. There are 4 girls and 3 boys and all of them are good looking, with pleasing personalities. They are all musical and have been in my choirs through the years, and several of them play musical instruments really well. Her son, Lucho, is the one for whom we brought back a flute this past furlough and he taught himself to play it and does really well. They are all talented in drama, art, sports, and are just really sharp individuals in general. They have been our counselors out at camp for years and we know we can always depend on them to not only do what we ask, but come up with some new and original ideas to help out in the planning of events.

They live in a rather bad part of town, known to be where much crime takes place. When I first saw their home I was depressed because it was just an adobe structure with dirt floors, and while it was very clean, it was dark and damp. I couldn't imagine a family like that coming from quarters like that. As the years have gone by and all of the children have reached college age, they have managed to score high enough on the tests to get into the national university, and 3 of the girls have studied to become nurses. The national universities here are free and the students are accepted on the basis of a test given each year. Those who qualify have their names published in the paper, and that is how one finds out if he will go to college or not. There is always much anguish or celebration after the publication of the names of those that made it.

Mrs. Davalos has volunteered to be our main cook at camp and has served faithfully throughout the years. There are some years when we have had money left over and have divided it among the cooks, but there have been many when the work was done without any pay at all. The work was done just the same and with the same sweet spirit. It is backbreaking labor, but those cooks put us to shame with their cheerfulness as they work those long hours to give the children the best they can from what we can provide. Sometimes it seems they produce a banquet from very little and I am sure it seems like that to some of those kids who have so little back in their homes. I remember being concerned because we serve only the traditional oatmeal drink, bread, butter, and jam for breakfast every morning, and one of the mothers told me that her child was so impressed because we not only had bread, but had butter and jam for it!

Just recently Mrs. Davalos and her friend, Hilda, another of our cooks, have started helping me with the buying and this has lifted a tremendous load. That is a pun, because I have been lifting market baskets until I feel like my arms are being pulled from the sockets. To have someone else take over some of that is a great physical relief, as well as a time saver. I still have to plan and buy a great part of it, but the strenuous task of buying vegetables and fruits every week is going more and more to them. I feel I can trust them, and it is an added help for all of us to let them make the necessary changes in the menus on the spot, if they find the needed ingredients are not available (which happens quite often). We have worked together long enough to know what is suitable and what we can afford. Also, this is training for when we can no longer be here; they know how to plan a menu ahead of time and carry it out according to plan. They have always been good cooks and have taught me many new dishes and things I needed to know about the food here. They have been invaluable in helping us find economical ways to make things stretch to feed a multitude. However, I have insisted on planning some basic menus and sticking to them, and not just getting up and wondering what we will cook today for 150 kids. It has been exciting, a most enjoyable experience, and a labor of love to get to work with our cooks during summer camps.

Rodolph's birthday always comes during camp time every year and he knows they are not going to let it go by unnoticed. Usually it is during the week that the smallest children attend, and the cooks and counselors plan a big celebration at night with a cake and balloons and games, etc. It is more to be endured than enjoyed, but they get so much pleasure in doing it that we can't forbid it. They play jokes and giggle and sing and make silly hats in craft time to use that night. The cooks always make an enormous cake that is decorated in what has to be the most original designs ever concocted for something that could be eaten. Each year they have tried to outdo the year before. We try to limit what they can do, but they bring from home and spend out of their own pockets if we say the camp can't afford extras.

NOTE: One year all the cooks dressed up like clowns and sang as they brought in the cake. It was adorable, but I thought it was a little too much at the time. I have heard them talk about it for years afterwards, though, and I realized that these occasions were more for them than for honoring Rodolph. They love a party and while Rodolph had to suffer through it, we allowed it to continue. Actually, I am convinced it would have continued whether we allowed it or not, because, of course, each year it was a "surprise!"

There is a tradition here of serenading you at midnight on the eve of your birthday. I know we are supposed to try to adjust to the way of life and the customs practiced in our adopted country, but this is one that is really hard to like. Imagine getting to camp after a hard day of inscribing 150 kids and bringing them out on the bus--you have them fed and settled for the night, get to bed and to a most welcome sleep, and then you are awakened by guitars and singing at your door. You are in your night clothes, you are dead tired, and the last thing you want is to open that door and let in a group of people who have brought you cake and jello and the ever present purple corn drink to enjoy at that hour. The festivities can last from an hour to forever; they love to sing and celebrate and have so little opportunity to do it. All kinds of emotions go through you at a time like this; I know everyone wants to be appreciated, but I, myself, would much prefer being appreciated at another hour during the day. It seems the more fuss you make over their not doing it, the more it brings it on, so we have found the only way to avoid it is to not be at home for your birthday and announce that fact publicly. I have to admit I have been guilty of announcing a trip during the time of my birthday when I knew we had not planned to travel! Poor Rodolph, they get him at camp each year.

NOTE: On our trip back to Peru in 2001, we visited with Mrs. Davalos. She and Hilda had cooked a wonderful meal for us. All her children came and we visited with them and our parrot, Chuckles, which we had given them when we left. The beautiful part to see now is that their house is all fixed up to be a very nice middle-class dwelling. They have the interior and exterior all very presentable and equipped. Three of the girls are nurses and one is the head of the public health system in our state. Another is a nurse in an international health organization. Her second daughter has graduated as a chemical engineer as has her oldest son, who has been working for a mining company. Another son is an accountant and the third was still going to school.

How's that for a good report of how the Lord blesses His faithful servants? Our hearts are thrilled to be able to see their enjoyment of some material things after so many lean years. They are still fun to be with and still laughing and playing their guitars and serenading. On the night before Rodolph's birthday just a few weeks before I wrote this (Jan. 2005), the phone rang and it was from Peru. He answered it and motioned to me to get on the phone, too. This I did just in time to hear guitars and the familiar singing of that birthday song; the Davalos family had gathered around the phone there to wish him the usual birthday greeting. I was just grateful that they did it around 9:30 p.m. instead of midnight!

MISSION FAMILY

Dear Mother,

The Charlie Brown School has been such a blessing as have been all those who have come to teach our children there. I remember the education of the children being one of my worst fears about becoming a foreign missionary, and they are all doing so well. Now that we have a building for our school, it has become the center for many of our mission activities and social events, too. We had our Halloween party there this year that included all the Trujillo mission station. As you know, the kids make their own costumes and require everyone else to do the same, and through the years we have had some really hilarious times just seeing the original outfits of our colleagues. (I think our outfits have given them a smile or two, also.) This year Spencer decided to go as a robot and he labored so hard on his costume. He worked and worked and got all dressed up to leave and as we started out, he realized he could not bend enough to get into the car. His siblings offered many very helpful suggestions like having him run along beside the car, but we finally had to help him dismantle and put it on again at the school. We discovered there are many lessons to be learned in preparing a costume.

Dear Mother,

We have found that doing simple things together help keep up our spirits, so we plan different activities like birthday parties to include all the station. Sometimes we have a program or play games or just eat and talk. We heard Gloria say that she had never been surprised by a party planned for her birthday. She said she always knew before hand and didn't think it would be possible to surprise her. So--we gave her a very quietly planned birthday party a full month before the date of her birthday. I can report that she was very surprised!

Another of our ladies here always says she can't stand the color purple and everyone teases her about it. So--we gave her a "purple birthday party," and everything that could possibly take on color was tinted some shade of that special hue. We had purple decorations, gift wrapping, and refreshments, and everyone who had something purple they could wear, did just that. The kids especially got a big kick out of it. The birthday girl expressed the expected disgust, but was a good sport and we all had a great time. If it weren't for things like this, life here would be so much harder. These times of fellowship give us a family feeling and it is especially good for the children to feel they are a part of an extended family with uncles and aunts like these.

Dear Mother,

We hardly know what we can do these days to protect ourselves from robbery or bodily harm from both terrorists and plain old garden variety crooks. During the session of the mission meeting here some of the families went to see the tourist attractions, and while they were out at Chan Chan they were robbed. Two men came riding up on a motorcycle with a machine gun and took their money and jewelry; they were so frightened. This is a common occurrence now.

Also, two of our families were planning to fly to Lima, but changed their minds at the last minute and went down in cars. This is very dangerous now because cars are stopped on the highway in that lonely desert, and we all tried to discourage them. They made it fine without any trouble, but the plane they were to have taken was hi-jacked by a man that they thought was a terrorist. He had a gun and grenades and held the passengers hostage for a long time on the ground in Lima. As it turned out, he was a mental case and the episode ended in a shoot-out in which he was killed and several passengers injured. If it is necessary to travel, one hardly knows what to choose.

Dear Mother,

　　We had a wonderful trip to the jungle to visit some of our missionary colleagues and see their work and the scenery there. They were very gracious to us and showed us a very good time and taught us quite a few things about another completely different way of life. We boarded a thatched-roof boat for a trip down the river to a native village, visited the Wycliff compound nearby, and just enjoyed being with them and seeing how they survive in these surroundings. They had a real menagerie of pets. One was a monkey that sat up in the tree right above where we ate on the porch and chattered at us the whole time. They named him Zacheo (for the little man who perched in the tree to see Jesus go by) and then had to change the name to Zachea when they discovered their monkey was female. ("a" is feminine, "o" is masculine) We loved to watch the antics of Zachea. They also had another pet that didn't appeal to me as much--a boa constrictor several feet long. If you like snakes (which I don't) I guess it was a pretty one. Their son loved to play with it and would let it wrap itself around him; one time I saw him let it go up under his shirt and come out the sleeve. He would lie there in the grass and let it slither all over him and laugh at our discomfort. Our kids all thought it was really "cool," and before they could ask, I said, "No, we will not be getting a snake." I can just see you, Mama, if we were to come home bringing a boa in a basket to keep in your house!☺

Dear Mother,

　　I have something to add to that story of the boa we met in the jungle. The owner brought it to mission meeting and had most of the children mesmerized each day by letting it slither round and about and carrying it over his shoulder and around his body. The family was leaving for furlough and they were planning to take it with them back to the USA. The mother had some trepidation about it, but the rest of the family were all excited about carrying home such an exotic pet. The report we get from their trip was that they carried it as hand luggage, in a basket of dirty clothes onto the airplane. They were getting ready to land in Miami when the mother said she just had a bad feeling about someone checking that basket in customs and getting the scare of their lives, so the son went to the bathroom on the plane, took the boa out, and wrapped it around his waist. He put on his windbreaker and kept his hands in the pockets holding the boa in place like that. Now what are the odds that something like that would work? Well, it did. And what are the odds that the customs officials would pick that very basket to check? Well, they did. Can you imagine the face of that customs official if he had run his hands down inside that basket and picked up that boa? I love missionaries and mission life; they are many things, but never boring.

Dear Mother,

A missionary lady spoke to us today and told us that she had been in an elevator recently when its cable broke. Her room was very high up in the building and it could have broken with her in it all the way up there, but it happened on the first floor. She said she wanted us to know that this happened on her birthday, and she knew her name was on the "Prayer Calendar" that day and people were praying for her. She said she felt that the elevator was on the first floor because of those prayers.

NOTE: Our convention publishes a list of missionaries' birthdays and asks that this be used to have a day of special prayer for each one. Many missionaries say they feel empowered on their special day knowing so many are remembering them and lifting them up.

Dear Mother,

I have something to tell you that you probably are not going to like to hear. Merry came home from school announcing that she has lice! I was horrified! I rushed to the pharmacy and asked if there was some kind of remedy for this and explained how embarrassed I was. The druggist informed me that he usually keeps a stock of a very good medicine that will take care of the problem quickly, but he was completely sold out right now. It seems that all of the children in the schools and in our whole neighborhood must have lice, not that this is any consolation. He assured me that no one here thinks any more of having lice than someone in the States would think of having dandruff.

I agonized over what to do and then I found out that several of the other missionary kids were infected, also. The mother of one of them called me and said she knew how to take care of it, so to just send Merry down to their house and she would treat her daughter and Merry at the same time. She had been here longer than we had and knew a lot about the culture and all, so I had confidence in her. She did give both of the girls a treatment that completely cured them of their cases of lice.

NOTE: In fact, I don't think Merry ever had another problem after that. One day I asked this missionary mom what she had used to do such a good job, and she told me the story. Since there was no medicine in the pharmacy, she went to the hardware store and told the clerk there that she had a tiny, delicate doggie that had a problem with lice and asked what could she use to get rid of them. The clerk told her to use DDT, and so she bought some of the powdered kind and combed it all through our girls' hair. She let it stay awhile and then washed it out. Merry had told me that this "aunt" had put something white in her hair and it smelled bad and made her dark brown hair gray. She said it didn't show too badly in her friend's hair because she is a blonde. I couldn't believe my ears, it is a wonder it didn't do permanent damage to both of them. (Actually, maybe that accounts for some of Merry's erratic behavior, huh?☺)

Dear Mother,

We want you to remember Ken Bowie in your prayers. He and a volunteer from the USA had a bad accident on the way back to Cajamarca from Lima. He went to sleep and drove over an embankment. He had been sick and taking medicine and left Lima at 4 a.m. and was driving straight through on what should have been a 2 day trip. They are in the clinic here. Ken has a dislocated shoulder, broken rib, and a badly cut eye. The volunteer, who is 60 years old, has 3 fractured vertebras. They are both in a lot of pain, but we hope they are going to be okay. The car was a total loss. Everything in it and on it was stolen before anyone of us could get to it. They were very fortunate that they fell only about 20 feet because the road climbs steeply up and up after that point, and any further along, the fall would have been so great that they would have had little chance of surviving.

There is a good chance that both men will be recuperating at our house after they are released from the hospital and until they can travel.

(NOTE: They did.)

Dear Mother,

We have wonderful news! You know how worried we have been because the volunteer teacher we had just couldn't seem to adapt here and had to leave. Since then, nothing has seemed to work out for the schooling needs of the children. (By the way, the missionary who recommended this teacher said she would never recommend anyone again for anything, "not even the Apostle Paul for a tent meeting!"☺) Well, the Lord has provided yet another miracle in the form of Mrs. Lillie Westmoreland who has offered to come and teach this year. She is a retired educator of sterling quality and we could not ask for better. We just can't believe she would volunteer to do something like this. God is good and so is she!

NOTE: Mrs. Lillie stayed a whole school term in Trujillo during the worst hot weather we have ever had and the floods that it brought on. She was a real trouper through it all and taught our kids not only the subject matter, but helped them develop study habits that they have maintained on through life. In our opinion she saved their education, and she certainly blessed all our lives. How do you thank someone for something like that? I do not have the words so I can only call her an exquisite "orchid," and hope she understands that I mean it as one of the highest compliments I can pay.

Dear Mother,

Your smallest grandchild got the bright idea that she would like to paint that playhouse that Rodolph made for our kids when we first moved here. It was a real work of art that he made from our packing crates, and it has seen quite a bit of use and wear throughout the years. We thought that painting it was a pretty good idea and gave permission, but she decided to invite the other MKs over to help her. Before we knew it, there were a bunch of little ones out there with brushes, blue and white paint, and really going at it. I am glad we checked with their parents beforehand because when I looked out the next time, they had painted not only the little house in a most unique way, but also both dogs, the patio, Amy's toys, their hair, the eye glasses of one child, and, of course, their clothes. It was rather hard to distinguish the original color of what they were wearing! I was really shocked at how fast they managed to do all this and dreaded having their parents see them. Thankfully, when the parents arrived to pick them up they thought it was funny and only laughed. I laughed, too, in relief.

Dear Family,

Things were so bad for our people this Christmas that we missionaries decided to make up a basket of staple foods, the makings for that traditional chocolate, and a paneton for each pastor's family. We suspect that this may be the only holiday food some of them have. We let our children buy little gifts for each of their children, and we plan to provide transportation out to camp and lunch, so we can all have a day of rest and relaxation together.

NOTE: This became a tradition for us and the highlight of our missionary families' Christmas each year since then.

Dear Mother,

We do have fun with the other missionaries here in the station. When birthday time comes around, we usually give a party that includes everyone, but the party we gave this year was special and has a little history behind it. At Christmas one year, as a joke, someone gave Max a really ugly tie and we all got a laugh out of it. Well, the next year he got another one just like it. He was told that everyone had noticed that he had not worn that first tie so they felt sure something had happened to it and he would surely want it to be replaced. Do you remember that on furlough we sent him a clown tie and put another missionary's return address on it? Well, that added to the fun because he was sure that the other missionary had sent it. Then also during furlough time, we collected hundreds of old ties to bring back to do craft work, and so we got the idea this year at his birthday time to let each of the missionaries here give him one of the worst looking ties we could find in all those cast-off ties from the USA . They wrapped them in beautiful gift boxes of all shapes, sizes and descriptions. It looked like he had made a real haul this birthday. (They had legitimate presents for him, too, hidden away.) Imagine his look as he opened ugly tie after uglier tie! We all laughed until I am sure any onlookers thought the missionary family had been into the wrong kind of spirits.

NOTE: Max got the last laugh, though, because for my birthday later on, he gave me two sofa pillows--made from the ugliest of all the ties! It was a cherished gift that I kept on the little sofa out at camp until we left. (Not very pretty, but cherished!)

Dear Mother,

Rodolph got back from his trip to Cajamarca with the other men from our mission. They say those mountain towns up there are unbelievably beautiful, but also unbelievably primitive. The highest mountains in Peru are almost 23,000 feet high and while our men were only up to about 14,000 feet, some of them could feel the effects of the altitude. Many people suffer from soroche (altitude sickness). I usually have a headache for awhile after arriving, but it goes away the next day. Some people cannot take it at all and have to get back to sea level as soon as possible.

The men had their meeting and then visited around in the area. They came upon some type of religious parade with very primitive, home-made musical instruments being used. The musicians were all quite drunk and hardly knew where they were staggering, and when these gringos offered them money for their instruments, they gladly accepted. Imagine my surprise to see our guys coming down the steps of the airplane with these! I couldn't believe what all they had in their hands. The first one had something like a bathroom plunger over his shoulder, but its handle extended nearly 10 ft. back over the shoulders of the next two men behind him. I thought I was seeing things. This is a clarin. It is a long hollow tube made out of a tree limb with that plunger-like thing attached to one end. It sounds like the mating call of a bull moose when you can finally get a note out of it, but it is one of the standard requirements for a mountain band. They also had a flute (which was a hollowed limb) and a drum (which was a tree trunk that had been hollowed out and had goat hide stretched over it). The drum was played with a stick broken off of a tree. Some of the "high class" musicians up there actually have guitars, harps, and pan pipes. All of these are hand-made and some are quite good. I was so glad that the clarin did not belong to Rodolph. (He had a drum and flute.)

Dear Mother,

Wait until you see us get off that plane! We will be the snazziest missionaries anyone ever saw coming home for their first furlough! We were pretty threadbare and so I found some material and had a dress made for both Merry and me, and then I found some more material at the pants factory that our Swiss friend runs here in town. We have a fine tailor in our church, who is also a personal friend, and he has made Rodolph a sport coat and pants. He suggested that there was enough cloth to make an outfit for

David, also, and we thought that was great. Then he said that there was still a little left over, and it was enough to make a tiny coat for Spencer. I can't decide if we will get attention like an Easter parade or a circus parade! The coats are a dark green plaid and the pants are gray. He suggested a suit with short pants for Spencer, but also that he make 2 pairs of pants for him just in case (since he is still in diapers). He was so excited over doing it and said he had never made a coat that tiny before. He has shown it to so many people that I told him I was going to charge him for advertisement. He didn't want to charge us anything for all that work, but of course we did pay him something. It wasn't anything like what it was worth. We have some really good friends here.

NOTE: One of the comical things about going home for furlough and returning was the interest in clothes. As the four year term went along we wore the same clothes over and over, and unless they got torn, stained, or we outgrew them, there was never a thought of how they looked. They were washed again and again in very harsh laundry detergent, bar soap, and bleach (even when the tag said "dry clean only"). I would look at the missionaries returning from furlough and think they were certainly spending a lot on being stylish, but then when we would return from furlough, I would look at the other missionaries and think how dowdy they looked in their worn and faded clothes. Later into the term those same clothes looked perfectly fine, just as they did before we left. When we would go home to the USA for furlough we would buy up quantities of clothes and other things that were hard to find in Peru. To this day I find it hard to pass a sale of deodorant without buying a couple dozen to stock up for future use (or anything else on sale for that matter). I still buy at the grocery store with the thought of the multitude of visitors we used to have, and I only realize what I have done when I have to give away or throw out much of it. I can't cook for just the two of us to save my life!

Another interesting thing is that when all our family get together for a holiday or anything that lets us eat together, they want to eat what we ate in Peru. That is understandable, but the funny thing is that while much of what we cooked there was authentic Peruvian food, we had to make up substitutes for many of the Stateside foods that we wanted as a part of our daily diet. Now that we are living in the good old USA and can buy the original thing, our kids want those things that we made up as substitutes. For instance, we had to substitute the Peruvian polenta for anything that required corn meal. It was what we used for corn bread or grits for us Southerners. I used it for turkey dressing, and now I have to search the stores and find something like polenta to use in our Thanksgiving dinner. (I discovered golden grits can be substituted for polenta which was substituted originally for corn meal.) I am constantly trying to get the right kind of peppers to make the Peruvian meals and keep on trying substitutes I find here to make it taste authentic for them. What a turnabout! Whereas in Peru a special gift for someone would have been a jar of peanut butter or dill pickles, here it would be an Inca Kola or a jar of aji molido. When one finds a Hispanic store or something Peruvian on TV or the internet, the word is passed around.

I constantly complained of what I couldn't buy in Peru while living there, and here I speak all the time about the fact that I miss the Peruvian food and that we had a better diet there than here. At least after proper cleaning, it was usually a healthier diet. If you could see the writer of these words, you would understand that the lack of food has not been one of the areas in which she has suffered.

Dear Mother,
One of our missionaries who teaches English here told this one as the truth and I don't doubt it. He related that one of his students said she could understand about powdered milk, powdered eggs, powdered sugar, baking powder, etc., but had a big question about baby powder? ☺

Dear Mother,
You know we have been trying to get rid of those puppies

that our dachshund, Lucy, had? Well, a missionary family in Lima said they would take one of them and Rodolph had to travel this week for a meeting there, so he decided to take the little black one on the plane with him. We were not up on the rules for taking animals, but it is a short trip and we didn't want to have the trouble and expense of buying a carrier, so Rodolph just put her in a box with holes in it and boarded the plane like usual. (We figured if those people from the jungle can carry all those things like chickens, etc., surely they would be understanding of just a little puppy!) He said he got along fine and no one even noticed the box at his feet until they started to serve the sandwiches. The puppy started to whine when she smelled the food, and people were beginning to give him some strange looks. He saved his sandwich so that every time a stewardess would come near, he could slip a small piece of ham and cheese through one of the holes, and the puppy would eat and be quiet. He said he hoped the sandwich would hold out until they arrived in Lima and it did, thankfully, so we are one puppy less. I hope we can find homes for the others.

Dear Mother,

There are times when I wonder if my children will ever grow up! We have enjoyed having David back for this visit so much, but he does the craziest things! He was asked to help with the smaller children during mission meeting, and when we looked out the window we saw them all covered with mud from head to foot. I couldn't imagine how they could get that dirty until I heard that your grandson had made a mud hole and hidden a "treasure" in it and invited them to find it. I was very relieved to see their parents laugh at them and not be horrified. Also, there was a discussion between two groups of parents as to whether it was too cold to go swimming and it was becoming quite an issue as to whether some should be allowed to go if all couldn't. Dave was asked to be the life guard and he appeared in red long johns with his swimming trunks put on over them. He said he didn't want to take sides, but wanted to be ready for whatever was asked of him.

It helped to defuse the situation somewhat.

There was another happening that really got our attention, also. One of our missionaries brought fireworks to celebrate the 4th of July and they were all Peruvian products. These are not known to be very reliable so I chose a vantage point to watch from the corner of a building, and I was teased about my timidity. Everyone else was standing on the cement drive that goes down into the soccer field (it makes a sort of natural grandstand) and they were viewing the proceedings from there. It went fairly well for a few minutes and then things began getting out of control; the rockets changed direction and began coming right at the group of spectators. There were missionaries running and jumping and dodging and diving and had it not been so dangerous, it would have made a hilarious cartoon! What a miracle that no one got hurt! I have to admit, though, we shall remember the excitement of this Independence Day celebration for a long time to come!

Dear Mother,

I hope you had a happy Easter and could celebrate it with the family. The mission here in Trujillo has become our extended family, and whereas they could never replace you and our other blood kin, we all find we really depend on each other in that role of sharing both our joys and sorrows. The fellowship we have here has meant so much, and the support of one another, both in our work and personally, has made the rough places bearable. When there has been a problem, we have known we could call on them to help us physically or emotionally.

This past Easter Sunday we decided to have our own sunrise service because the churches here have not latched on to that gringo tradition of ours, (yet☺). You know how I have been carrying on about how hard things are for us all right now, so we decided it would do everyone good to celebrate Easter in a way to which we are all accustomed. We met at our house early and I had breakfast for everyone. We asked one of the missionaries to bring a devotional in English and we sang our traditional hymns. This missionary brought just the right message for us all at this time. He said it was not original with him, but perfect for our time and situation. He described the anguish of Christ's followers on the day of His death, but talked about the fact that this was Friday and "Sunday is a comin'." He applied this to the tough times we are experiencing and admonished us to not give up hope and remember God's promises for tomorrow. We all thought it was very timely and it really spoke to us to keep things in perspective, stay strong, and wait for the triumphs in God's time. I have heard more than one missionary refer to it and say, "Remember this is Friday." It has sort of become a rallying cry for us during these tough times.

MISSIONARY LIFE

Dear Mother,

So many people there at home ask us what we do as missionaries. They want to know how we decide to go about our work, etc. Rodolph says he thinks that so many times his day is determined by whoever rings the gate bell first in the morning! We have a parade of folks each day who come asking for help.

One man came with the most pitiful story of how he had come to Trujillo looking for work and had found none and only wanted enough money and food to get back home. He seemed very sincere; he said he was a member of one of our churches in Lima and he mentioned names of pastors that we knew, so we ran around getting him what he needed. Rodolph gave him a new shirt (his was ragged and dirty), and I fed him and went the "second mile" by putting together a package of food to last him on his journey. We sent him on his way with enough money to get him there and some to spare. We felt like we had done a really good thing. In a few minutes the girl who was house-sitting for the Methodist missionaries who live nearby, called us and asked us if we knew a young man who was a member of their church and down on his luck. He knew their pastors etc., and she repeated the exact same story he had given us. We told her to tell him to wait right there, and the Dixons would be there shortly to see about his needs. We went immediately, but he had gone. She said as soon as she mentioned our names he remembered he had business elsewhere. He had really done his homework for such a small amount of larceny.

We never throw food away. Not a crumb or drop is wasted. We buy more bread than we need in the mornings and we have regulars who stop by to get it. Some are a little more particular than others. There is a sweet little lady who will never ask for anything, but she goes through the garbage when it is put out each day. She is embarrassed if you offer her anything, but she always checks the trash when she thinks no one is looking and takes away in her basket or sack anything that might possibly be usable. (The family accuses me of "gift-wrapping" some of our leftovers for her.☺)

Then there is the little old man who arrives periodically. He has on clothes that are patched so many times and so dirty that a forensic scientist could not tell what was the original material that started out his attire. His hair is long and gray and matted and he has on an old half-rotted-away straw hat that thankfully covers up most of it. His face is dark and weathered and he has one tooth left in front. He shuffles along slowly supporting himself with a gnarled stick worn smooth with years of use. In spite of this description, he has a certain air of dignity about him. He and I formed a rather odd friendship based on his asking for bread and my giving it to him, and sort of treating him like an invited guest. It gave me a laugh yesterday when he arrived for his handout and I was not here. The girls gave him some bread and he was highly indignant to be treated like a common beggar. He informed them that the Senora always gave him hot coffee with his bread and he expected that when he came. They were furious at his audacity, but it tickled me; there is just something appealing in the spunk of such an old man in such dire circumstances.

There was one other rather noteworthy beggar at our gate, or maybe I should call him a "demander" instead of a "beggar." This rough looking young man told me he was recently in prison and I didn't ask how he got out! He said he was asking for help and he was trying that first before robbing what he needed. He certainly looked like he could make good on his threat, and while I did not at all approve of his approach, I must admit it got results.

Dear Mother,

Knowing how you don't care for live birds, I think you might appreciate this story more than most. As I have told you I have had laryngitis for nearly 6 weeks and while I seem to have gotten over the worst of the cold that started it, I just can't seem to get my voice back. It is really hard to teach and especially lead the choir at the seminary and church.

Well, yesterday at church the very poorest lady who attends came up to us. Now this lady has absolutely nothing in the way of material wealth. She lives in a dirt floor shack, has practically no teeth left, and her non-descript clothes are very worn but clean. She is very faithful to attend every church service; she not only is always there, but is always very friendly and cheerful. Every now and then she has given us eggs, usually 2 or 3 at the time telling us on each occasion that she has raised her hens in her own backyard so these are special. As I was saying, yesterday she approached us as we were getting into our car and said she had something for me, and she thrust a huge squawking chicken right into my arms. Now, to tell you the truth, I don't much like live chickens, either, and here I was in my Sunday finery clutching that big loud dirty bird like it was the most precious thing on earth, and frankly, it WAS pretty special at that moment. It was even more so when she explained that she wanted me to have that so I could get some nourishment into my body and get well. I pictured all we have each day and all she lacks each day, and I looked at Rodolph and said, "We can't take this from her." He said, "We can't NOT take this gift in the spirit it was given." I gave that thing to Rodolph as soon as I decently could and since he is an old farm boy he didn't mind, even with his good suit on. As you can imagine, we will find some discreet way to make this up to her in the future so it won't be such a big loss. The Christian love and generosity of our "hermanos" (brothers and sisters) here is always overwhelming!

(NOTE: Who would have ever thought a chicken could be called an orchid?)

Dear Mother,

There is an interesting phenomenon here--almost everyone calls me "little sister." This is from young and old alike and I am a head taller than most any man in the church except Rodolph. Since it obviously is not physical size nor a matter of age, I choose to think it is a term of endearment. (I hope I am right!)

Dear Mother,

We had a cute thing happen this past week. It seems that our Peruvian brothers are getting smarter all the time. One of the single ladies that teaches kindergarten at the Heraldo Church came up to us at camp and began by telling us they wanted us to be the "padrinos" (godfathers or sponsors) for their "graduation" in Dec. Rodolph had done this once and had given each child a New Testament. She said that one of the parents thought it would be a good idea to have that "nice man" back again. While we were both thinking of how to say a polite but firm "NO," she went on to say that they had decided to invite us and would it be okay if they named their class after our first grandchild. You should have seen Rodolph putting on the brakes and breaking out into a big smile and accepting! So, the name of this year's 5-year-old graduation class will be "Nicolas DeBord Dixon." How about that?

Dear Mother,

Just out of curiosity I decided to keep a register of the overnight guests we have had here and I counted them up today. From Jan. 26th to June 6th, we have had 78. Now remember, many of these stayed over a week and some were just for the night. Some were families and some were singles. Some were people we knew and some were not. All had meals here plus many more who ate but didn't spend the night. We have not had a single day without house guests during this time. Thankfully we love having company and most of them have been a joy to have. It is a little strain on the budget sometimes, though.

Dear Mother,

I'll bet the folks back home never dream of the enormity of the gift when they provide a car for missionaries. So far we have used ours as an ambulance, a hearse, a taxi, moving van, transportation for the bride and groom to the wedding, and a bus for all the guests to return home. I think the record number of Peruvians packing into our old suburban is 26. This was after a wedding the other night and it was so late that all the public transportation had already stopped running. They had no other way of getting back to the city and they just kept piling in. Rodolph was driving and I had a seat, but I had a couple of kids in my lap. We tried to be nice until some of the first ones in were having difficulty breathing and the bottom of the car began to drag on the ground. We then had to call a halt, or I think we might have had a calamity. I really think a few more might have managed to get in somehow!

Dear Mother,

Remember the "tons" of clothes we brought back to give away? Well, we decided to have a garage sale for our WMU ladies and we gave them buttons to use as money. It turned out to be great fun and a wonderful way to distribute evenly what we had. (However, I did see a few of the craftier ladies doing some shady deals on the side with trading and borrowing buttons to get a little more than their fair share.)

Dear Family and Friends,

Saturday night three of our churches had a youth conference and asked us to be on their program for a panel discussion. It was funny because the panel was on courtship and marriage, and Rodolph has a real shiner of a black eye and a cut nose. He fell into the front door last Wednesday and really did it up right! His face was all swollen and he was hobbling even worse than usual because he hit his knee also. We put ice on it and finally got the cuts to stop bleeding, but he was a mess and the bruises continue to look bad even though he is okay now. I just told the group of young people that if their husbands didn't shape up you could always have "husband improvement sessions" like some people I know, and that this was the result of our recent one. They liked that! I'm not sure anyone believes "running into a door" anyway!

We attended two birthday parties this week--the first was the usual with ceviche and goat meat and was really good, but the other was distinct! The daughters of the little blind lady who comes to our church were giving this party to celebrate her 85th birthday. Many people were invited but only a few of us went. I hate to admit it, but I am afraid that the reason for the poor attendance was that this home would not be on the list of the more desirable ones to visit, and also, there was another party at the same hour in one of the wealthier homes. These are sweet people, though, and are very faithful to all the church activities. So we went and we talked and sang like usual, but then they, too, served a plate of food. We had some kind of meat that was served over fried potatoes, and a very spicy, greasy sauce was poured over the whole dish. I thought the meat was really tender and the taste was not too bad, so I was on my second piece when the lady said, "This is the tongue of a bull or cow, I don't know which." Now this was the first time for me to eat this (knowing what it was) and it just seemed to grow and grow right there in my mouth. I looked at Rodolph and the rest of his face looked as bad as the bruised part-- sort of green. It is amazing how much stuff one can hide under a lettuce leaf on one's plate! I know he and I must have the record for that. He had to make a quick trip home soon after, but my old asbestos stomach saw me through it with little effect. (Of course, I have been known to be guilty of slipping some of my portion on his plate when he was not looking.)

There surely can not be many people on this earth who have the privilege of such friends as our family has. Actually, you people are our family whether you like it or not! You have done so much for us that there is just no way to express how and what we feel. You are truly our lifeline that keeps us here.

Dear Mother,

Rodolph was baptizing out at the puquio (spring) near camp, and I think he is beginning to show his age, too. They dammed up the spring to make a pool, but it still was not deep enough, so they dug a hole for the pastor and the candidate to stand in. Rodolph baptized the first lady--a rather good sized one--and when she started to back out of the hole, she slipped on the side and grabbed him and they both went down again! I just missed it with my camera! I also wanted to take a shot of the dressing room where he went to put on dry clothes. It was a sheet that two men were holding up for him right there in front of everybody, and since he is taller than they are, you could see his head above the sheet when he stood up. It would have made a great picture, but I decided it might not be too polite in a church service. It probably wouldn't have bothered anyone at all except me; they would have all just posed and tried to get in the photo. It is hard to get a solemn atmosphere when you attend a Peruvian baptism indoors, but when you are on the side of a mountain under overhanging cliffs, seated on the ground around a clear crystal stream, birds singing, sun shining, blue sky, friends surrounding you, and watching one of your own take this step of faith--it definitely IS praise time! And they express it in a happy fiesta way. It is so natural and I love them for it.

Dear Mother,

I have just learned first hand how missionaries are unjustly blamed for all kinds of things. The dentist down at our church's medical clinic told me that the little daughter of our caretaker out at camp came in with a cavity in her tooth. While admonishing her to be sure and clean her teeth and watch what she ate, the little traitor told the dentist that her having cavities was, "Hermana May's fault," because I gave her candy. The dentist was laughing about it and we both recognized that it was only a little girl trying to make an acceptable excuse, but it made me wonder how many others of our sugar-coated good intentions go awry and become a stumbling block instead of a stepping stone.

Dear Mother,

We are enjoying our classes at the seminary this year; the students in this new group seem to have a good spirit. I invited a couple of them home for lunch after church and ended up with 15 here to eat. I don't have any help right now either, and Merry said she surely was tired of washing dishes by the time we cleaned up after them. I had to divide up the rice and other things into smaller portions so it would go around, and while no one went away hungry, I don't think some of them got all they would have liked to have eaten.

This past week I had to give a test for Rodolph in one of his classes and it was just before their break time, so I took some buns and butter and jelly to share during that period. You would have thought that I had given them something really special. I know they get coffee and bread for breakfast, but apparently the jam and butter is a luxury. It makes me feel bad that they are so appreciative for so little; I forget they don't have much chance to enjoy many of the little extras like that. What is even more sobering is the fact that they have so much more than most of the people with whom they are working on the weekends.

Dear Mother,

We had a real rain Sat. night, and I guess it would have been funny to see if we had not been so tired and it had not been so bad. We wondered when it would stop and wondered about so many people living in houses much worse than ours. We woke up with the door bell ringing at 3:00 a.m. It was shorting out with the rain running down the wall and into the wires of its mechanism. Water was running under the front door, the hall door, the French doors in the living room, and the kitchen door. Since everything is flat on the ground, any accumulation just comes right in. Spencer's room outside was under water, rug and all, and Rodolph's office up on the roof was the same. It started running in the kitchen window from the roof, and then through the roof and ceiling into the kitchen and dining room. We began to stuff towels under the doors and wring them out and stuff them again and repeat the process over and over. We swept the water out of the house, then we went upstairs and began to sweep the roof. When we swept the roof, it came in the windows and under the doors worse than ever and was filthy dirty!

I was in my night gown and Merry was in a shorty one. Amy changed three times because she fell down in it. Spencer was in short pajamas, too, and only Rodolph was decently dressed. The helper got up (fully dressed) to assist, but we were all a sight and worked like mad until 6:00 a.m. when it finally slowed down. It was what would be only a good shower back home, but it really tore up the place here and not just in our house. There are no drains anywhere and so the water just collects until it runs to the lowest level and if your house happens to be in the lowest level-- too bad! We are planning to build a raised entranceway and put on a new roof because they are predicting more rain, with the worst to be in March yet to come.

The heat is bad and it is sticky and humid without the good cool ocean breeze to which we have all become accustomed. We depend on that to be our natural air conditioning. The Humbolt Current has moved out to sea and the warm current from up north has moved in bringing hot air and hot water and sharks and heaven knows what else! It happened once like this in 1925 they say. What a mess!

Dear Mother,

I think I could write a book on how to have a safe, enjoyable trip to Lima with a large family and friends. It would be a short book of only one sentence. It would read like this--"Don't go!" I think you might agree when you hear my tale.

For once in our lives, we packed the car ahead of time, had our lunch ready, and all we had to do was get up and go out to the car and take off. We planned to leave at 5:30 a.m. which should have put us in Lima between 1 and 2 p.m. From there we would travel one more hour up into the Andes to the mission camp which is near a beautiful little resort village that we all love. We were going to our annual mission meeting and were leaving a day early to relax and have some family recreation time before the meeting started. We got everybody up and dressed, and our friend who was going to caravan with us arrived right on time. When we went out to the car, we noticed the smell of gasoline and a pool of liquid underneath the car. We pushed the car away from it before Rodolph tried to crank it. He had filled the gas tank the night before and the gauge was sitting right on empty then. It didn't take a quiz kid to figure our trip was going to be delayed. There was nothing to do but unload all we had packed and let Rodolph take the car to the mechanic. We waited, wondering if the trip would be possible at all. I opted for just trying again tomorrow, but my stubborn husband said that he was sure he could get his friend, who was a mechanic, to fix it right away. We wandered about the house in our traveling clothes walking around all those suitcases, sleeping bags, toys, boxes, and bundles that were scattered everywhere. The wait was almost more than some of us could take, but finally, about the time we should have been arriving in Lima, he called to say he was on the way home and it was fixed. We did a record job in repacking the car and we were on our way.

We never like to leave in the afternoon for a long trip in Peru because you need enough extra daylight time in case of a problem. No one plans to be on the roads at night, and you certainly don't want to be stopped beside the road for any reason. You go through long stretches of nothing but desolate desert where there is no sign of habitation. It is more dangerous in the darkness because many people are hit by another vehicle whose driver just didn't see them. Also, you are at the mercy of robbers in an isolated place like that. So I was nervous about leaving at that hour, but like the good obedient wife and indulgent mother that I am, (stop smiling!) I yielded to the majority and we set off.

We had not gotten out of sight of Trujillo before we had to

have a bathroom stop for our driver who had drunk too much coffee. There were still a few trees and bushes along the outskirts of town that took care of this problem, so we were on our way again. (I think it was about then that Spencer asked for the first time how much farther it was.) We had not gotten to the first town down the way, which we consider about a fourth of the way and our usual first rest stop, before we realized we had a flat tire. We had to stop and unload enough stuff to get out the spare tire and jack and take care of that. Well, we didn't want to travel over those roads without a spare, so that meant finding a place to repair the tire. We found a little mechanic shop beside the road just as we came to the first town, and they did our work under the shade of a little Poinciana tree.

As we began again, we noticed the trunk lid of our friend's car begin to bounce and then spring up. Since Dave is 15 and has learned to drive, he was helping out in that car as "co pilot" and companion for the other missionary who is a single lady. Dave jumped out and ran around to the back of the car and shut it tight. This was a scene that we saw repeated at least 42 times or more between that point and reaching our destination. We tied it down with everything we could think of but it had a life of its own--it would rise again. It was so irritating but so improbable that it became funny, and we would die laughing to see Dave run around and slap the trunk lid down. It became a game to see how much longer they could go before it opened again.

We made it to the halfway mark and the sun was beginning to get a little lower in the sky, but I thought that not much more could happen on one trip. (This does not speak well for my thought process!) Well, this little service station is where we always fill up the car again to be sure we have enough gas to arrive in Lima. Rodolph started to fill the tank and discovered he could only get a little bit of gas to enter the tank. It ran out down the side of the car. The men there helped him rock the car, blow into the gas line, and offered many more completely useless suggestions. The only thing we could do was take a chance that he had put in enough gas to get us to the next service station. We took off again, with the good wife and mother shifting into the "I told you so" mode. As nervous as I was, their faith won out and we arrived at the next service station and the whole process was repeated. They shook and rocked the car as they tried to get the gas to enter the tank. The conclusion at which they arrived was that there was a kink or a bubble in the gas line that would not let the gas flow into the tank. But the cause of the problem was not my interest--I wanted the solution!

We continued on to Lima, stopping at every service station we came to, and closing the trunk lid of the other car every few minutes. I wanted to find a place to stay in Lima and not attempt the trip out to camp. I was just so glad to see civilization again! I had support from the children in this, but the logic of the argument won out that it would be too much to unload all that stuff and find a place to stay at that hour. It was getting on toward midnight by then, so we continued on to camp.

I wish I could report that the adventure ended there. We arrived at the mission camp well after midnight and managed to finally wake the caretaker who let us in and showed us to where we could stay. We carried in what we just had to have that night and what was too valuable to leave in the car. We threw our sleeping bags on the beds, and those of us who were not asleep already, were out almost before our heads touched the pillow. The lady missionary was in the room next to ours.

I awoke with what I thought was our door rattling and like a good wife, I nudged Rodolph and asked him if he heard it. He said he thought he heard something and we listened. It was pitch-black dark; you couldn't see your hand before your face. We decided it was Amy moving around in her crib which was made of metal. We thought she had kicked it or something and it had made a sound like that. Just as we were settling back down, we heard the single missionary yell, "No!" Rodolph jumped up and ran out to see what was going on. We heard footsteps speeding down the stairs from our building. He ran down the other staircase which was closer to our room and he saw a man running away. Just then the lady missionary came out and that's when Rodolph realized he was in his underwear. He ran back for his pants and returned, but of course, there was no sign of the intruder then.

We discovered he had entered by way of the stairs that go into the room of the lady missionary and was trying to rob her purse when she woke up. He threatened her to be quiet and pretended to have a pistol, but she yelled and that is what we heard. He apparently had tried to enter our room first, but was scared off by the movement of the baby in the crib. There was another missionary couple already at camp, too, and they got up and joined in our consternation about what had happened, but most of the children slept right through it all. In spite of no locked doors, we all went back to sleep after awhile. Now I know we have been assured that the Lord will not put more on you than you can stand, but don't you think that in our case, He comes rather close at times?☺

Dear Mother,

The names of some of the mission cars around here have given us a chuckle. The Methodist missionaries have a pitiful little car that looks so bad and limps along like it is sick and they have named it "El Poderoso" (The Powerful); another is called "El Chalenger" (The Challenge) because of the challenge it is to get it to run. One green mission pickup truck is named "El Sapo" (The Frog) because it jumps and bounces you about. Our truck, which is bigger and bounces you even more, is named "El Canguro" (The Kangaroo) and our little red car is called "La Ormiga" (The Ant) because it does the work of the big ones, but is so tiny. You take your fun and laughs wherever you can find them.

Dear Family,

Last night at the unified meeting of the churches of Trujillo a new missionary spoke, and as weak as my Spanish is, I was surprised at his lack of a command of the language. It was so bad that the thought crossed my mind that he needed an interpreter. I wondered if any of the people could understand what he was trying to say. When he finished an invitation was given, and at least a dozen people came down to accept the Lord. I felt I had been taught a lesson, or maybe even several lessons in this. I am not proud of my Spanish, but I don't think about it very much now; it has become a way of life and simply the medium we use here to communicate. However, there was a time when it was agony for me to be in a session where nothing but Spanish was spoken, and we have told you of the blunders we have made in wrong usage and grammar (and still do). So have I forgotten so soon, or who am I to judge? Does my compassion extend only to our nationals and not to a missionary brother? Then, there is the encouragement that God can use even the puniest efforts for his glory. It is not about us, but God working through us as pitiful as we are--as pitiful as I am. He brings the harvest in His own time, in His own way, and sometimes He lets us be a part of it. What joy that is!

(NOTE: This is what I mean about orchids in jelly jars.)

They announced at this meeting that there are now 26 churches in the Trujillo area (not counting the ones way up in the mountains) and over 40 annexes, which are places where a work has begun but has not yet organized into an official church. When we arrived, there were 3 churches here, and Rodolph, as Missionary of the Area, began with those and has worked with all of the churches begun since then in one way or another. He not only has worked with many churches up in the mountains but over into the jungle, also. It is mind boggling but gratifying as we look back over the years and see the struggle that has gone on in most of these groups, and to see they have not only survived, but in most cases have flourished and started annexes of their own. It is almost comical to see such tiny churches plan to sponsor another little group. We love it and we love them for their heart for missions. I wish we could carry some of these dear folks back to the USA with us when we return; they could teach us all a real lesson in how to live your Christianity.

Dear Mother,

Fifteen minutes to midnight and the phone rings! It always makes me squirm to hear it at that hour. It is a man from a nearby settlement who needs $50 so his wife can have a Caesarian operation at this moment. She is in labor and has complications. He has no money and no way to get it at this hour. Thankfully we had it on hand. (He was one of the few who came a week later to pay it back. Of course Rodolph let him keep it.)

Many of our people asked for government help through the Catholic Church and were turned down because they are Evangelicals. We help those in need without qualifications or obligations of any kind.

Most of the people in Shiran have never seen the ocean. They live less than an hour away and have never been. We plan to take them in the new truck this coming Saturday; it should be fun.

NOTE: This was done to the delight of all. Each time we said it was time to go, they begged to stay just a little longer. It was a great day except that the missionary who took them (Rodolph) got so sunburned that we almost had to take him to the doctor.

Dear Mother,

The other missionaries have been kidding me about "Loca Carlota." We have been warned about the many mental cases that are wandering about our streets. Some are just pitiful and harmless, but others can be violent. We are told that people in one town or village will gather them up and take them to another and put them out because there are no facilities to take care of them. It is rare that you go to the downtown section of Trujillo without encountering at least one or more, and many times we have them come to our houses. They are seen in various unusual attires, and many have not bothered with clothes at all. There is a crying need for government aid for these poor souls.

"Carlota" lives near the corner of the main plaza downtown. She has made a dwelling out of cardboard boxes and sleeps there at night. The story is that she was at one time a nanny for one of the important families who lived near the center of town. As she aged something happened to her mind, and this is the result. She is a tall thin lady with very dark skin (from the Caribbean area I think) and really short, white, curly hair. She stands in the street and uses a stick to tap on the cars that stop there for the traffic light, and she demands money. If you don't give her something, she bangs your car rather hard. Everyone knows her and everyone seems to respond in a positive way. Sometimes she seems more lucid than others, but she always stands there in a regal manner like she is doing you a favor by letting you give her something. Sometimes she speaks a few words and sometimes just accepts in silence what you hand out before letting you pass by.

The thing about which I have been teased is that Carlota will not accept anything from me. I have offered her money each time I pass, but she will nod or bow or pat my hand and smile and let me know in some manner or other that she cannot take my money. My friend says she nearly beats her car to death before she can get her money out, but she will not hit my car, and will stand back and wave me on through the intersection. I have never had any connection with Carlota, but obviously she relates me with something or someone in her past that she treated with respect. Of course, it could be like my missionary colleagues say--that even Carlota feels sorry for a poor old missionary type like I am.☺

Dear Mother,

There was a headline in our newspaper today that lamented the condition of the country with all these strikes and shortages. The latest is a shortage of wheat and it read, "It Looks Like Our Daily Bread Will No Longer Be Daily." Sadly, this is all too true of too many people here.

There has not been any gasoline or cooking gas for two days either, because of high seas. The ships couldn't offload their cargo, but they say they have arrived in the harbor and are waiting for the surf to die down and there should be a supply after that.

One never knows what necessary item will become scarce or disappear completely at any given time. I try to keep a supply of what we consider really necessary to our existence here, but it is a hard task sometimes. I've gotten really good at substitutes and innovative menus to use the things I have on hand. There has been little complaint from the family and there is nothing that ever goes wasted because someone will take it and find some use for it. (I suspect that some of my culinary experiments that were given away may not have been eaten but used as building materials like mortar or cement.☺)

Dear Mother,

I heard something the other day that tickled me and really spoke to me of our feelings about things we don't find to be exactly like that to what we are accustomed. Rodolph said the odors are hardest for him to take and I have to admit they are quite pungent in some places, to say the least. There is a really bad one on our back road shortcut to the airport because we have to cross the spot where they let raw sewage flow into the ocean. We have learned to take a deep breath before getting there and not breathing again until we pass it. There are others that really bothered me at first and now I don't even notice them. (I am not sure if this is good or bad.) Anyway, the cute little poem I heard goes like this--

"I have the nicest garbage man,
He empties out our garbage can,
He's just as kind as he can be,
He always stops to talk with me.
My mother doesn't like his smell,
But then she doesn't know him well."

I have no idea where it came from, but I like it. It tells me I should give others the same grace I expect for myself.

(NOTE: I guess I was trying to say even then that sometimes one has to look hard for the orchids, but they are there if we take time and effort to find them.)

FAMILY LIFE

Dear Mother,

There are some really great things about being a missionary in a place like this. What little bit one can do or what little talent one has is multiplied and appreciated. When there is nothing at all, or nothing with which to compare it, what I can do is pretty good! There is a certain sense of satisfaction in that. For instance, when I fry up a batch of my special greasy, soggy donuts and powder them down with sugar, and maybe add some cinnamon, or ice them with other exotic flavors that we substitute here--why, it's party time! There are no other donuts anywhere, much less Krispy Kreme or Dunkin' Donuts, to have as competition. And when I play the piano--I am a concert artist!

Dear Mother,

You are not going to believe what I did yesterday. Merry and I went to buy groceries at the main market there in the center of town. It was filled with more crowds than usual because of the holidays, and we both were carrying two huge baskets to buy what we needed. We had bought vegetables and some meat and fish and only lacked the fruit which I always buy last to put on top. Merry left me to go to the front of the market to buy some thread.

I was in the process of paying the lady and had just raised up my hand with the billfold in it, ready to take out the money, when someone hit my hand hard enough to shake my billfold free, grabbed it, and disappeared--all in an instant! I looked up to see a burly young man running away with it and melting into the crowd. Without thinking, I took off after him. I guess he thought because of the many people there he could attract less attention by just being a part of the crowd, and he slowed down to a fast walk. He also thought an old gringa lady would not be able to do anything about it. Since he thought wrong (and I was not thinking at all), imagine his surprise to look over his shoulder and see me bearing down on him! He took off again with me right behind him yelling that he was a thief and had my purse. We continued that way right on through the market, out the door, and down the street. It must had been a curious sight for the onlookers. I kept up with him until he threw my billfold to another man standing on the street. This man saw me coming and gave it back to me. I stopped then and let him go.

It scared me when I realized what I had done, and I have no idea what would have occurred had I actually caught him, but at the time I could only think that he had taken my billfold with my Peruvian driver's license inside, which had taken 2 years to obtain at great cost to my emotional health.

On the way back to the fruit stand where I had left my basket, people came up to me and shook my hand, patted me on the back, and told me how proud they were, and I was feeling pretty good about myself. When I arrived there to retrieve my basket the little lady vendor was no exception, she said, "Senora, you surely do run fast--for someone your age and size!" That sort of cut short my moment of glory.

Merry was really surprised when she returned to all that commotion and found out I was the cause of it. Some of the folks in the market chased the man down and brought him in later with a policeman and were very upset about the robbery. It was amusing to hear their account of it and also to hear that the major cause of their anger was because he was from out of town. I guess if he had been one of the local crooks I wouldn't have gotten that support.

Dear Mother,

I don't think we have to worry about Spencer becoming a professional soccer player. He came home from school this week and announced that his kindergarten class was to have a big soccer game on Friday. He had to have a blue shirt and short white pants for his uniform because they were to play the other team who would wear red shirts. We managed to get him dressed and all set for his game, but I had a class at the seminary at the hour of this grand event, so Rodolph was elected to attend and see this "world championship competition" between 4 and 5 year olds. (Peruvians take their soccer very seriously!)

Rodolph arrived late as usual and his report is that all he could see was a blur of red and blue clad kids running all over the place. It was hard to distinguish the playing field from the spectator area as there were quite a few family members who had come to cheer for their own special little one. He located Spencer who greeted him with, "Daddy, Daddy, I scored a goal!" Rodolph was impressed and just as he asked him what the score was, the game ended and it was all over. Spencer proudly announced, "They won us one to nothing." (For those of you who are lacking in soccer savvy--our son had made an "auto goal"--the only point in the game and in favor of the other team.)

Rodolph has already used this as a sermon illustration, and I foresee many more because it has unlimited possibilities in speaking about being sure of your goals and direction, etc. I just may use it myself.

Dear Mother,

We lost Amy for a short while one day this week, and when she nonchalantly walked back into the house, we asked her where in the world had she been without telling us. She said she had only been walking around the "apple." We were completely puzzled and could not think of what kind of Peruvian custom she might have encountered. We kept on questioning her until it finally dawned on us. "Manzana" is the word for "apple" in Spanish, but it can also mean "block." Amy had just chosen the wrong one to tell us she had just taken a stroll around our block in the neighborhood. Not only our kids, but more often their parents, do this kind of thing quite frequently and we do encounter some strange looks from time to time. When I see a quickly hidden smile (or sometimes not so hidden) I know I have said something I didn't mean to say.

NOTE: I still remember our classmate in language school who tried to give a talk about his ancestors being from Germany. His efforts convulsed our teacher and through tears of laughter she asked him, "And where is your head from?" We were all perplexed until she explained that he had just used the word for his hind end and said it came from Germany. I decided to choose my words very carefully after that.

Through the years we have had a lot of chuckles over our bloopers in Spanish. Rodolph's first memorable one was in Costa Rica when he asked for the horses' room thinking he was asking for the men's room. I am sure all of the preachers have at one time or another spoken of the "fish" of the world instead of the "sins" of the world. I remember giving a whole 10 minute devotional at church where I spoke of the apples, pears, bananas, oranges, etc. of the Spirit instead of using the proper word for that kind of "fruits."

Even after years of speaking and understanding, a slight change of usage or a one letter difference can convey a completely different message from which one intended. Our Peruvian brothers were very gracious and forgiving, but it helped to keep us humble.

Dear Mother,

Please tell the ladies at the WMU this one; I think it puts a new light on the missionaries' birthday calendar they promote so faithfully. Last week the family asked how I wanted to celebrate my birthday and I opted for a family outing where we could have a meal and play some tennis afterwards. We went to the Country Club (where we are members and pay a fee of $5 per month--just in case this does not fit your idea of the missionary image). It was very pleasant and David decided he would play Mom in a singles game. I was flattered that my teenage son would be seen playing with his mother and recognized the sacrifice for what it was. Well, we began and continued on and on for quite a long time until I finally beat him. This obviously was not what either of us expected, and he walked off the court mumbling that he should have known better, because this never would have happened if all those people back home had not been praying for me on my birthday! Somehow I doubt many of the prayers going up for me on that day included my tennis game.

Dear Mother,

   We had a new, exciting, and rather upsetting happening since I last wrote. I looked out the window the other day and saw a man walking across our back yard. He was coming from the back wall and walking toward our patio area. He looked like the stereotyped caricature of a crook; all he lacked was the striped suit. He did not seem to have a weapon and had nothing in his hands, so I jerked open the back door and asked him what he was doing there. He said he wanted out and started coming toward me.

   There was no way he could have gotten into our back yard without coming through the house or coming over the wall, so I knew he was up to no good. By that time both Bertha and Gladys had joined me there in the hall, and I told Bertha to open the front door and Gladys to stand there and not let him go anywhere but out. It was only a few steps from one door to the other. I thought about all the things out there on the patio that he could steal or even use as a weapon, so I told him to come in and I would let him out through the house.

   All three of us were frightened because he was one tough looking fellow, but I couldn't think of anything else to do. He came right on in and hurried out. He asked for us to open the gate and let him out of the front yard, and I told him to wait just a minute and we would get the key for him. I shut the door after him and Bertha went to get the key. Before she could get the gate open, he was up and over that 8 ft. wall in a flash. As he left, however, he told her he would be back, and knowing Bertha, I imagine this will be the source of several sleepless nights for her. We heard a car racing off just as he was leaving.

   When Rodolph came back, we went to all the neighbors whose property borders our wall and asked them if they were missing anything. All said no except one family who said they were just returning from an outing about that time and had not had time to look around yet. When they checked they found quite a few of their valuables all bagged up and ready to be carried off. Apparently they had returned just in time to scare him away and he jumped their wall into our yard. We called the police who didn't even bother to come out. It makes one feel well protected by our officials!

The neighbors are all going together to hire a guard. Having a thief in your house at 3 in the afternoon puts a rather bad light on things. Anyway, I have faced down yet another bad guy!

Dear Mother,

I had my first experience with a Peruvian dentist this week; it will be the last experience with this one! He pulled a wisdom tooth, and when he gave me the anesthesia he hit a nerve that shot up to my eye and turned my face yellow. I had to go back to have a cavity filled, and when he gave me the anesthesia this time my heart started beating wildly and I couldn't breathe and almost fainted. When this spell finally passed off, it had not deadened my jaw at all. I questioned what had happened and he said, "Oh, Senora, you are just very nervous." I thought that rather strange so I checked with our family doctor on our next visit to him. He said the dentist had done just what I suspected--put the anesthesia straight into the bloodstream and it went through my system to my heart, and luckily my heart was strong enough to handle it. He said that many people have been killed in a dentist's chair. I told Rodolph that I truly understand that an accident could happen to anybody, but either this dentist didn't know what happened, or he knew and lied about it and did nothing to help me; and either way, I was not going back if all my teeth rotted out!

Dear Mother,

We were out walking along the watering canals near the camp with Amy this week and I think she may have learned that parents can give good counsel at times. She was walking on the edge of the canal and we kept telling her that she was going to fall. Like most little ones she thought she could make it, so she ignored our advice, lost her footing, and slipped. As she fell she turned over a big rock with her foot, and underneath that rock was a huge nest of fire ants. Before we could run to help her the ants had swarmed all over her little body. She was screaming with the pain of it. We grabbed her and dumped her into that muddy water as fast as we could while jerking off her clothes. Thankfully, this washed all the ants off quickly, but even so, she had bites from her toes up to her neck. She was miserable for a long time after, but miraculously, seems to have had no lasting effects from the experience. (She's not more obedient, either!☺)

Dear Mother,

This volunteer group really put out the work. They did all kinds of construction work like roofing, electrical wiring, making tables, repairing worn out, broken down appliances, etc. One really great thing they did was take 2 of my old washing machines and one of another missionary's and make one out of them that actually works. It has a green top and white bottom, but it sure beats washing by hand!

The first night after they left we were too tired to even take notice of what was going on, but the second night after closing up and getting all the staff back to their homes, etc. we sat in the den and pigged out on the things they had left behind for us---I had Vienna sausage, Little Debbie oatmeal cakes and a Fig Newton; Rodolph ate Beenie Weenies, Oreos, and Chips Ahoy cookies. It is a wonder we both weren't as sick as dogs! Oh yes, I forgot to tell you--I can now enjoy Trujillo as much as the USA--we now have "Pepsi Max" (diet Pepsi)! If they were to take a sample of my blood right about now, it would be 95% Pepsi Max! They just arrived and are the first diet drink to come to Trujillo. Life is worth living now!☺ Actually, I only bought one at first then I bought three more after I saw that I liked it, but one missionary bought a dozen at first sight.

Dear Family,
        We are well and alive even if our news is not earthshaking--Oops!--wrong choice of words for this section of the world! We survived camps and are now trying to survive the post-camp time when everybody has waited for us to get through so they could put in their requests for help. They are varied and sundry, many are very original, and all are very insistent! My capacity to say, "no" has always been a little more well-developed than Rodolph's, but he has put that word into his vocabulary more and more lately. The requests for money never stop and the money does, so when it gives out we just have to say, "There is no more." However, the requests for personal help from individuals and churches seem to increase all the time. I forget how we are "experts" on every subject and expected to go and hold conferences on things I know nothing about (and am not interested in learning). I told a lady yesterday that she could read the book as well as I could and she could certainly tell it in much better Spanish, and she just looked at me as though she couldn't believe what she was hearing. (It didn't work; I had to do it anyway!)
        Our new helper isn't working out too well. We were out at camp and the current missionary visiting at our house in town came home late one night. She was sleeping and didn't hear him ring and ring the bell. He couldn't get in and had to go to another family's house to spend the night. We thought that was pretty funny until she double-locked the front door while we were out and we couldn't get in either; we had to climb over the roof so we could get in the back way.
        I was so pleased the other day when I found some beautiful green asparagus in the market. It is a rarity and we love it, so I carried it home and she decided to cook it for us while I was gone. She remarked that it was hard and I wondered about that, but I saw what she meant when we began our meal--she had cut off all the tender tips and thrown them out and cooked the stems! If the

garbage hadn't already gone, I think I would have tried to rescue those tips! We are saving money on vacuum bags, though. We use these over and over because we have to empty them so often to find our handkerchiefs, socks, jewelry, etc. that we are missing, and also see what new things she may have encountered and just sucked up as she goes along.

Dear Mother,

We had incredibly good flights back; especially since we were delayed because of Hurricane Andrew. We couldn't see much from the airport in Miami, but as we flew over south Florida, the houses looked like a giant's foot had splattered every one of them. We left the USA on time and even the trip from Lima to Trujillo was on time.

The folks have discovered we are here now and the visits have started. Some have stayed 5 hours. Some go and others come with their visits overlapping. Yesterday they began at 8 a.m. and lasted until 6 p.m.--not even one minute without someone here. Mrs. Davalos brought us a lemon pie and another lady brought some fruit, but the rest just brought themselves. I was as exhausted as if I had plowed all day! It would have been bad enough to have that many visitors just to welcome us home, but all wanted to talk about the problem they have had in the church while we were gone and were very emotional about it. Well, I guess I can truthfully say we feel needed! I hope we are up to the challenge. I guess if nobody needed us, we would feel bad, but I really wouldn't have minded waiting a week or two for us to get settled in again--I think I could have handled my feelings that long!☺

Rodolph really misses our queen-size bed at home, he fell out of this one. He forgot how small it is and when he rolled over to get up, he fell flat. When I realized he wasn't hurt we both nearly died laughing! I told him today I would call the carpenter and get him to make rails for us.☺

We have discarded the idea of moving out to Shiran because the news of El Nino is so bad for this year that we think it could be dangerous, and most certainly we could be isolated because of roads being washed away. Our news says it is predicted to be the worst of the century and will last longer than any other. We will be the only missionaries in Trujillo during the worst months (Dec.-Mar.) so we will need to be here I guess. When it all begins we have decided to drive the "Canguro" (truck) leaving the "Ormiga" (car) here at the house so we will have transportation here if Shiran gets cut off.

The local people here are really trying to get ready for the rain by repairing their roofs, or in some cases, putting one on for the first time. I expect there will be a lot of plastic sold in these days. Village people in Shiran are building little shacks up on the mountainside in which to stay if needed. It seems that what happened in 1983 made believers out of a lot of us. One bright spot is that there is talk of getting a phone in the neighboring town; that would be a blessing to have some means of contact back to Trujillo.

NOTE: May I say here that the predictions were true. It was a terrible time, but the worst flooding in our area in all recorded history was during El Nino of 1998. There were many lives lost and an incredible loss of property. One cannot believe the destructive power of water unless you see it. The whole landscape down the valley was completely changed. When we went back for a visit in 2001, we did not recognize some parts at all. One just would not think it possible that such a dry desert area could ever have that much water pass through it.

Dear Family,

Guess what! Burger King has arrived in Lima! We both had a committee meeting there last week and we got to try out both the Pizza Hut and Burger King. It was like a visit to the USA. Burger King imports all the ingredients for its food from there and you cannot imagine how GOOD it tasted here! (We went 3 times.)

It has been rainy this week out at camp, but off and on--not a steady, scary one like last week. The river continues to rise and fall as the rains continue up above us in the high mountains. We can hear it as it throws big boulders around and crashes rocks together and rushes by, then calms down again. This is quite a country! It never ceases to amaze us.

Dear Mother,

Rodolph took Spencer to Lima so he could take the SAT test at the American school there. It will be interesting to see how his grades turn out. They got in 3 hours late on the plane because the Trujillo airport was under siege by people from the jungle who had been waiting 3 days for a flight and were taking over any plane that came in.

Amy has lost weight, cut her hair, and grown fingernails--it is wonderful to see what an interest in the opposite sex can do for one! She is funny; we love her.

Dear Family and Friends,

We had the usual eventful trip back--one flight canceled, one delayed 8 hours, and one piece of luggage lost. It was Spencer's new suitcase with all of his and his dad's suits and good shirts. They both cheerfully offered to not wear a suit and tie again until returning to the USA in 4 years, but your prayers for us resulted in yet another miracle and the suitcase arrived 2 days later.

We found the house and things in reasonably good condition except for water problems, 2 broken windows, and a shredded lamp shade. It seems that a little mouse had taken up residence in our absence and the damage was done trying to kill it with a broom. Rodolph set a trap for it, but that resulted only in catching the tail of our dog which ran around our tile kitchen floor banging the metal trap and barking amidst the running, jumping, screaming, and laughing of us all. I thought again that somehow this was not the way Lottie Moon modeled missionary life for us.

As we arrived in Trujillo there were about 70 or more of our church people there at the airport to meet us and they formed a circle around us and sang "Bienvenidos"--a song of welcome. Many had walked a long distance and others had to spend money on 4 buses to give us a welcome back hug. The warmth of their Christian love really touched us.

We miss you all so much, but we feel the Lord's leadership so strongly in being here at this time.

Dear Family and Friends,

Some of you have inquired about the children. David lacks one year of finishing seminary and Merry is a sophomore at Furman now. Spencer just turned 16 and we are concerned about his schooling and his military status. He was born here so he has dual citizenship and this makes him eligible for the Peruvian draft if he returns to Peru after our furlough. The Foreign Mission Board says he will be a test case for the Peru mission since he is the first with dual nationality to reach this age.

The reason this is a problem is that Peruvian military service is mandatory, and anyone who does not report for duty can be picked up off the street and hauled away. We see trucks all the time filled with young boys from all walks of life being taken off. You can see the consternation and fright on many of the faces and some are even crying. Many of them call out or try to throw a note to someone passing by to let their family know where they are. If taken in this manner, they are not even given the opportunity to notify their parents. When a young man does not come home on time around here the first question asked is, "Were they picking up fellows for the military today?"

We certainly would not want to forget Amy. She is now at the ripe old age of 11 and is enjoying life, and we enjoy her. She and Spencer are very close, but you would never get either of them to admit it.

Dear Mother and Amy,

The news on our crate is that it may be in Lima, it may be

140

in Paita, or it may be in Japan! Seriously, the boat has docked in the port of Callao and has off-loaded half of its cargo and the other half goes to Paita. The other missionary here has all the papers for her shipment coming through just fine, but our papers are for someone going to Japan! I have tried to be patient, but I really could use some of those things in that crate about now, especially that generator in these times of no electricity. If this is the Lord's way of teaching me patience, I hope I can pass His test. (I'm pretty sure I have already failed His tests on attitude, criticism, and humility!☺)

Dear Mother,

Spencer is so funny; he came in with a testimony of how one needs to be specific in his prayers. He got up late and so he was left to get to school on his own. He said he went to the corner and prayed for a taxi to come quickly and it did; he just forgot to pray for an empty taxi to come. So he prayed again and this time for an empty one, and it came and went right past him. He then prayed for an empty taxi to come and stop for him and it came and did. Only after reaching school did he remember that he had left his books and homework at home. Each of our children are a real piece of work! Magna, the lady who took care of Spencer when he was little, sent him a gift she had crocheted for his birthday. She had his initials in it (the "S" was backwards). He didn't exactly know what to do with it and neither did I, but I assured him it would be nice to keep.

We were out at Shiran the other day and when we came home that night, Spencer was as animated as I have ever seen him. He was almost in the middle of a robbery right there near our house. He had a "very-soon-after" eye witness report. It seems 3 robbers entered a house a couple doors down from us, and someone called the police who came and parked in front of Spencer's friend's house. The thieves shot at them and the police returned the fire. There were 5 shots in all, enough to startle the neighborhood. The police killed one of them and he fell off the wall right into the street and they captured another, but the third one got away. That kind of thing is happening more frequently here now. Before the last couple of years I don't think I ever heard of armed robbery. There was blatant thievery everywhere, but the criminals were not usually armed.

Spencer is a regular miser with the little money he gets; he doesn't spend a cent needlessly. He is surprisingly generous with others when he does decide to spend it, though. Amy always spends hers before she gets it!

Dear Mother,

It takes all of us awhile to get over our homesickness each time we return. Amy said on the plane, "I just miss them so much," and then she just wept. With big tears running down her cheeks, she looked at me and asked, "Why can't we stay one place or the other?" Although I knew the correct answer, it was a hard question for the moment.

Dear Family and Friends,

We are still reaping the benefits of Spencer's baptism a few years ago. He made his profession of faith during a church service and we knew it had not been the custom of this church or pastor to baptize children, and so we did not insist on it. However, Spencer was so enthusiastic about his decision that Rodolph asked the pastor if he could attend the classes he gives for new members. We understood he would not be baptized, but he wanted to learn. The pastor welcomed him into the group and after a short while came to visit us and asked us how we would feel if they presented him as a candidate for baptism. He said Spencer fully understood what he was doing and he felt like he was ready. Of course, we were thrilled and Spencer became the first child under 16 years old to be accepted into the church as a member. Most of the new members were in their late teens or adulthood. This opened the door for others and many of Spencer's friends have now been baptized as a result of his being the "test case." One of these friends was Omar. It was not too much longer after that when we received word that Omar had drowned somewhere up north on a visit to see his grandparents. This had a profound effect on Spencer and his peers.

There was a little 9 year old boy who was baptized the other day and he is the youngest so far. Amy said, "If he can, I can, too." She accepted the Lord about a year ago and went down to see the pastor, but was not encouraged to join a class. After this, she went to see the pastor again, joined a baptismal class, faithfully did the homework for 8 weeks, and yesterday, she and 15 others were baptized. We were so proud of her. It was quite an impressive service (and quite long).

In the evening Rodolph and I went to another church where he had to preach. This was a different experience. The church is adobe with dirt floors and the "pews" are planks laid over 3 bricks on each end, which lets them sag in the middle (especially when I sat on it). These are not high enough to let you put your legs up under you, and with a dress on, it is hard to find a place to put them. There is no back, of course, and the "pew" in front is so close there is not room to stretch out. By the time he finished preaching I was pretty tired. The people are so nice and friendly, though, and when our car got stuck in the sand as we were leaving, half the church helped push us out, grinning all the time. It was quite a contrast between the a.m. service and the p.m. service. But then I have always maintained that Peru is a "Land of Contrasts."

Dear Mother,

We have really enjoyed David's visit and I think he has enjoyed being here too. He went over into the jungle with a missionary up north to help teach guitar lessons and they traveled by car. That was a new experience for him. He was also asked to translate the mission meeting minutes into Spanish because it is a government regulation to have a record of them. It hasn't been done for quite a few years, so he has found some things to do that have been really helpful. One of the not-so-helpful things he has done, though, is buy a parrot. After he did that Merry wanted some little birds, and so we now have 3 birds to clean up after. He was so sure his parrot would talk, but it only squawks and dirties everything it gets near. It throws out its corn and water and even eats up the cups we feed it in. Somehow it got the cup caught on its head yesterday, and we found it walking around in the cage wearing the water cup like a helmet. There is the ever present danger of getting bitten, too, so I don't know how this experiment will turn out.

Dear Mother,

Amy pops out with how much she misses you at the oddest moments. She prays for the family so much and so long that if we are in a hurry, we don't ask her to say the blessing. She loves and enjoys Snoopy so much, yet the other day a little girl came to our door trying to sell two little puppies and when I said we could not have 3 dogs here, she offered to trade Snoopy for them. I told her she should be ashamed of herself!

When we were at mission meeting she came in and said she was going to be a good girl from now on. I readily endorsed this decision, but I had to ask what brought this about. She said that she didn't want God hitting her. Of course, I had to question this statement a little more and she elaborated by telling us that her teacher for Bible School had told the class that Adam and Eve had been bad and God "punched" (punished) them! (Her teacher has the standard Southern accent that most of us here share.) After we had gotten our laugh out of that, I teased the teacher about the theology our child was learning from her, and she came back with her own question about what we were teaching her. It seems that she asked the class if they knew what happened after a person died and Amy had the answer. She said, "If you are good you go to heaven, and if you are not you just stay right on there in Trujillo." I hope her concept of Trujillo has improved since then.

It is gratifying to see the love these children of ours have for one another. They don't show it as often as we would like, but every now and then it expresses itself in a way that makes us think there is some hope for each of them. Spencer had two friends over to spend the night in the tent for his birthday, and David thought they might get scared (I did too)--so picture that lanky, six foot, 15-year-old sleeping with three 8-year- olds and 2 dogs out there in the back yard in a not so large tent. The girls wanted to heckle them some, but I wouldn't let them.

Dear Mother,

Did I tell you we are getting a new car? Our jeep has given its life to missions. It would seem that its life is over for sure. Karl and Rodolph went to the mountains in Karl's car and it broke down. They had to leave it there and come home and get parts off of our car to go back up and fix it. Thankfully, we are in line for the next available mission car and we just got word that it has arrived in Lima. Spencer is so excited he can hardly stand it. He and his dad are going down on the plane together and return in the new car. He will have his own daddy all to himself to enjoy this exciting event. He has just finished up 4th grade too, so life is good right now.

Dear Mother,

David is really serious about his work this year and is turning in beautiful papers and getting wonderful grades. He even got a seal for neatness, imagine! Merry had perfect grades, too, but got a note from the teacher saying that she needed to be neater! Doesn't that sound like her? Spencer is still making us laugh with his way of expressing himself. For example, he said they had to sing two songs in their Mother's Day program, "A long one and a short one. The long one is longer than the short one, and the short one is shorter than the long one." David, especially, just falls in the floor laughing at him. Amy is still the boss of the house, making everyone jump when she wants something. She is so cute, though, that no one seems to mind. We are blessed.

Dear Mother,

Merry had a traumatic experience this past week. You remember the rabbits I told you we had tried to raise? Well, our caretaker out at camp had given the pair to us and had kept a pair for himself. He let the children pick them out and Merry chose a black one with a white spot on its forehead that looked like a star, so she named it "Star." David had a white one. We kept waiting to have little rabbits, but had no success. Finally the caretaker said that he thought maybe one of us had two males and the other had two females, so maybe we should switch one of them and then we could have little ones. So it was decided that Star would be the one to go. Merry was not at all happy about this, but the other rabbit arrived and finally we did have some baby rabbits, but did not have much luck in raising them. When we would go to church, Merry would go over and visit Star next door at their house on the sand mountain. The caretaker's wife invited us this last week to a birthday party for her little daughter. We had provided some classes in cake decorating at church, and she wanted to show off what she had learned. She had done a good job and not only had cake, but also tamales and lemonade. We admired the good work she had done on the party and complimented the food, and she told us that she had made the tamales out of rabbit instead of the usual chicken. After we ate, Merry went out to play with the children. In a few minutes she came running back in, crying as if her heart was broken. With a face that was almost green in color, she exclaimed, "I have eaten Star!" She had seen the rabbit skin hanging on the clothes line and had noticed the distinguishing mark of white on the black pelt, right where the face would have been. She was inconsolable for quite awhile, and I didn't feel so good myself!

Dear Mother,

I got quite a surprise this week. I was not feeling well and had gone to lie down for awhile back in our room. I was dosing off when I heard the piano and called out to Rodolph to please tell whoever that was that I needed a little quiet for a short rest. He came to the room and I could still hear the piano going. I asked, "Who is that?" He said, "We have a concert artist here today that has come to practice." I didn't think that was too funny, and he said, "No, I really mean it, there is a concert artist in there playing your piano." About that time, there was the sound of a Chopin waltz that brought me out of the bed. I was stunned by what I heard. I asked again who it was and got the same answer. I had to go and see for myself, sick or not. It seems that a neighbor was hosting this internationally famous concert artist from New York who had a program scheduled for the municipal theater that night. The technicians were tuning the piano at the concert hall and he had no place to practice, and since our neighbor knew I had a piano--he just brought him over. We never know just whom we might find in our house at any given time. I might add that my piano has never sounded like that before or since!

Dear Mother,

Just as I was thinking, "well, another child settled into gainful employment, independent, and mature," I get this card from Merry that says, "Mom, whenever my priorities become confused, and the pressures and ambiguities of life raise my stress level, I just want to lift up my head and shout.......I WANT MY MOMMY!" She can always make me smile.

Dear Mother,

Guess what we have at our house now? Snakes! Right, we all feel the same horror! Before you write the Board for me to come home, let me explain. I saw on the floor in the kitchen what I thought to be a large fishing worm. It looked just like one. It was a pinkish cream color and about the same size, but it wriggled a little differently. When I investigated I discovered it actually had a little head and tail. We immediately dispatched of it and, other than wonder where it came from, thought no more about it. Then one appeared in David's room, outside across the patio. We began to get a little concerned when we saw a couple more, and we noticed we usually found them near the doors.

When the gardener came we questioned him, and he actually found one and assured us they were harmless. He confirmed that they were really snakes and said there must be a nest of them somewhere. Even though they are harmless, hearing the fact that we could expect more was a little unnerving. I noticed the children were a little more careful about wearing their shoes. When we saw one there would be a minor panic for awhile until someone did away with it. In fact, there were some really new and unusual dance steps practiced by our Baptist missionary family when someone yelled, "Snake!" Wouldn't you know that in the desert where no one ever sees a snake, a whole family of them would take up residence at our house? David came in one morning and was laughing at himself. He said he got out of bed and didn't have his glasses on and did a real jig around his room until he realized that what he thought was a snake was his shoestring. Missionary life--it is never boring.

NOTE: Periodically these little pests would appear and we almost got used to them. Instead of yelling, "Snake!" someone would calmly indicate one had come in, or just sweep it out or kick it out and step on it without comment. The gardener finally found the nest they came from and got rid of them for good. We were not unhappy about that.

Dear Family,

Forgive another group letter, but the time is just getting away from us and I spend even more time than before reminding and nagging and heckling Rodolph about the things he's forgotten to do!☺ No kidding, as we both get older and more forgetful, I go around cutting off things he's left on like the TV, CD player, cassette player, lights, etc. and collecting up his coffee cups from the patio, deposito, and sala--but I do this after HE has found my glasses so I can look!☺

I had the station over Fri. night for supper because 4 of the ladies have birthdays in Oct. They are all in their thirties and constantly remind us of our old age--so I made a cake celebrating their "140" years. (I added all their ages together.) It gave me a little satisfaction to see their "young" faces when they read the cake.☺ It was a nice evening and I enjoyed doing it.

Last night at 10 p.m. the doorbell rang and it was Bertha and Nancy and others of their family bringing us goat meat and yuca and tamales, all piping hot in one of those enamel lunch pails that stack one on top of the other. We had already gone to bed, but got up and ate goat at 10:15 p.m. (and went to bed again smelling of goat!) When there are just two of us here, we can do as we please!!☺

Dear Mother,

These kids are going to make me old before my time. Merry came in yesterday with her lips and all around her mouth tinted a bright blue! I was horrified and asked what in the world she had been eating. She nonchalantly replied that she had eaten some little things off the trees in the park. I nearly had a heart attack! We got her to take us to where she had gotten the fruit and she couldn't find the place. I flew around the neighborhood asking everyone I saw if they knew what she could have possibly eaten. I finally found someone who said they knew what it was and it was okay, because their children had eaten them too. I got the feeling they were laughing at me. I had to hope they were right, and since she is okay, I guess they were. You never know what Merry will do next.

Dear Mother,

We have been so proud of David's basketball team this year. They have done really well and are in the playoffs down at the main coliseum where the professional programs are put on. We attended the game last night and were astonished to see the referee call a halt to the play and begin to talk to Dave. We wondered what he had done. We were even more puzzled when we saw all the players begin to look at the floor and step around ever so carefully, and some of them began crawling around on their hands and knees. Then all at once, the referee blew his whistle and the game commenced again. After it was all over, we quizzed David about the strange happening and he turned a little red as he admitted in embarrassment that it was all his fault. He was not too accustomed to his new contact lens and had lost one during the scramble under the basket. He told the referee to please give him a moment to find it because they cost so much that his parents would kill him or at least make him stop playing basketball if he lost it. The game was stopped and all the players helped him look, and then to his great mortification, he found it stuck to his cheek! It seemed to bother us a whole lot more than anyone else; no one even mentioned it to us or teased him about it. He would have never lived that down in the States. Of course, they probably wouldn't have stopped the game in the States, either. Life is always interesting here.

Dear Mother,

Your newest grandson is so sweet. He doesn't look much different from the others even though he is a Peruvian.☺ I hope we pleased you by naming him "Spencer" after Daddy. He has reddish blond fuzz for hair and is skinny and has a really fair complexion, so I don't guess we will get him mixed up with any of the little Peruvian babies around. I am fine and he is fine, and we will send pictures as soon as possible.

A few days before the birth, my doctor was sick and I had a bout with pleurisy. A friend recommended another doctor who came to the house and listened to my chest with his bare ear. He didn't even bring a stethoscope! Needless to say, I was glad that MY doctor recovered in time for Spencer's birth. He is great.

Dear Mother,

We have evened up the score with girls and boys now and while we are all so proud of Amy and think she is wonderful, I, for one, think maybe 4 children might just be enough, especially when one reaches the age of 40! There were only two babies in the nursery at the clinic--ours and one little preemie in the incubator. Since Amy is a gringuita and weighs over 9 lbs., there is not too much trouble in distinguishing which is ours. The other kids are ecstatic over a baby sister, especially Merry. I have to admit she is a pretty baby and I had a rather easy time of it; I surely do like my doctor. The clinic leaves a little to be desired, but I was only there a short time.

Dear Mother,

Let me picture you a vignette of missionary life at its purest. I heard a great commotion and went to see what was going on. Somehow, a little bird had gotten into Chuckles' cage and Chuckles was screaming, "Out, out!" and "Hello." Gladys and Bertha were there trying to extricate the bird and Gladys' little boy was also yelling, "Out, out!" The three dogs were barking and jumping on the cage and it was bedlam. It sounded like WW III had begun!

Dear Mother,

Spencer had a very traumatic experience the other day. The three children were out on the patio and a huge cucaracha ran across the tiles. David told Spencer to stomp it! David and Merry were barefooted, but Spencer was dressed as usual with his little shirt buttoned right up to his chin and also tucked into his "Frontier" jeans which have all kinds of pockets and flaps and zippers and loops. This is his standard everyday dress, completed by his little cowboy boots. He made several valiant attempts to step on the bug before it disappeared. Then, after a few seconds, he began to jump around and to shake so violently that the others couldn't make out what he was trying to tell them. David finally understood what he was struggling to say and ran over and jerked off his pants to find that the cockroach had run up his leg! Spencer was completely overcome with panic and his big brother and sister could do nothing but laugh.

(NOTE: And they still laugh every time we speak of it today.)

Dear Mother,

They had a going away service and party for David last night. It was so sweet. They said so many nice things about him and told him how they were going to miss him, expected great things of him, and were hoping to welcome him back one day.

I, myself, don't know if I will live through the experience of letting my child go. I know this is the natural and the right way of things, but it is harder than I ever dreamed it could be. I have heard missionaries speak of this, but it was one part of missionary life I chose to ignore for as long as possible. I know the Lord will not ask me to do anything for which He will not give me the strength, but I am thinking this might come pretty close!

I was proud and surprised at David's response when they asked him if he would like to say something. He expressed himself very well in thanking them, and then he said something that caught the attention of us all. He was trying to explain how much he loved them and Peru, but he was excited about going to the USA to college. He summed it up well by saying, "I don't know if I am leaving home or going home." I am sure that will ring in my heart for years to come.

Dear Mother,

Happy Mother's Day! We will certainly be thinking of you. I hope some of my kids can be with you since I can't be with you, and they can't be with me.

Merry, right front, and her class at Ridgecrest orientation.

David, back row and second from right, and his class at Missionary Orientation in 1967

Our first Christmas in Peru and the "Charlie Brown Christmas Tree"

Our "Home" in Trujillo
Los Laureles 263

First of our two Peruvians, Spencer, at three days of age.

Four "Dummies" – Merry, David, Amy, and Spencer

Spencer and his first-third grade teacher, Missionary Journeyman, Pam Hicks.

Amy, in center, and MK Rachel Armstrong, with teacher and MK school administrator Career Missionary Gloria Brinks.

Amy and her volunteer teachers, Doris and Bryan Stone, on a field trip.

Arrival of Volunteer teacher, Lillie Westmoreland, to teach Merry and Spencer.

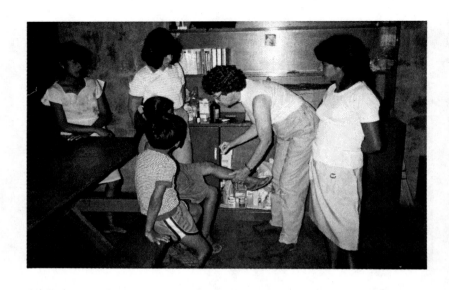

Volunteer Nurse, Sue Forrester, during Summer Camps.

Missionary Volunteers Ralph and Gloria Beatson and daughters, Jennifer and Shannon being greeted by their new Peruvian friends.

Chapel at Camp.

Arrival of new campers.

Eleven cabins and two dormitories provide housing for 250.

Pure water from two deep wells at Camp drilled with missionary volunteer assistance.

One of the long lines of campers enjoying the pure cold water from the wells.

Evening Vespers at a youth camp.

A group of counselors with the Directors

Learning to ski on grass?

"Walking through the Bible" summer camping activities.

Camp Cooks – Mrs. Davalos, Hilda, Anita, Leonor, Maria, and Alicia

One of my many Seminary Choirs.

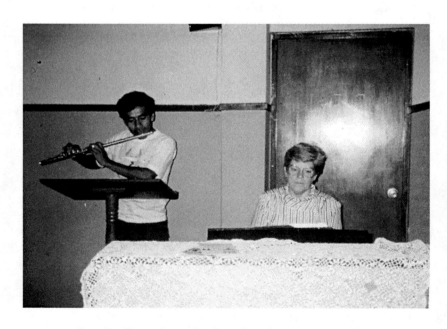

Lucho Davalos playing for church worship.

164

My trusty "field" pump organ – without the hound dog.

My "back yard" WMU group.

Acteens sleepover.

My kids at San Antonio.

"Coal miners' convention."

**Rebuilding after the earthquake. This is the mother of the
young man who thanked us years later.**

The small hands are Spencer's, and his guinea pig was as big as everyone's.

Kindergarten class named after our grandson, Nick.

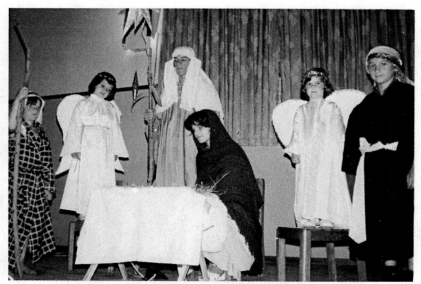

"And Amy was an angel."

Julio Villar family.

Julio receives a new believer during the invitation.

One of our many "mass" weddings. This is Gladys and her husband, Julio.

"Normal" baptismal service.

Watering her red geranium plants. "Where do you get that water in this desert?"

54,000 2-liter plastic bottles bring the water across the desert.

TRIPS

Dear Family,

Can you stand another travel story? This one is different, I promise, and is quite funny in retrospect, but not at the time it happened! Our trip was great until we got nearly half way to Lima from Miami. We were lucky (we thought) to have the first two seats in the coach section, just behind first class at the big exit door. On this type of wide-bodied plane there is no dividing wall, there is just an open space that the crew uses for a serving area. There was a little activity, but nothing so disturbing that we couldn't stretch out our legs as far as we liked and really relax.

Well, we were dozing off and BOOM!--Something hit our seats and Rodolph gave a little yell and tried to get up. The liquor cart from which the stewardess had been serving had been parked just in front of us, and we must have hit an air pocket or something because it rolled into us and tipped over right into Rodolph's lap! He was drenched with liquor of all sorts; it poured into his seat along with the ice cubes from the ice buckets. He was soaked from just below his head to his feet! They came running up and moved the cart and helped him up and tried to brush him off. I was splattered a little on my shoulder and hair, but he was soaked through to the skin all over.

We were stunned at first and it took a little while to realize what had happened. They were very solicitous and took us up to first class and brought us all the goodies that one receives there. They asked Rodolph if they could get him anything else and he said to please bring him a blanket and some hot coffee. It was there in a flash. They asked him if he wouldn't like to change his clothes and he said he sure would, but he didn't have any more in our carry-on luggage. His sweater was so soaked that we had to put it in a plastic bag; it was dripping. His pants are ruined I am sure, because they are dry cleanable only. They were extremely nice to us until they realized we were not going to be ugly about it and then they just left us alone. I would have left us alone, too, because we smelled like a brewery!

The rest of the trip would have been really pleasant except for the smell and the fact that Rodolph felt like he was freezing to death. I am just glad that the cart didn't hurt his legs or the bottles break and cut him.   I'll bet everyone thought that we (and especially Rodolph) were some kind of special drunks when we walked through the airport. We were waved on through the customs area and I think that was the reason. They wanted us out of there. When our friends met us, we didn't say anything and we noticed them looking at us rather strangely. Finally, one of the missionary friends whispered to me and asked if something had spilled on Rodolph. We broke out into gales of laughter and told them about it. They said we should sue the company for that. I could just see us suing a Mexican owned Peruvian airline, can't you? Needless to say, when we arrived at the apartments that night, we washed EVERYTHING before going to bed, even if it was late.

Dear Family,

We have another volunteer couple staying with us in our home who arrived here yesterday at 5:30 pm. They had spent the whole afternoon in the Lima airport waiting for the plane to Trujillo. We heard on the news tonight that the airport was bombed around 8 p.m. It was a car bomb and it knocked out every pane of glass in every window, even 10 stories up in the tower. Amazingly, only 1 was killed and 31 seriously injured. It was right at the international side entrance, so this couple had a close call. We always feel so much extra responsibility when we have volunteers. We want to keep them safe and comfortable while they are here, and we try not to take chances that would put them in harm's way.

Dear Mother,

Let me give you some background before I tell you about our latest adventure. Last term one of our missionaries was driving home and a drunk man ran out in front of his car. He could not stop in time to avoid hitting him, but he picked him up and drove him to the hospital. He even got him to a hospital in Lima, but the man died. This missionary was devastated and did all he could to help the bereaved family. Upon taking the body back to the family's home way up in the mountains over practically nonexistent roads, he came to within 18 km. of the village only to find that even this rocky trail ceased and there was only a path for walking, or for horses, mules, donkeys, and oxen. These people make their living by selling their milk and what few items of produce they can coax out of the earth at that high altitude. (It is 14,000 ft.) He saw the predicament they were in, and he promised to build them a road so they could get to market with their milk before it spoiled. It took quite awhile and some backbreaking work with not very adequate equipment, but a beautiful 18 km road was finally finished. It is an incredible deed of death-defying dexterity, determination, and dedication. It is a work of originality, sweat, tears, genuine sympathy, and Christian love! It is astounding!

We were invited to the inauguration of this road and Rodolph was to have the invocation. Let me tell you about our trip. We left early Thursday morning and picked up one of the local pastors who wanted to ride with us. We listened to him for the whole 6 hour trip until we arrived at the missionary's house. We found there that the missionary wife had just received the news of her mother's death, and she had left for the USA. She had worked so hard on this celebration, and while tragic news like that is never welcome, it could not have come at a worse time for her or us. Several of our VIP group had arrived and they were staying in the missionary's home, so we were banished to the volunteers' quarters a short distance away. They are not too bad; we slept in our sleeping bags, and we did have a bath all to ourselves in which there was water sometimes! The electricity up there has a different schedule from ours; they are without light from 3-7 both a.m. and p.m. (It is a better schedule than ours which is being off 8 hours without a break and at a different time each day.) Since our hostess was not there 2 of the other ladies decided not to make the trip, but I did not receive that information, so I was the only missionary lady to take that long trip back into the mountains for that dedication. It was something I am glad that I didn't miss, but something I wouldn't want to repeat anytime soon!

We left Cajamarca at 7 a.m. and it was about 3 hours on the dustiest, bumpiest roads you can imagine--5 men and me! Rodolph and I had eaten only a scrap of bread (literally) and gulped down a barely warm cup of coffee, and we were off. No bathroom facilities were available until we reached an outhouse 2 ½ hours up the mountain at the "base camp." (Interpret "base" as you will.☺) He has made a camp out of two metal shipping containers that his equipment came in and has them rigged up in a most original manner. I took both of our cameras to get great pictures and neither of them would work in that altitude. I was sick over that, but someone promised to make copies of theirs for us. I hope they remember. After two and a half hours without stopping on those roads it would have been funny seeing folks trying to get to the outhouse first, if one had been in a condition to laugh!☺

We went on up the mountain another 20 min. or so, and as we crossed a huge ravine and went around a curve we could see all the campesinos (country folk) coming to meet us--a parade that stretched out for several curves around the mountain there. They were dressed in the Sunday best of those colorful clothes of that area. Most had on ponchos and all had big hats. Some were dressed in white shirts and red skirts and they stood out. (Pun! ☺ The skirts were all those wool ones with what looked like a hundred petticoats underneath.) There was an arch made of cedar branches and other leafy boughs. (Where they got that I don't know!) The band of drums and flutes and the devil dancers with the bells on their legs came out to meet us. Later the ladies danced too! It was all very authentic except that I didn't see even one drunk, and Rodolph says he only saw two that were being led away!

At the ceremony beneath the arch, they unveiled a plaque that was carved into the rock beside the road. It was dedicated to the man who was the victim of the car accident, and it also contained a Bible verse about Jesus being the "camino al cielo" (road to Heaven). From there we had a parade into the schoolyard of the pueblo. They had decorated the road-building machinery with flags of the USA and Peru and put flowers and cedar on them. We rode into town with the people standing on each side of the road the whole way, clapping for us and throwing flowers. It was very impressive and I felt like the Queen of the May! These people were so appreciative of having this done for them. It had cut their 5 ½ hr. round trip down to 40 minutes.

After the initial inauguration in which Rodolph had the prayer, followed by the parade to the pueblo, they then began a program which lasted 5 hours. Now get the picture--I got up at 5 am, I had no lights or water, I traveled 3 hours, stopping only at the outhouse for a short break, (for which I was very grateful!) I took part in an inauguration ceremony, rode in a parade, and then I attended a 5 hr. program. We were standing on top of the world at 14,000 ft. with 2,500 mountain folk milling about everywhere and no bathrooms and no trees and the ground was too wet to sit on even when your legs gave out!

It was after 4 p.m. before we had "lunch" and the pachamanca was served. There were 4 of them--big pits where hot rocks had been cooking the food all day. They had killed 4 animals (courtesy of the mission) and put them, along with potatoes and sweet potatoes, into these pits where the hot rocks were. They covered them with alfalfa, then dirt, and let them cook. They then dug it out of the pit and gave us a chunk apiece. We were served first, but it was almost too late for me! We ate and finally started out to return to Cajamarca. This is an area that gets a lot of rain this time of the year, but it didn't begin to rain hard until we were leaving, and when we looked back as we went around the curve, we saw the people were still standing in line waiting for their food. When we arrived at the base camp and outhouse, there was a repeat performance of the stampede to get to the outhouse first. Being the only lady did have some advantages.☺ After all the experiences of the day, I was ever so glad to get back to Cajamarca and our rustic quarters--they looked like the "Sheraton" to us after where we had been! It was a beautiful day in spite of the discomfort and I am glad I got to be a part of it.

We took a tour of the city and the work there, and again I was the only lady, but I went and saw and enjoyed! Rodolph spoke in two churches on Sunday and one of them has as its pastor a young man we have known almost all his life. He has worked as a counselor at our camp for many years. He paid us a nice compliment and said he was in the ministry first of all because of the Lord, but second because of us. Knowing Tito well, I am still thinking about that. He also said we had been in Peru 22 years. I corrected him and said it was 25 and he said, "Caramba, you have been here longer than I have." We all got a laugh out of that.

Dear Family,

I am writing you all the same letter so that I can tell you about my trip to Chile. We really had a good conference, a good trip and good time. We all returned quite tired and well received by our husbands and children. We think maybe it was worth it just so they could appreciate us more around here! We left Trujillo on Friday afternoon and the trip to Lima was the most "interesting" of the lot! We made it in 35 minutes from the time we took off until the time we were on the ground in Lima. Normally it takes around 50 minutes. We had two "bumps" about half way there that were just like hitting a hole in the road in a car. At that, the plane started down and the lights blinked off and my purple corn drink spilled in my lap. (And I had on the suit I was going to wear to Chile.) I said to my friend that the steward had a panic stricken look on his face, and she said, "Well, wouldn't you, too, if you had all this going on while you were juggling a full tray of that purple corn stuff?"

Oh yes, I forgot to tell you, when we got on the plane (the Santa Teresa) my friend said her seat was broken so we moved. As we sat down in a new place I reached for my seat belt and it came off in my hand and the arm rest fell off into the floor. That really gave one a sense of confidence to start off with! Anyway, we made it to Lima and all of us were together in the apartments there, and we all went out to eat and shop. We almost spent all of our money before we even got to Chile. It surely was fun!

We left for the airport around 1:30 a.m. and the plane was due to leave at 4 a.m. I was the first of the group to check in, and Gloria and I were to sit together. The flight originated in New York and when we got on the plane someone had our seats, so we had to wait and take what was left. We were on a DC-10--one of those wide-bodied planes that they don't fly in the USA anymore because of their bad safety record. That unnerved me a little more, but it was a good flight and we arrived almost on time, but had a long wait until everyone got checked through customs. The Chilean missionaries met us and had a bus for us to go to a hotel. The Chilean countryside is lovely and it is springtime there now. The trees were just budding and all the flowers we are accustomed to seeing at home like iris and peach blossoms and wisteria were all about. It is a beautiful country; the city is full of parks and so clean, and the people are very courteous and well dressed. They have shopping malls and super markets like the States with so much available at really good prices. We were all about ready to change our fields of work! But one of the cab drivers told us, "You see it very tranquil now, but underneath it is like a seething cauldron, boiling and ready to bubble over!" We believed him when we heard bombs explode and gunshots beneath the windows of the hotel where we were staying the last night there.

We visited a park in the middle of town that has cable cars high in the air to carry you from one hill to another. The mountains all around the city are covered with snow and are beautiful! The weather ranged from hot to very cold. It was like South Carolina in the spring--you could expect anything and usually got it--even rain. We wore short sleeves one day and sweaters with a poncho on top the very next day. On the last night there we went to a restaurant on the 17th floor of a building, and it revolved around once every hour to give you a perfect view of the city. The moon was full that night and it was a lovely sight! I heard more than one wife express a desire for her husband (and family) to enjoy it with her. (I have to admit I was one of them.)

I think the wildest we got was when we saw the shopping mall--three floors high and a city block long--full of good things to buy! It was modern and had trees and fountains, and I decided at that moment that I needed about a week and a lot more money to do it justice. It was fun to look, though. Our last night there the airline paid for our stay in a swanky hotel right downtown. We were on the 12th floor and since we had a tremor the night before and bombs in the street below while there, we didn't enjoy it quite as much as we might have under other conditions. They even paid for our breakfast the next morning before leaving. All in all it was a fun trip.

Oh yes, the conference--well it was great, too. We were about an hour south of the city in a Catholic retreat center run by nuns. It had a beautiful view of the mountains. We were going from 6:30 in the morning until after midnight most nights. It was a really full program. The best thing was the fellowship with others who are having some of the same problems we are having and in some cases much worse. It also helped to build a real sense of family among our own missionaries here. It was good to go and good to be back.

Dear Mother,

Just when I think I have seen all the laws and regulations here that could make me scratch my head and think I am not reading right, there comes another that keeps our lives interesting. We were told we must go down to a notary's office and have an official copy made giving OUR permission for OUR children to travel out of the country with US. I could understand having to give our permission to travel with someone else, or even just one of us, but with both parents present? It has to be done within a month of our travel and must be presented with all our papers, or they would be detained. We could leave, I suppose, but they couldn't. Actually, I'll bet I could leave this bunch of characters we have with them right there at the gate and pretend to walk away, and they would obtain special permission for them to travel with us pronto!☺

Dear Mother,

Your daughter is now qualified to be registered as a "real live missionary"! The sweet little couple, who live next door to the church and whom we helped after the earthquake, have accepted the Lord and want to be baptized. He has done much in helping to rebuild the church and seems to be such a fine man. He came to us and said they wanted to be in full fellowship with the church there, but felt they must get their lives in order before they could ask the church to accept them. As he continued with his story and request, it seems that he and his wife are not legally married and they want to go back up into the mountains to their home to do it up right. I thought that was great until I heard the part where we come in. They wanted us to take them and be their witnesses. Now Rodolph has made several trips up there and all of them have been noteworthy in odd happenings to relate when he returned. So I was not sure if I was prepared for this, but how does one say no to a request like that?

We left our house in time to be at their house at 6 a.m. only to find that they had overslept and we had to wait for them to get ready. They finally came out to get into the car with their 3 children and a huge German shepherd dog that they wanted to take to a family member. I nearly died when I saw that fierce looking thing, but as it turned out, he was the best passenger out of the 6 of them. We discovered they were not used to traveling much when all but one of them got carsick. (That one was the dog.) The baby wore cloth diapers and no plastic pants, and I think that is enough to say about that.

Our trip was to take us up the Pan American Highway for a couple of hours and then turn off onto a dirt road for another couple or three hours. The highway parallels the Pacific coast and even though it is paved, it is a narrow road and not in good condition by any means, but it seemed like driving on velvet in comparison to the road we took that climbs up into the Andes. I couldn't decide which bothered me the most, the bone-jarring bumps or the thick heavy cloud of dust that covered us, getting into our eyes and nose and mouth. After awhile I almost looked forward to a call from the back to stop quick so someone could be sick outside the car. (Sometimes we stopped quickly enough and sometimes we didn't.) We continued on up the mountain in this fashion.

We passed over a narrow ledge where the road hugged the side of the mountain going straight up on one side of it, and dropped off down a huge cliff into the valley on the other side. We were commenting on the scenery and the gorgeous view, when we noticed a commotion up above us. We looked up just in time to see a large rock coming toward us which bounced off the road just in front of our car. Our first thought was a rockslide and we were in terrible danger, but as we looked closer we saw a woman, or what I assume was a woman, dressed in what appeared to be tons of colored tissue paper. It was wrapped all around her body and head, and she was throwing rocks at the cars below. Our passenger calmly told us her name and said she was the local "Loca" (crazy woman) who lived there among the caves and boulders, and her main activity was throwing rocks at folks passing by. He seemed placidly unconcerned with what was going on, but then the car in which he was riding, and which seemed to me to be in grave jeopardy at that moment, belonged to us and not to him!

We continued on until we arrived at the town where the mayor was to perform the ceremony. We had to locate him and get him to the office, and after what seemed an eternity to me we finally got the family assembled there, too. I held the baby and kept a watchful eye on the two older ones while the couple went through the nuptials. It was a disinterested dry reading of the legal terms of matrimony according to Peruvian law by the mayor, but all parties concerned signed the proper papers, and our couple had now set things right before God and the government of Peru. I was proud of them and ready to go home.

Then came the surprise they had for us! They had planned for us to pack several more family members into the car, which I thought was full already, and take them on up the mountain to their home place where a wedding dinner was being prepared for us all. We managed to arrive at that location via a smaller dirt road that was only one lane; if you happened to meet oncoming traffic someone had to back up to a place wide enough to pull aside and let the other vehicle pass. This is no small feat on a mountain road that has steep drop-offs down into the valley hundreds of feet below. Actually, I don't remember seeing a car, but we saw several burros carrying loads and oxen pulling carts. It was like we had stepped into another world completely alien to anything I had ever seen. The scenery was unbelievably beautiful, but the lifestyle of the inhabitants through these gorgeous vistas was more primitive than anything I had experienced before. Yet, there was a tranquility in that natural setting that was akin to something holy. As physically uncomfortable as I was, I found myself tuning in to whatever it is that draws someone to live in an isolated place like that.

We drew near to the home place which we could see now in the distance as they pointed it out. It was a small adobe hut with a lean-to kitchen attached. They cooked over a wood fire, and the wedding banquet china consisted of chipped enamel bowls and tin cups. They had set a table for us outside beside the front door, and as I was admiring this work they had done for us, I saw a cat that had climbed up on the bench and was drinking soup from one of the bowls that had already been placed there to cool. (They like their food and drink lukewarm.) I took mental note of which plate it was and determined to sit elsewhere. After the soup they served us rice and stewed chicken on china plates, and we had lemonade to drink. After the dusty ride the lemonade tasted especially good even though it, too, was lukewarm. Rodolph asked for a refill several times and the last time he requested it I could see the pitcher was empty. They said it would be just a few minutes to make another pitcher. We watched while the lady went down to the watering canal right there near the house that is shared with all the animals (cows, pigs, chickens, dogs, cats, and burros) and dipped in the pitcher. She came back up to the house to squeeze a few more lemons into it and add some sugar. She stirred it good and brought it over to fill up Rodolph's cup again. I noticed that his thirst seemed to have been quenched somewhat, because from that point on he didn't ask for another refill, and I saw him glancing several times at the cows wading in that same water.

As I was wondering how I could get everybody loaded up and on our way again, the lady who came with us brought her baby over to her brother-in-law who lives up there, and told him she thought maybe the baby had fever and would he check and see. I wondered what he was going to do and was astonished to see him get a raw egg still in its shell and pass it all over the baby's body. He put it against her forehead and under her chin and around her neck and under her arms, etc. He moved it about ever so slowly, and I looked about to see everyone watching intently. It gave me an eerie sensation, and I wondered if we were about to see something of the mountain practice of witchcraft. After about 10 minutes of doing this they gave him a glass of water, and he broke the egg into it and looked at it very carefully. He pronounced that the baby had a little fever, but nothing serious. He showed us that the egg had a little streak from the heat of the body which indicated a temperature, and he said that if the fever should happen to be extremely high, it would practically cook the egg. I guess there is some scientific truth in that, but I think I will stick to our trusty thermometer back home for the time being.

It was very hard to get the families to let us leave because I think none of them wanted to say goodbye. This was a rare occasion for them and it could be a long time before they would see each other again.

We did finally begin our return trip home, though, and this time we were at least minus the dog. I was tired, dirty, and filled with more adventure than I could assimilate in one day, and I had visions of my clean comfortable missionary house waiting for me back in Trujillo just a few hours away. I was counting off the hours and the kilometers, and just when I thought we might be nearing the Pan American highway and the bliss of pavement, we saw a long line of vehicles parked along the road. We stopped at the end of the line and asked what was happening. We were told that there had been an avalanche that had taken the road off down into the valley, but the equipment had arrived and they were making a new road to get around it which should be ready in a few hours. I do believe that here in Peru I will be learning that patience is not only a virtue, but it is a means of survival. (I think that you, of all people, Mother, will agree that I am going to have a hard time surviving if this is true.) We waited until we could pass by the site on a freshly made path over the fallen mountain. We finally retraced our route, deposited the family at their home, and arrived at ours. You can believe that my prayers of thanks that night for being home again were some of the most sincere of my life.

Dear Mother,

People are beginning to tease Rodolph about his plane trips. They ask him if he is planning to fly anytime soon, and if so on which plane-- because they don't want to get on the same flight that he boards. It really is scary to have had so many unusual things happen to him on the many flights he has had to take to so many different places.

NOTE: He has had bomb threats where he has had to get off the plane and let them search for the bomb. He has had to change planes because of bomb threats. He has had to turn back after takeoff because of a malfunction of some mechanical part. One time on a flight to Lima a window that was just two seats behind him blew out, and they had to take emergency security measures for that. The plane had to dive to get low enough to relieve the problems of a pressurized cabin and oxygen, etc. and all the passengers had to move to the back of the plane. The pilot managed to fly into Lima with his wheels almost touching the waves of the ocean and landed safely there at the airport which is thankfully right at the seashore. We, as a family, have been bumped off international flights (to save 6 seats at once), been caught in the edge of a hurricane, had to turn back and make an emergency landing because a passenger had a heart attack, been given first class accommodations because they didn't know what to do with so many in one family, been scattered throughout the plane in different seats because they didn't know what to do with so many in one family, and have been detoured through many different airports and even countries. We have waited more hours than I like to remember in airport waiting areas, and we have also had to run with luggage in hand to try to catch a plane that was leaving before the indicated hour. When I wonder at the color of my hair, I think I have found a clue in writing this.

One very poignant incident happened on a trip home for furlough. We were leaving during the time when a military dictatorship was in power and it was illegal to have dollars in the country. Everyone was checked going in or out of the country and we were not about to do something to keep us from leaving at the proper time. So we left Peru with our four children (the baby was still in diapers) and not a penny to our name. We had been gone for 4 years so we did not have a valid credit card either. We arrived in the Miami airport only to find that one of our flights had been canceled, and the attendant informed us that we would have to pay extra for the other flight they were substituting. Rodolph offered to pay the extra by writing a personal check but was informed that they did not accept personal checks. Well, here we were--a family of 6 with no money and no way to get any right away. Remember this was before the time of ATM machines, etc. I was beginning to go into panic mode again, but Rodolph managed to be calm as usual and explained that this problem was not one we caused and they should honor our tickets. They finally put us on another plane without charge. (I think it was just to get rid of us.) Then a sweet thing happened. A lady, standing behind Rodolph in line while all this was going on, reached over his shoulder and handed him a $20

186

bill and said she didn't want us traveling with all those little children and no money. She was a perfect stranger, and when he protested, she told him it was for the children and put it into his pocket. We were a little embarrassed, but this show of concern by someone who didn't have to get involved in our dilemma really touched us. We never knew who she was, but we remember her kindness to this day. Then we boarded that other plane, a new 747 which fascinated us all, and we settled back to enjoy the flight and had to sit there for 3 hours because they couldn't get the door closed. I hear people speak of "Murphy's Law" being in effect, but when it has to do with airplanes, we call it "Dixon's Law." The good and happy thing about it, though, is that we have always arrived safely and for that we give thanks and consider the inconvenience a minor thing and another lesson in patience.

Dear Mother,

I think I had one of the scariest airplane moments yet this week and I was on the ground. You remember how Grandmother used to say that if she was killed by a plane it would have to fall on her? Well, it seems like it came pretty close. I went out to the airport to pick up Rodolph who was flying in from Lima, and the fog just kept coming in from the sea until it was as thick as I have ever seen it. I just knew they couldn't land here in Trujillo without radar, but they kept saying it was coming in and I couldn't go home in case they somehow managed to land, so there I sat. I finally went out and sat in the car and watched to see what would happen.

I was sitting right in front of the control tower and I began to hear the roar of a plane overhead but couldn't see it. Just then a plane came into view and was headed straight for the tower (which is not too tall as you know). From where I sat it looked like there was no way a collision could be avoided! The plane made a terrible noise and roared upward, barely skimming by just a few feet above the tower and me! I couldn't believe what I had just seen! It was the Faucett plane that Rodolph was on and it was flying around up

187

there in a fog as thick as the proverbial pea soup.

I thought after that near miss they would surely give up and go to some other airport to land or back to Lima, but they announced a plane coming in and I was so relieved. As it was landing I could only see the blur of it when it passed the terminal. I could barely make it out, but I saw enough to realize it was red instead of orange and that meant it was an Aeroperu plane that just touched down. Rodolph was on Faucett and was still up there somewhere making rounds of the runway. I was horrified to think that there had been two planes making those rounds without benefit of radar and no visual contact. I prayed for all those passengers on that plane still up there, and the pilot and crew trying to bring it in, and especially for my husband who had to be petrified by the near accident he had just experienced. After a few anxious minutes more for everyone in and around the terminal, the Faucett plane came in and landed safely. When I finally saw Rodolph and gave him a big hug, I asked him how he had managed to stay so calm through all that danger and excitement. He asked me, "What danger?" When I related all I had seen and felt he was truly amazed. He said that he knew they were circling around a lot and had made 4 attempts to land before they finally touched down, but those in the plane couldn't see anything and had no idea they had come that close to hitting the tower. It made the newspapers the next day and I think he began to believe it then. They reported the plane missed the tower by 15 feet.

Dear Mother,

Julio and Rodolph decided to take a trip to Julio's home town over in the jungle to have an evangelistic campaign. Julio's son, Marcos, and David were to go with them, and while I doubted their ability to be of much help, both fathers and sons seemed pleased and excited about the prospect of a shared trip. They arrived in the town after traveling by plane, bus, and jeep, and began their presentations of films, preaching, handing out tracts, etc. The Catholic priest there was very friendly and even offered to let them show their movies on the wall of his church nearby. On the very first day while they were doing this in the little park beside the church, the police arrived and told them they would have to leave. The officers apologized, but said there had been a military coup in Lima and the news that they had received was that the government had been overthrown and all public gatherings were prohibited. They said they realized this was a religious meeting and not of a political nature, but to meet out in the open in such a public place like a park, could not be permitted; it would get them (the police) in trouble if it were allowed. They sort of hinted that if they could find a place to meet indoors, it would be okay. Imagine the surprise when the Catholic priest, who had already been so kind, friendly, and helpful, offered to let them meet in the Catholic church for their evangelistic campaign!

The police had to check the documents of all people coming and going through their town during this time and especially those of foreigners, and would you believe that neither Rodolph nor David had their papers with them. (Our carnets and passports were in the mission office in Lima for renewal at that time.) Our fellows could have been in very serious trouble, but the authorities there were very understanding and not only helped them during their stay in the town but in getting their passage back home.

In the meantime, this poor missionary wife was back at home with the other 3 little children. (Amy was a newborn at this time.) The media informed us in Trujillo that all of the population of Peru was under a curfew from 8 p.m. until 6 a.m. and all citizens had their guarantees suspended. We were worried sick about the fellows because we didn't know how things were over there in the jungle during this coup, and we didn't even know for sure exactly where they were. We knew they had no way of contacting us, either, so we just prayed a lot and were especially glad to see them when they returned. We realized this was yet another way that God has shown His special protection during scary times.

Dear Mother,

This trip I just took was a first for me, and now I know a little more what Rodolph goes through when he has to travel to unknown and out-of-the-way places. My seminary choir was invited to sing at a church over in the jungle, and since that includes the whole student body, the rector made plans for us all to go for the weekend and have an evangelistic campaign, too. This was a real turn-about for us to have Rodolph stay home and keep the children while I traveled alone. I have to admit I felt a little funny about going and, also, about leaving him in charge of the house and 4 children (one in diapers). I can't imagine how he felt about it, but he was a good sport and encouraged me to go.

To my knowledge there are only two roads that go over into the jungle--one up north and one out of Lima. We were to go to the northern part and not travel into the real rain forest, but to what is called the "eyebrows of the jungle." You have to cross over the Andes which are bare rock on our side, and then as you start down on the eastern side the vegetation begins. It gradually gets denser as you travel along down the mountain until you are into the actual rain forest and the area around the Amazon River. The high part where the rains first begin and greenery appears is called the "eyebrows." There are only a few places that the Andes can be crossed because of their great height. (Almost 23,000 ft. at the highest) Most of the jungle towns can only be reached by plane or boat. This particular town is called Bagua, and it looked like jungle to me and surely was hot enough, but they tell me it is still considered the "eyebrows" because of its elevation and not true rain forest jungle.

We started out in mission vehicles until we reached the town up the coast where we were to begin our journey into the interior. We have a strong church there and they let us park the cars on their property and have a rest stop before we boarded the buses to take us to Bagua. When we all got on the bus, we occupied almost the whole seating area. It was a good feeling for me to have so many people that I knew to be close by on what I considered a major adventure. We were to travel all night and arrive in Bagua in the morning. The entire trip took 16 hours. We stopped around midnight for a rest stop and found there were no bathrooms, so the girls lined up on one side of the road and you took your turn behind the line. You then took your place back in the line until each lady had taken her turn behind you. The fellows had their "rest" somewhere else in the pitch black dark, so it wasn't a major problem to have a moment of "privacy," it was just a little different from that to which I was accustomed. We were informed we could get some refreshments here if desired and I had visions of a cold coke, but they only offered lukewarm soup that had chicken feet and heads in it. Some of the students indulged and said it was great, but I passed it up.

The students were having a great time and sang and talked, and from midnight on some of them actually slept a little. I think I felt every bump and curve and narrow bridge that went over and around things that could only be imagined because they could not be seen. They told us when we passed over the highest point and were beginning our descent down into the jungle. It was not too much longer after that when the rains began and the people who know about these things began to get worried about the road being washed out or encountering a mudslide. Thankfully, I didn't know enough to be that worried, I just tried to stay in my seat while we careened around the mountainsides and wondered how much longer it could possibly take.

As day began to break and we could see a little of the surroundings, we were told it wouldn't be much longer now as we were nearing Bagua. I had traveled enough with Peruvians to know that when they say that, it only means there is still quite a long way to go. Sure enough, it would have been bright daylight when we finally arrived if it hadn't been so cloudy. The rains had let up some, but had left behind the most mud I have ever seen.

The church people in Bagua came to meet us and some of the men carried our luggage for us older ladies to the church several jungle blocks away. These men had their pants rolled up and were barefooted. We soon saw why. The streets were not paved and the mud reached to the calves of their legs in places.

We all had to take off our shoes and wade behind them holding on to each other to keep from falling. I was so grateful for their taking my bag because I would have never made that hike carrying something heavy in my hands. We shared these muddy streets with pigs, dogs, and almost every other animal you can name. The most prevalent, though, were the hogs running loose everywhere and they looked pretty fierce to me. I tried to keep a distance between them and me at all times.

The houses were interesting. They were different from the coast because they had to withstand the rains, but there were still a few made of adobe and I wondered why they didn't melt down completely. Most of the houses had tin roofs or corrugated cement or tile ones, while the ones on the coast have just straw covered over with mud. We immediately felt the heat. It was oppressively humid and sapped what energy we had left after that trip.

They showed us to our quarters and not for the first time I wished for Rodolph because the married couples had nice places nearby, but all the rest of us "girls" shared one room at the side of the church. I had my sleeping bag and some of the others did too, but most had only a quilt or blanket to spread on the floor. There was one double bed in the room, but it only had springs on it and no mattress. The single missionary, who had been banished here also, and I claimed this and put our sleeping bags on it. The others didn't mind because their blankets were too thin to put on just springs. As it turned out, this was a stroke of genius on our part because in the night we discovered this room was the location of what must have been a rat convention. They were everywhere and there was the expected squealing and screaming from both animals and girls alike! Being on the floor was to put yourself in a little more vulnerable place than elevated a little like we were. Even there, though, it was not a good feeling to think one of those things could crawl over you or drop onto you at any minute. There was little sleep enjoyed by anyone during the nights there.

There was one crude dirt floor "bathroom" at the side of the church. It was a hanging pipe "shower" and a commode inside a picket fence enclosure and it was to serve all of us--both men and women. There were about 20 of us expected to use it, as well as all the church people who came to cook, help, or attend the meetings.

The "kitchen" was set up at the back side of the bathroom wall and it consisted of a long log that was burning at one end. The pot of whatever was to be cooked was set over it. As the log would burn down, it was pushed along until a new part reached the fire. This would continue on until the log was completely burned up and then another would be brought. This was a new concept for me.

I noticed a barrel of water beside the bathroom and asked what it was for and was told it was for anything we needed. It was for drinking or washing, and it looked like someone had been washing in it already. It was dirty and had things floating around in it. There was a hose beside it from which it was filled, and so another lady and I decided we would clean it and fill it with fresh water. We spent quite awhile doing just that and when we finished and filled it up again, it looked just like it did before. We asked where the water came from and were told it came from the river. We had looked at the river and knew it was muddy and that both animals and humans used it for everything, and we felt a little sick at the knowledge we had just obtained. We felt even sicker when we saw that the plates and utensils were washed in this water and the lemonade and other fruit drinks were made from this water-- straight out of the barrel. As thirsty as I was in the heat, I drank less there than on any trip I have ever taken.

The food was interesting and quite different from the coast. We had no butter for our bread, but we were given ripe avocado to spread on it and it was delicious. We had a lot of fried bananas and rice. We truly appreciated what they did for us. It was a real hardship for them to cook for a crowd like us, especially since most of our group were hungry young people.

We had our services and the choir sang really well considering how tired everybody was. The people were very appreciative, and the way they thanked us made us feel like real celebrities. They expressed to us what seemed like a genuine gratitude for our coming and they begged us to come back.

After another almost sleepless night due to rats, we took the bus back to the coast. The people in the church there had a meal for us, but I noticed that most of the students did not have as much interest in the food this time as they did in finding a bathroom. I was told that this interest in bathrooms continued for almost a week after our return to the seminary because of stomach ailments, which I felt was due to their water consumption from that barrel.

It was a great experience--looking back on it. However, I think I will keep the children next time and let Rodolph go and never again envy his taking a trip while I am at home changing diapers.

Dear Mother,

We had a caravan of cars going to mission meeting this year. It made us feel better for the safety of it, but it was hard to keep all those personalities driving at the same speed and needing rest stops at the same time. There were 5 cars of us, and we each carried lunch and had one big picnic all together. That part of it was fun, but we had to stop for flat tires, over-heated motors, and all sorts of troubles that always happen to old cars on these Peruvian roads. The children all loved being together and rode first with one family and then another. It helped make the trip shorter and more enjoyable for them.

Well, we stopped in the desert where there were a lot of sand dunes for a big rest stop for everyone. The ladies went one way and the fellows another. Spencer, modest as he is, went farther than anyone behind his own private dune. After everyone got back into their cars we looked around and the area was vacant, so we took our place in the caravan to continue the trip. We assumed Spencer was in another car since the kids had been changing around all day, and they assumed he was with us. As it turned out, he got left in the desert. Our colleagues in the last car in line happened to see him in their rear view mirror and went back to pick him up. We did not even know we had left him until we got to the next stop. We have taken a good bit of teasing about trying to get rid of some of these kids of ours.

Dear Mother and all,

      We just got back from Cajamarca to visit the Bowies and their twins. The little girls are really precious! They are still thin and much smaller than others their age and slower in talking, etc. but are doing fine. The doctors told the Bowies when they got them that they were suffering from malnutrition, and the smaller one of the two just might not make it. She was so weak that it could possibly be too late for her. She seems to be doing fine now, though, and they eat all the time. Linda can't keep them filled. They are still very skinny and delicate, but really loving and friendly. The girls came from the jungle and they still don't have the final adoption papers, but they hope to get it done within a few months. The Bowies have certainly taken on a lot of responsibility, but those little girls are surely fortunate to have such good parents. I'm glad the Board no longer has rules that prohibit adoption.

      They have a nice place in Cajamarca. It is a rented house right near the "Inca Baths," and they have a huge swimming pool in the front yard with hot water from the thermal springs that come up all through that area. Their house is steam-heated, too, by one of those hot water canals that runs right by their wall. You can look out of the windows and see vapor rising all across the countryside where the little streams (and big ones too) are flowing with almost boiling water. They say you can cook an egg in it, and I know for a fact that you can't stand to touch it with your hand when it first bubbles up. The little mountain ladies go down to the streams and have plenty of free hot running water to wash clothes. The majority of the people still wear typical mountain dress there and it is very picturesque.

Dear Family,

      We have some news to share! Rodolph just received a call and an invitation to go to Paraguay and help them develop a master plan for a camp there. They have just received a tract of land and want to build a camp from scratch, and Rodolph was recommended to help. It was already approved and his expenses will be paid to do it. I am invited, too, and approved to go, but at my own expense, and it would also take my vacation time. I figure one doesn't really have to have an official approval under those circumstances. It is so gratifying to be a missionary WIFE--at least it has kept me in this humble spirit that I have maintained all these years!!!☺ No kidding, I am really glad that he can go.

Dear Family,

Remember Rodolph's invitation to Paraguay to help in the planning of two camps there? Well, I was invited to tag along, but at my own expense. When we checked into the cost we found it beyond our reach (over $800 round trip). So he made his plans to go alone. Just before he left the office secretary called to say that there was a new flight and Rodolph could fly for $470, and a second person could fly for $235. We decided that it must have been meant for me to go since that flight was to begin on the very day he was to leave. (One can rationalize most anything if one wants to badly enough!)

Anyway, we both went for a week and had a wonderful trip. It seems this particular flight was the inaugural flight of Aeroperu to Bolivia and Paraguay, and all the ambassadors and their wives and officials of the government and officials of the airline were on this flight--dressed to the teeth! We had the smoothest landings and takeoffs I have ever experienced on a Peruvian plane, and the best food, and a choice of 8 video programs. (They had little screens in the back of each seat.) They gave us gifts of every kind--pens, pins, 2 key chains (one in a little velvet bag from a jeweler), cigarette lighters, little wooden carts, and long stem red roses. In both airports where we landed they had a reception with a huge buffet and drinks and more gifts. We didn't stay for the one in Paraguay, but in Santa Cruz, Bolivia, I chatted with the ambassador's wife. She was dressed in the latest style, high heels, etc. like a fashion model, and I was in my Shiran camp clothes. (I was the most comfortable!) Rodolph went in his tie and coat so he wouldn't have to pack it and he looked okay. I saw him talking to all the "wheels" and he came back with some business cards. One of them was the VP of the whole Aeroperu Company and I thought we ought to tell him about the incident with the liquor cart, but I decided it probably wasn't the most appropriate time to bring that up.☺ It was truly one of the best trips I have ever had on whatever airline!

On the flight returning home there were only about 15 of us, plus the crew, on that same plane. We really got good attention then, too, but I doubt that flight will survive without more passengers soon.

We stayed the week with our missionary friends, Ken and Linda Watkins, whom we have known since orientation days and enjoyed being with them. Actually, it was being with them that made the trip such a pleasure! We saw quite a bit of the country traveling from one camp to the other, and from where we landed in Asuncion to the far side of the country where we were staying (right on the border of Brazil.) We did get to take one day off for seeing the Iguazu Falls which were about 30 minutes from the house of our friends. They are incredible! I have some wonderful pictures you won't escape seeing. I am not sure how much we helped them, but we two surely learned a lot about many new things. Also we really felt like world travelers since we at least touched the soil of Paraguay, Bolivia, Brazil, and Argentina on this trip.

Dear Merry, (and Mother and Dave)
(This is a letter I started to Merry and it got so long and involved, I decided to send it to all three.)

I am writing this above the clouds on the way to Lima. We go there tonight on our way to Iquitos, where we are scheduled to arrive tomorrow night. We just hit a big air pocket, so I thought I would write a letter to keep my mind off the flight--you DO remember I am a white knuckle traveler!☺ I will write you along on this trip so you can enjoy it with us, okay? I won't get to write you many more letters before you get here. I surely hope everything is going well in your dorm, in your studies, with the financial aid problem, boyfriend situation, and well, just with everything. We do pray for you every day and think of you and talk about you. Spencer and Amy are out at Shiran Camp and it has been so quiet at home. We are landing, so will stop for awhile.

Dear Mer,

Guess what? I am now in a "white knuckle" taxi ride! Remember Lima taxis? I think I prefer the planes!☺ More later-

Dear Mer,

We are now on the plane to Iquitos and our fellow passengers are loaded down with vegetables, fruit, chickens, guinea pigs, and Heaven knows what all! I had to stop writing to play my game of Bingo--we had to fill up the whole card to win a free plane trip and I only had one number to go when someone else yelled, "Bingo!" I am looking out right now on a huge brown river that is curling around and around on itself as it flows along. (I think the pilot follows it to Iquitos!☺) We were a little late taking off because some people got on the plane thinking it went to Pulcallpa. They had to announce that we were going to Iquitos and invite them to get off. It looks like we may get wet there because there are a lot of clouds about and the plane is beginning to bounce around a bit as we begin our descent. I think I'll exercise my knuckles some other way than writing until we land. I'll write a description of where we go and what all happens on our return trip.

Dear Mer,

Do I have a lot to tell you! First of all, when we arrived in Iquitos, there was no one to meet us. We waited over an hour while the sun went down and darkness descended. We had no idea where to go. Finally, the pastor of the church arrived on a motorcycle! We had a huge suitcase, 2 carry-on bags, a huge movie film case, my pocketbook, and your dad's briefcase. We didn't know whether to laugh or cry. Could you imagine coming to pick up us and all of that on a motorcycle? We suggested we take a taxi and follow him. This we did and went off into the jungle somewhere about 10 miles or more from the airport. We got out of the taxi in pitch black dark and entered the gates of the camp. We could hear dogs barking, big insects buzzing, and all kinds of indistinguishable sounds, but none of them of human origin. As far as we could tell, there was no one else there at all except us and the pastor. We weren't quite sure how we felt about this.

Then the pastor said he must leave us and go to see what happened to his group. He helped us to get to the "kitchen-dining hall," and he left on that motorcycle--the light of which was our only source of illumination up to this point. This eating area was a small shack enclosed in plastic mesh to help keep out bugs and whatever else was out there. It had a few tables and benches and the kitchen consisted of a kerosene stove. We couldn't even see this at the time, though, because it was too dark. It was also creepy. Finally, the full moon came up and we could see shadows and images like silhouettes; we couldn't decide if this was better or worse. Our imaginations were working overtime and I was beginning to anticipate a whole night spent out there alone--just the two of us--not knowing where we were or what to expect. We tried to joke about being taken on a "snipe hunt," but we were beginning to feel a little too uncomfortable to laugh very hard about it.

Then after an interminable wait, three hermanos arrived on a motocycle with a sack of rice. We finally found our flashlights and we held them so the men could see to prepare our supper--rice and fried bananas. Eventually, the pastor arrived with the truckload of participants. (The truck had a flat tire on the way and so their normal half hour ride took them two hours.) When the pastor tried to turn on the generator for lights, the caretaker, who arrived about then, informed him that the motor was not working and there was no one who could fix it. We only had candles and flashlights. Finally, (and thankfully) Rodolph offered to pay for renting a generator, and later on in the evening we had lights. In the meantime we had unpacked enough to prepare our beds without really being able to see, and you know how I feel about spiders, etc. I didn't even know what the place looked like or where I was until the next day. We had a full program that night and got to bed at 12:30 a.m. I was SO TIRED I actually slept some.

Now let me tell you about the bathhouse. It was a tin shack with two stalls for showers and a trough for a lavatory and two holes! I was aware that this was not the best of accommodations but it got a lot worse when I found out that both the men and the women had to use it, and there were about 40 of us! I only went 3 times in 3 days!! I made your dad go with me then! Actually I was so hot and sweated so much I was too dry to go!☺

Just outside our doors there was REAL rain forest. It looked like a set from an old Tarzan movie. I saw some of those gorgeous, gigantic blue butterflies fluttering about and there were trees and flowers and even fruits all around that I had never seen or heard of before. The second night we had rain and lightening and thunder, and I do mean RAIN! WOW! We were across the camp in a meeting area when the rain began. It started all at once with a loud BOOM! When we tried to leave we found we couldn't walk in it, because it was almost hard enough to knock you down, and you couldn't see where you were going. So those who knew what to do helped the rest of us to get beneath a chalkboard, portable tables, and some wide planks that we found, and ushered us back to our cabin. All the babies were there with their mothers (and therefore with me) and they cried and did what babies do. I snored, though, so I got even! There were about 15 children ages 3 and under. One mother handed me her darling little girl of 8 months to hold and I snuggled her in my arms. She had on a precious little sun dress and frilled socks and shoes and nothing else. She was as bare behind as the day she was born. I finally gave her back and she immediately wet the next person--I did have some good luck on this trip!☺

After the camp was over we went into Iquitos and walked around. The Amazon River has overflowed it's banks, but the flooded houses are being used anyway--the two story houses that is. They simply move up to the second floor and use a boat to get in.

We tried to get a taxi to return to the airport and the only thing that came along was one of those 3 wheeled motorcycles with two seats in the back. We put all the luggage we could down where out feet should go and held the rest in our arms. We had to put our legs over the luggage to help keep it from falling, but also because there was no place else to put our feet. Here we go for the half hour drive to the airport. We get to about a mile from the airport and are just beginning to think we have made it, and we notice the front tire is going flat. The poor driver kept watching it with a sick look on his face. I imagine our faces pretty much mirrored the expression on his. We got slower and slower and just as we arrived at the entrance to the airport, it went completely flat and stopped! I felt sorry for the driver, but I had used up a lot of my sympathy on myself by then, and I was just anxious to get back to where I could take a real bath and have privacy to enjoy it.

I am writing this on the plane as we return. We just had a Bingo game and they announced it in German, Spanish, English, French and another language we think may be Japanese. We had to fill the whole card, and by the time they called all those numbers in all those languages, we hardly had time to be served our chicha (purple corn drink) and "plastic" ham and cheese sandwiches before arriving in Lima. I never thought I would be anxious to get on a plane, but to get home and get a real bath sounds like heaven. I only got one bath in the camp and had to cover myself immediately after with bug repellant. Since that makes the dirt stick to you worse, it didn't help a lot. I don't think I will fuss about anything at home in Trujillo for a long time if I can just get back there to it! I'll try to finish this later; we are getting ready to land in Lima.

Dear Mer,

Well, I am seated once again on good old Faucett--"Santa Ana" this time. We are on our way home at last. I hate to admit how much I miss the "Dummies"! (Merry's name for Amy and Spencer) When I got in to the apartments in Lima last night I couldn't decide which I wanted to do most--bathe, eat, or sleep. A bath won out, and your good old Dad went to buy chicken while I bathed, then we ate, and he bathed while I slept. I forgot to tell you that the third occupant of our seats last night returning from Iquitos was a quite large lady with all kinds of loose luggage--rice bags, cookie box tied with string and one large open tote bag containing several pots or buckets of something. I thought one time I saw something crawl past me and I brushed at my pants. A little while later we heard a commotion two seats behind us and the steward was killing a huge black something on the wall of the plane. It looked like a tarantula to me. If it had been MY seat, I would have probably bailed out the emergency exit. Well, we just took off and are now above the clouds once again and getting ready for----BINGO!☺

Dear Mother,

Well, I have another story about a trip to Lima. It is getting so that no one asks us how our trip was anymore, they just ask, "what happened this time?" We were about half way, out in that desolate part of the desert. There is one truck stop there where someone has leveled off a bit of the desert and built a little adobe hut from which he sells a few products like lukewarm bottled drinks and stale crackers. He has a barrel of gas for those who are in desperate need, and it is pumped in a most unique way. We approached this little oasis and saw a huge number of cars parked there and a policeman who was waving us down to pull in also. We did, of course, and upon inquiring about the problem, he assured us that we would only be detained a short time. A ship was being moved up the highway on some sort of transportation and it was so large that it was taking up the whole road. No one could pass it coming or going. We waited and waited. This was another time when we had gotten up at first light to get to Lima at a good hour, and here we were only half way and nothing to do but wait or go back home!

The "short wait" turned into hours. By now the area had filled up with cars and a line was backed up on the highway for quite a distance. We ate our lunch, played games, walked around, talked to others in transit, and even slept a little. We had one terrible scare when a truck pulled up and couldn't stop and plowed into a bus parked there. It caused a chain reaction that stopped only a short distance from where we were parked. For a few startling seconds we thought we, too, would be involved in that. Thankfully, no one was seriously hurt, but there was some serious damage done to cars and personal property, and so a lot of Latin feeling was being expressed quite freely. It began to escalate and we were getting worried a riot might break out. The lone policeman did all he could to placate the crowd, but soon he felt it might be best to distance himself from all this and he left. When he left one driver decided it was time for action, so he took off in his car in the direction of Lima. There was a little hesitation and then others began to leave, and so finally, we got into our car and left, also.

We traveled quite a distance before we came to the huge boat. Sure enough, it was there, blocking the highway on both sides, and it seemed to be stuck because it was not moving at all. The first cars had managed to make a path in the desert around it and were on their way. There was a long line of cars in front of us and we had to wait our turn. It was not an easy thing to do and we wondered if we might be stuck there along with the boat. Rodolph was able to navigate the path around it, though, with only a few breathless moments of spinning wheels and flying sand, and then we, too, were on the way to Lima. So here we were, 6 hours later than we planned, but finally on our way to the big city, and hoping that dumb boat would be moved before we had to return to Trujillo!

Dear Mother,

Rodolph came home with yet another hard-to-believe story of his plane trip to the jungle. He was REALLY glad to get home this time! Actually, I think he was glad to get anywhere with his feet on the ground after that. He and Julio decided to take a trip over into the jungle to do some evangelistic work. Rather than go all the way to Lima and then fly to the jungle from there, they found there was a military plane that went directly from Trujillo over the mountains and into the jungle, which would be much faster and also cheaper. They couldn't drive, because there are only a couple of roads that even go to the jungle and usually they are impassable. When you can drive it, the shortest time would be about 5 days one way, and I am not sure if there IS a road going into the place they were heading.

Anyway, they got their tickets and I carried them out to the airport for the usual long wait. They definitely would not be traveling alone for there were all kinds of people waiting with them. There were a couple of rather unkempt "hippie" types with the stereotyped long hair and knapsacks who were obviously tourists. They were chatting with an official looking man in a pilot's uniform. Most of the rest of the passengers had to be returning to the jungle after a visit to the coast, because they had every imaginable type of produce and animal that they could stick into a bag, bundle or box and carry it as hand luggage. I saw one man with 2 fighting cocks, one under each arm. There were buckets, cheeses in cloth bags, vegetables and fruits that don't grow well in the jungle, clothes, and toys, etc. It was a sight!

Finally, this long awaited, highly praised military plane arrived. Instead of the sleek jet I expected to see taxi up to the boarding area, there lumbered up the oldest, dirtiest, most pitiful looking cargo plane you can imagine! It was one of those types that let a huge door down at the back so it can be loaded from there. There was another wait for the pilots to refresh themselves, and then I told our fellows goodbye with an extra hug and prayer for their safety. Rodolph did not look too chipper about boarding, but Julio was in his element. (He was born in the jungle.) I prayed very hard that whole week they were away. There is no way to get a message from there, and I figured that not hearing anything at all was good news in this case.

Rodolph said they boarded through that big door and discovered they were to sit in little canvas sling seats along the sides of the fuselage, and the whole center of the plane was filled with cargo. He sat down and strapped himself into his little seat and looked around. Julio was seated on one side of him and the man with the chickens was on the other. He saw that the cargo was well strapped down and was relieved because he had heard tales of planes crashing due to shifting crates and boxes. He reached down to test one of the straps and it came loose in his hand. He tested another and it also came loose. The straps were just tossed across the bundles and not tied down at all!

Just about then they took off, and the adventure began. They had to climb high enough to cross the Andes which are about 23,000 feet at this point, and so there was quite a quick, steep climb to reach a sufficient elevation to do this. That is when he discovered the plane was not pressurized. He noticed a lot of tubes dropping down from the ceiling, and it wasn't until he felt a shortness of breath that he realized what they were for. He also realized that there were not enough for every person to have one of their own and they had to share with their neighbors. They put them in their mouths and then handed them back and forth until they could begin the descent and get enough oxygen to once again breathe naturally.

At the first stop they took off the cargo, and everyone got off while they put on another load of something. Rodolph was curious as to what it would be this time. When he got back on, he was shocked to see that it was a load of freshly slaughtered meat. It was not wrapped, just placed there as it was, full of flies and smelly in that jungle heat. It, too, was not strapped down and Rodolph couldn't believe his eyes and nose.

At the next landing he wondered what else could happen, and once again all the passengers got off the plane. Rodolph said he wasn't too anxious to get back on, but the guard motioned for him to board and so he did. As he was boarding he saw the guard arguing with a lady who said her husband was already on board and had her ticket. The guard told her he was sorry, but she had to have her own ticket in hand. Rodolph was the last one getting on, and he could hear her banging on the door as it shut behind him. When Rodolph got back to his seat, he counted about 30 people standing around the plane with no place to sit. They had bought passage with standing room only! Many people in the jungle do this because it is a cheaper rate and they don't have to buy their ticket ahead of time.

Here they were, raw meat, standing people, and horrified missionary ready to take off. Just as the plane lifted up above the tree tops some of the people standing began to scream. The pilot stuck his head out of the cockpit and yelled, "What's the matter?" A crew member at the rear yelled back, "The door came open." The pilot yelled again, "Well, close the door." The man yelled back that it was done and they only lost two, and held up two fingers. Rodolph says he never found out what those two things were, but he had visions of two people or, possibly, his luggage.

After another landing and takeoff, Rodolph noticed the pilot back in the passenger area chatting and walking around. He had a short moment of panic about who was driving the plane and looked around into the cockpit and saw one of those hippies sitting at the controls. At that, his panic increased. He rubbed his eyes and pinched himself to check if he was seeing things or dreaming. He wondered how many rules of aviation had been violated on this one day's trip.

When they finally landed in the town of their intended destination, Julio said they must hurry down to the ticket office and purchase their passage back to Trujillo. Rodolph told him he was not returning on that plane even if it meant he had to walk back. He looked up the commercial flights and booked the tickets on a jet going to Lima and then on to Trujillo. Like I said at the beginning of this letter--he was mighty glad to get home! I know the apostle Paul had some adventurous missionary journeys, but I think this one may rank right up there pretty close.☺ They did have a good week over there, thankfully, and feel like they reached a lot of people with God's message of love.

NOTE: Rodolph has used this trip as a sermon illustration many times. He speaks of security, sharing the "Breath of Life," being sure of who your "Pilot" is, the necessity of having your own personal ticket, planning ahead, God's protection, etc. There were so many times that our experiences showed up in his sermons that after an unusual happening, our kids would comment on the type of sermon we could expect to hear soon. He was pretty good about asking their permission before using their personal experiences, though. Maybe I had better add here, too, that they all gave permission to write about them in this book (even before knowing what all I might relate).

HARD TIMES

Dear Family and Friends,

     I have wanted to write each of you a note, but Gloria's death has just upset us all so much that I haven't been able to pull myself together to do my usual letters. We still just can't seem to believe or accept it. We are going to miss her so much--the nationals as well as the missionaries. I, especially, am having a hard time with this because I depended on her for so many things. For those of you who may not know, Gloria Brinks was killed in a car accident on Oct. 30, 1987, in California where she was furloughing. She was due back here the end of Dec. She was our children's teacher and one of our very dearest friends. She lived a block from us on our same street. We had a memorial service for her at the little church she helped to organize, and it was held on Tuesday at the same time of her funeral service in California. She was killed by a drunk driver who came around a curve on her side of the road. She was returning from speaking at a WMU luncheon where they gave her a surprise shower of Christmas presents to bring back to Peru with her. She was only about 30 minutes from her home. Please remember her family there and us, her family here, as we adjust to this tremendous loss in our lives, personally, and to our work in Peru.

Dear Mother,

     Gladys' mother is sick and she went to the mountains to bring her down for an operation. We have been helping them to get her to a doctor and into the hospital, but that is not as simple as it sounds because all the hospital beds were full. Rodolph had to pay the bill for a senora who didn't have the money to pay what she owed, so that she could be allowed to leave and let our patient have her bed. Then the doctors went on strike and did not operate, and Gladys' mother had to leave. Now we are waiting for the strike to be over so we can start again with the process. I hope the poor thing can hold out until then.

Dear Mother,

It seems Christmas always brings unusual excitement to us and not the kind one normally thinks of with the yuletide spirit. We like to have cinnamon rolls for Christmas breakfast, and the yeast in the stores nearby is usually pretty stale. We have found a place that sells fresh yeast, so Rodolph went there to buy us a cake of it on Christmas Eve. It is not in a very good section of town, but we have never had trouble there before and the storekeeper is very accommodating. Well, Rodolph saw a group of men bothering a young girl as he got out of the car, and he went to help her. They, of course, attacked him and wrestled him to the ground and took his wallet. There were 3 of them, and they took the money out and threw the wallet back down on the ground, so he didn't lose his papers. He was not really hurt, just roughed up some, so it could have been a lot worse. He came in telling me that was the most expensive yeast we have ever had, so those cinnamon rolls had better be good.

He didn't fare quite as well this time as he did on the occasion when two men tried to take his watch. One snatched his watch off his arm and the other tried to detain him while the first one ran away. Rodolph knocked one aside with his briefcase and chased the other who looked back, saw him coming, and threw his watch on the sidewalk. It would seem that unusual happenings bring about unusual reactions in my normally mild-mannered missionary husband.

Dear Family,

This political situation is something else! Everybody is complaining about the takeover of the banks. We don't know where it will all end, but something funny took place these last two days in Lima. A group of the workers in one bank loaned themselves the money to buy the bank, and the way they managed the legalities of it was in perfect accordance with the law. It would put them out of the reach of the government because it is a group and not an individual or a few individuals that own it. I don't understand it all, but it has thrown a monkey wrench into the plans for taking over their bank to the delight of the general public. Today's paper said that the police had closed the bank; we are waiting for further developments. Where else but in Peru!

Everybody is really nervous about the terrorist activity. One of our neighbors told us that they were sitting in their church (Catholic) and a lady put a bundle under her pew. Everyone got so nervous that they made her open it up and the poor thing only had some detergent and oil that she had just bought at the store. Everybody is watching for bombs. One of our ladies who lives across town, received a note which said it was from the "Shining Path" and threatened the whole family if they didn't get $10,000 right away. She found a fuse attached to a rolled up piece of paper with a bullet in it. No one knows for sure if it is a joke or not. Personally we have not felt much pressure, nor reason for fear, but maybe we just don't know enough of what is going on. Of course, we have the security of knowing that we can leave if things get too tough, and our people here have to stay to live with it--whatever comes. Do remember us; these are difficult days for many. We need to know how best we can help and where to direct our energy to the best advantage.

Dear Family,

I am more distracted than usual because the mechanic has been working on our car in our driveway. He has been here 3 days now. (He eats his meals here so he may never finish.)

Things are pretty bad right now. We were in Lima last week when all this mess broke out, and I thought that if I could just get home I would never leave again! We got there on Tues. evening to discover that the new president of Peru had made a big announcement that there was to be a massive devaluation of the

Peruvian money among other drastic changes in governmental regulations and restrictions, and it all was to be put into effect on Wed. morning. Everybody was in a panic, and you haven't lived until you are in a city of over 7 million people in a panic! We had nothing to eat in the apartments so we had to go to the store for coffee and bread, etc. We managed to get into the store, but we found it difficult to move about or even get back to the exit. There was a long line to get milk and there seemed to be very little of it left, and the butter and bread were already completely gone. Actually, quite a few of the shelves were already empty. The people were pushing and shoving not only in a rude manner, but in a frightened manner. It finally got to me so badly that I told Rodolph that if he wanted the few things we had struggled to gather up and put into our basket, he could stand in line and buy it. I had to get out of there--which I did. Bless his heart, he stayed, and with what he bought and what Sylvia loaned us and fed us, we managed for the few days we were there.

At least during all this confusion nobody was going anywhere, and we could get in to see the dentist on short notice. It was a little scary getting to the offices, and we did an awful lot of walking. We made the mistake of going to a sandwich shop and buying one sandwich for Rodolph and 2 cups of coffee. I then decided I could have a milkshake (because my mouth was numb) and our bill came to $14. (I was numb all over at that!) Needless to say we didn't eat out again. Actually, we did forget and ordered 2 cups of coffee and a coke in the airport and that cost us $6. When we checked in at the airport, they charged each one of us 5 million intis extra, and the original round trip only cost 4 million intis. We had the choice of paying or staying. Thankfully, we had that much money with us (many times after being in Lima we don't), so we got back home to find everybody startled into a state of shock and depression.

Our gasoline is the highest in the world right now at $4 a gallon! That means all products made from petroleum like plastic products, as well as anything to do with transportation, have just gone sky high! This week the prices of some items like produce (things that are spoiling) have been reduced and people think that is a good sign. It is not enough yet, and people are hurting at all levels of life. Some of the rich folks have had their wealth completely wiped out, and we have heard of suicides and mental break-downs. The poor, who didn't think they could get any poorer, just found out that they can.

There have been blockades of the highways to rob the trucks and people in transit, and there has been looting of stores and markets. We heard last night of a church member whose shop was wiped out. He is a butcher and they stole everything he had. So many places have just locked their doors and have not opened up to the public yet. They prefer to lose business rather than chance a robbery. I didn't have as much food on hand as I usually do, but I always keep something ahead for times such as this, so we didn't have to get out right away to buy. We just stayed in until we could see how it was going to be. It really isn't as bad as it probably sounds to write it down like this, but it does sort of get on your nerves sometimes. In the midst of all this, life goes on pretty much the same; we just keep an extra eye and ear on things. As one of our missionary wives said, "I am getting a hump in my back from keeping a low profile."

Dear Family,

Have you got your crying rag out? Here comes another chapter in "The Perils of Peru"! I didn't get to mail part one of this "saga" because they blew up the Post Office-- or tried to. They managed to damage the foundation and blow out all the windows and doors, but it is still standing and I hear it is ready to get back in business soon. If this gets to you, it will be by courtesy of friends going to the USA who will mail it for us there.

Rodolph went to pick up a man from Cajamarca who came here for an operation and was being discharged from the hospital. He parked in front of the hospital where there is a guard and hundreds of people passing at any given moment, and he was gone only a few minutes. This was long enough for someone to steal our new CB radio, his jacket, the truck jack, the antenna and all the cassette tapes he had left there on the seat. Amy was especially pained by the loss of the tapes! We still have a radio at camp and one at the house, though, and those are the most important I guess. I still would like him to have one on those dangerous roads, so I can know where he is in case of a break down or other delay.

Also--last night after church Rodolph and Amy were talking to friends outside and I was talking to Maria in the entrance way, when we heard and felt an explosion very nearby! Too near, because the church just shook with the concussion, and Rodolph said he could feel the "wind" of it on his face. They exploded a bomb in the next block from where we were, and that is getting a little too close for comfort. Needless to say, the conversations terminated rather rapidly after that and everyone scattered home. An account of it in the paper today says a guard at the place where it exploded, kicked it out from under a truck where it had been placed. He ran and dropped to the ground before it exploded and was not hurt. It was about 8:20 p.m. and in a place where there are always groups of young people. It is a miracle no one was hurt. Some of our church young people were walking home that way about that time, too.

There is one house between us and a bank, and on Fri. Amy told us that she heard something like an alarm from there. We didn't hear it and thought nothing of it, but apparently it was robbed again for the 6th time in these last few weeks. They are building something out there today that is going to make it look like a fortress--can't say as I blame them.

Dear Family,

Things continue on here in a normal fashion--There is a volcano near Arequipa that is throwing gas and ashes 12 k. up into the air and planes have been re-routed around it. They say it may erupt at any moment and has already caused activity in other volcanoes nearby. There have been two earthquakes in the jungle plus many aftershocks. We have had a strike of all the hospitals in the country except private clinics, and this is entering into its 3rd month now. There has been no gasoline for 4 days at any of the service stations, there is no wheat, and many places are without bread already. We have had the lights cut off on an average of 3 days per week, sometimes more, and for several hours at the time-- sometimes the whole day or night. It comes and goes all day everyday. There is now a shortage of water and people are lining up in places like parks with their buckets to get water for their homes. Prices continue to soar; things can double in price from the a.m. to the evening. We are doing okay, but can you imagine what this is doing to people who barely make it during the good times? I just heard an interview of Carlos Garcia (VP of Peru) on the TV, and he said his government is planning to issue a silver coin that will put an end to inflation. I certainly feel comforted in hearing that!☺

Our family continues to function just as usual--yesterday we managed to flood the house with about 2 inches of water. Rodolph had put in a new pump which gave us such good water pressure that it broke something in a connection in the bathroom. The result was all of us sweeping water and taking out soaked carpet, shoes, etc. Amy and I were here when it happened, and when Rodolph and Spencer came in I remembered my WMU meeting and left them with it. What a blessing WMU is!

When we bought this new pump Spencer carried it in its box as hand luggage through the airport in Lima, and we almost had an incident with the security there because of it. They asked him what he had, and he answered without thinking, "Una bomba." There was an immediate reaction from the guards, and he thought just in time to add, "Una bomba de agua." The same word in Spanish is used to mean "pump" and also "bomb." He added very quickly the words to describe a water pump before we all got detained and put in jail.

Dear Mother,

The new helper is really good and works all the time, but is

215

so set in her mountain ways that it is really hard to teach her something new. I still have to do all the washing, most of the cooking, and all of the baking. (She had never seen an oven.) She keeps the floors really clean, but doesn't clean the furniture and other stuff like that, and we have so much dust. She is really faithful to water the yard, though, and does many things that others don't want to do. Every morning around 6 a.m. she gets up and sweeps all around the house, the driveway, and the sidewalk in front of the house (in front of the wall on the street). She sweeps the house at least 10 times a day I think. She never stops to rest and never walks when she can run, but spider webs hang from the pictures and lamps. Sometimes I think she is just so tiny that she just can't see that far! She is 39 years old, so I guess that has a lot to do with learning new ways. She has finally learned to dial the telephone, but is scared of it and will only use it in case of emergency; she walks down the block to tell her sister something. She is a surprisingly good cook of the few Peruvian things she knows, but somehow our tastes haven't yet gotten accustomed to chicken heads, etc. in a stew. (I am really generous and let her take all that home to her family.) Maybe we could send you a bowlful home by David when he leaves, if you think it sounds like something you might want to share with the family?☺

There has been so much sickness among our people and everyone has come to us for financial help, but there is no extra money around to help them. We have given away about $300 this month to people in dire need. I don't want to sound selfish, but I told Rodolph that we just can't keep on doing that each month because there is just no end to it, and there is an end to our ability to help like that. You know him, though, he can't say no even when it is the only thing left to say. The wives of two of our pastors were sick this month, and Segundo's daughter has to have her tonsils out and a lot of treatment for a sinus condition. A complete stranger was robbed and Julio asked Rodolph if we could help, and he "loaned" him $60. Mrs. Davalos asked for money to start up a little business and many others have asked for things like that, and we had to turn them down and just give to those in the worst condition like in the hospital or needing food or medicine. If you know of anyone who has won the lottery and needs a place to spend some of his money, I think I could direct him to some worthy causes.☺

Dear Mother,

I had a foolish thing happen to me. I slipped playing volleyball and tore the ligaments or tendons or something in my ankle. It swelled and turned blue up to my knee, and I can't walk. Rodolph tried to buy me some crutches and was told they would cost $38 and they would order them from Lima. He went to pay and they said they would give him a discount which would make the bill $65. It seems the price was for only one of them. We learn new things all the time!

The Furrs' car was stolen from in front of their house around 8 p.m. the day before Max got home from the USA, so Rodolph had to help see about things. When he talked to the police they said they would go and look for it that night, but only if he would buy them gasoline for the patrol car! They also wrote him an order for an "official capture" if he found it. Can you believe that? We haven't heard a thing from it, so I am afraid it is gone for good. I wonder if we will ever get used to this kind of thing, and then I ask myself--should we?

Dear Mother,

I have some sad news to relate. Rodolph and I decided on the spur of the moment to visit La Esperanza Church this Sunday. Hermana Guillermina met us at the door and we hugged and talked awhile. Later during the morning service, she brought the message and it was very good. I remarked to Rodolph that she looked really good and in better health than before. We had a nice time visiting with the folks there after the service and came on home to eat lunch. We were still eating when her husband called from the hospital and told Rodolph that she had died. It seems she and her

217

two year old grandson had walked to the little market there nearby to buy something for lunch, and she passed out in the street on the way home about a block from her house. When they got to her she had no pulse and was DOA at the hospital. Her son, David, now an MD, was on duty there when they carried her in! (This is Tito's mother, too). It was a real shock for us and a real loss for the Christian community. I counted on her so much for mature, stable counsel and support. She will be greatly missed.

Dear Family and Friends,

Last night as we were on our way to pick up our new puppy (a miniature dachshund we named "Teeny Weeny" and call "TeeWee") we saw a commotion on the main avenue as we turned onto it. My first impulse was, "Get though this quick!" I thought there was a riot or demonstration in progress and we would be caught in it. Then we realized they were trying to stop someone to take a little 9 year old boy to the hospital. He had been hit by a car that had fled the scene. We put the boy in our car and waited until his father arrived running and scared to death. Amy and I both got out to make room, and Rodolph took them to the hospital. Then the mother came running up with a tiny baby in her arms. Amy and I walked her home and told her we would return (which we did). They are an extremely poor family and new in town; he is working as a watchman for a very small brickyard. The first question their oldest little girl asked was, "Is my brother dead?" Then, "Does he have a broken leg?" Then, a statement made with a face filled with agony and desperation, "This will cost money."-- And of course, they don't have it--no insurance--no hope.

This is when we receive assurance of our calling to be here. We can help in cases like this. We can show love and share the hope and peace that is only available through our Lord.

Dear Family,

One of our pastors was returning to Trujillo on the bus and

saw a package under a seat that looked suspicious. He showed the bus driver who quickly picked it up and threw it as far as he could. It exploded, blowing out all the windows of the bus and pretty much destroying it. Thankfully, no one was killed. Many of the passengers received bruises and cuts from flying glass and debris, but they were saved by the alertness and brave action of both our pastor and the driver. This is a daily occurrence and our normal life here. Hardly any of this makes the papers; you only hear of it when it happens to someone you know, and that happens far too often!

Dear Mother,

This electricity going off and on gets on your nerves. One of our missionaries said they received a video tape of a movie they wanted to see and it took them 2 days to see a 2 hour movie! The whole family ran to watch it every time the lights came back on. You have to laugh; it's all you can do.

I had my butternut pound cake in the oven last week and the electricity went off just as it was beginning to rise. That's when I discovered my new gas stove has an oven that works on an electric spark.

Then as if that was not enough to fray my nerves, when the electricity came back on I discovered someone had left the faucet in the bathroom open. It would be easy to do because if the lights are out the pump doesn't work, and without the pump there is no water to tell if the tap is on or off. So when the electricity came back on, the water ran until it overflowed the lavatory and flooded almost the entire house. This has happened more times than I care to remember, but at least we have had very clean floors for awhile after each inundation!☺

Dear Mother,

Do you realize that this post office strike has lasted 5 months? No mail, coming in or going out, is tough. I am just glad we can get friends and their friends to carry mail out for us. There are so many unlikely things happening that it seems like what is normally unusual, has become unusually normal--like no gasoline, no lights, no water, no bread, but increases in prices, crime and terrorism. However, we are still able to enjoy a good joke about it. A fellow missionary remarked about the water shortage here in Trujillo and said she was glad that we didn't have foot washing services in our churches, because if we did, we would have to dry-clean them.

Rodolph was out of town the other day and left me with the car, but also an empty gas tank. I had to wait in line 3 hours to get some gasoline. Well, one of our friends waited even longer than I did and it gave out just as she got to the tank, so it could have been worse. Sometimes it's hard to remember that we are supposed to have a sense of humor about all of this.

Dear Mother,

Poor Bertha, I have felt so sorry for her and have not known how to help her. She got word this past week that her mother, who lives way up in the highest Andes in the most primitive conditions possible, had an infection in her leg. She had stepped on a stick which punctured her foot, but she thought nothing of it. Many times these people walk barefooted even in that extreme cold of the high altitudes, and the rocks and rough places don't seem to bother them. However, this time proved to be different. Even the villages up there don't have access to much medicine, and this family lives in an isolated place way off from the nearest settlement. Someone did manage to get word to Bertha and her family by a truck driver who was passing through. They got together what they thought she needed and we helped them pay for it. They sent it up to her, but it arrived too late. The next word they got was that their mother had died. They were devastated and there was little we could do to comfort them. Most of the people here mourn and express their grief more emotionally than that to which we are accustomed.

Dear Mother,

    I had an experience this week that didn't scare me so much at the time, but now that I have had time to reflect on it, it does frighten me. I think I have learned a lot from it, too. Rodolph and I left all the children for the first time to do some shopping for ourselves and, also, fill the requests of our station which turned it into a shopping trip for almost all the missionaries in Trujillo. We drove down to Lima for a two day stay and carried a bunch of stuff from the folks here. On the way back we were to be practically a transport company for bringing them the things they ordered or had left in Lima to bring back at the first opportunity. Apparently we were the first opportunity, because we had the biggest load of just about everything you could think of in that car! We had not only groceries and suitcases of clothes, but a TV set, a water pump, a set of silverware, and you name it; we had it. Now I have told you that our car is the oldest in the mission and I don't know if the strain of such a load was just too much for it or what, but half way back, right in the middle of the desert, it stopped. Here we were, the two of us, that vast wasteland of sand and rock, an empty highway, and a tantalizing array of products all for the taking. We knew the nearest town was over an hour in either direction, but we weren't quite sure how far. Rodolph managed to get the car to the side of the road, got out, and checked under the hood. He determined that it was something like a fuel pump (I don't remember exactly) and he fiddled around awhile before he decided it had to be replaced. I think I suggested something silly like looking under some of the rocks and seeing if he could find one there, because I knew what was coming next. Sure enough, he said he must hitch a ride back to the next town, buy the part, return, and put it on. I said, "Okay, I will go with you." He said, "Oh no, you have to stay with the car because we have so many things belonging to other people in there, and we can't leave those here without anyone to guard them."

    The Pan American Highway, beside which we were stopped, is a ribbon of asphalt reaching from Ecuador to Chile through the whole length of Peru, and it is the only route from north to south in the country. One would think that maybe it would be well traveled, but many times we travel for miles without seeing another vehicle. This was one of those days. Finally, the oldest truck you have ever seen lumbered up at a snail's pace, and Rodolph flagged it down. Actually, he sort of ran beside it while he talked because I think the driver was scared that if he stopped, it wouldn't start again. An agreement was made to take him and he hopped on and left me, just like that. He did manage to yell back to me that he would return in two hours maximum. When I heard him I remember thinking, "Two whole hours, by myself, at the side of the road--this is going to be an eternity! I hope I can stand it!" It's a good thing at that point that I didn't know just how long I would be there alone!

It was a beautiful day. The sun was brilliant, there was a cool breeze, and I could actually see a little bit of the ocean in the distance. If I strained to look, I could see it crashing up on the rocky beach. I admired the scenery for awhile, read a book I had in English, studied my class plans, and walked a little bit--but always keeping the car in sight. I ate my lunch and eyed his. I searched out a bathroom, and did edifying things like singing to myself, watching the lizards and other little creatures of the desert, and thinking bad thoughts about husbands who always move so slowly. A few cars went by on the highway and a few more old trucks, but they only slowed down and the occupants stared at me with strange looks on their faces. A couple of vehicles looked like they might stop, and I thought my heart might stop, too, if they did.

The two hours passed and I began to look for Rodolph's return. Three hours passed, then four, five, and six. By then the sun had traveled completely to the other side of the car and was getting a little low, and a little panic was beginning to set in. Thoughts now of what has happened to my wonderful husband, the father of my children, the one I love so much, were put ahead of concern for my own safety. I forgot all his faults, I just wanted him back. At this point, my activity consisted of just one thing-- praying for his safe return.

After 6 hours had passed, I saw a vehicle in the distance

through the rear-view mirror and watched it approach and saw it was going to stop. I held my breath, and then I saw Rodolph jump down and start over to the car. He was dirty and exhausted, but he had a bundle in his hand. I just can't describe my feelings at that moment, and maybe it is better that I don't try, because mixed in with all those of praise for God's protection were some that are not worthy to be mentioned. He began the job of replacing the part under the hood somewhere, and I prayed very earnestly that he had the right one and it would fit. While he worked he related his adventures. It seems he had to go from one town to another until he could find what he needed, and that included finding transportation from one place to the other. He finally finished this missionary "assignment" as a car mechanic, and asked me to start the engine while he watched. I held my breath, and you can bet I prayed hard before I turned that switch key! When I did, the most beautiful sound in the world followed--the engine started! We got on home only about 7 hours later than expected, but it never looked so beautiful as when we drove into our driveway. God is good.

Dear Mother,

Last Friday when we were downtown, we turned the corner and came face-to-face with two big military tanks that had their guns trained on a group of demonstrators right in front of us. We decided it was time to be elsewhere fast. We pray for a peaceful turning over of the government, but have no idea how it will all come about. I am buying up food today so that we can stay in if we have to.

Dear Mother,

It is hard to get used to these crazy rationing laws we have here. The latest is that you can only buy beef for 15 days of the month. It cannot be sold in the market, stores, or served in restaurants during the other 15 days. I think the idea is to try to build up the herds of cattle which are really poor, both in number and in quality. It is impossible to raise herds here in the desert because of the lack of pasture lands, and so they raise them in the mountains and have to walk them down to the coast to sell. We have seen those cattle walking along the road from camp, and while they may have been fat when they left the mountains, those we saw were really skinny-looking by the time they reached here. We only eat beef when it is ground up anyway, because it is so tough. There are a few cuts you can cook in the pressure cooker until it is edible, but doesn't have a great flavor. I am glad that we have enough electricity right now to run my freezer, so we can have meat during the other 15 days if we want it. I think I might feel like someone could come in and arrest me if I ate it then, though!☺

Dear Family,

Julio was on the bus to Huaraz at night and 5 armed robbers stopped them and stole everything but the clothes the passengers were wearing. They were looking through the luggage when another bus arrived. The assistant on the other bus took the pistol of a policeman riding the bus and began a shoot-out with the men. There were bullets flying everywhere! They finally fled. Poor Julio! This time they got Maria's watch! He had borrowed hers because he had his watch stolen the week before walking to church. His car has been stolen twice and he has been robbed countless times! I told him he was like a magnet attracting robbers.

Dear Mother,

To give you an idea of the economic condition here now, an article came out in the paper today with a picture. It showed a long line (over a block long) of children that had been waiting there for days and sleeping there at night to receive a plastic toy promised by one of the political parties. That pulls at the heartstrings.

Dear Mother,

It was so hard to send Merry off, but the anxiety of Rodolph's illness took the edge off of our homesickness for her. First we prayed a strange prayer, "Lord, please give him hepatitis," because the alternative option was a tumor in the liver. Then we prayed, "Thank you, Lord for typhoid." The doctors still don't agree as to the diagnosis that he has both hepatitis and typhoid at the same time. They said he definitely has typhoid, but now he has turned a bright Easter egg yellow, so there is no doubt that he has hepatitis.   NOTE: We had gone to Lima to see Merry off on her trip back to the States when Rodolph felt ill. We were so fortunate to be there where he could get good medical attention. This was Rodolph's 2nd case of typhoid and 3rd of hepatitis. When he had typhoid the first time, we almost lost him because it took the doctors in Trujillo 2 weeks to diagnose it and then give him the proper medicine. It took months for him to recuperate fully. This time, he got proper care in the hospital. We were in Lima 16 days with clothes for 3 days, so we were very grateful for the mission apartments where we could be safe and wash clothes and cook our meals. God provides.

Dear Mother, Clyde, and Dani,

I have tried and tried to write and somehow, I just can't, but I am going to get this off someway. How are all of you doing? We think of you constantly and wonder how you are managing. I am doing okay, but don't feel too good sometimes, guess that is to be expected at this stage of pregnancy. We finally heard the tape of the services yesterday and thought they were so beautiful and appropriate. Please do thank Rev. Vaughn for sending the tape and also for the service, itself. I plan to write him when I can. It was certainly a tribute to Hampie, and he sounded like he really knew her well. It helped me to hear the service, but frankly, I just haven't felt like I could stand it right lately. Not being able to be there with you all, did something to me, I think. I don't mean that you should worry about me or anything like that, but I loved that crazy sister of mine, and it hurt more than I thought possible to not have seen her for so long a time and then not to be able to be there with you all for the funeral. Also, by not being there, our way of life here is not affected like yours and it is just hard to accept yet that she is not there anymore. Is Dani okay? Everyone here asks about her. I don't think I have received a card or letter from home but that they don't mention how strong you have been during it all, Mother. I know that has been a help to you, too, Clyde. I just wish there was something I could do to help you all. We do love you so much and think of you all the time and never forget to pray for you.

Dear Family and Friends,

The most difficult experience of this four year term was Papa's death last February. (Rodolph's father) It was very hard to be away from the family at that time, but as in every other experience we have found the Lord providing the grace that is more than sufficient to meet our needs. We were in our camping program at the time that it occurred, and the counselors had a very meaningful memorial service for us during the very hour of the funeral services back in the States. They expressed their love and appreciation for Rodolph and his Christian witness to them, and it was at this camp that several made their decision to go into the ministry and began making their plans to attend the seminary. This meant so much to us and gave meaning to our decision not to return to the States for the funeral. Rodolph agonized over that decision, but because he had just gotten back from a visit to see his Dad a few months earlier, he felt like this was the right thing to do. It apparently was, because these young men speak of his strength during this time as being a deciding factor in their lives.

This is a letter from Merry after the death of Rodolph's father:

Dear Family,

Dad, I just want you to know that I've been praying for you in a special way. I know it really must be hard with Papa's death and all. The service was truly beautiful, and I almost felt like I had taken a quick trip to heaven and back. I know Papa is fine now, and I know Granny was surely glad to see him! We really will miss him, though; I guess that selfish human part of us just wants to hang on. I'm just so glad I got to know him, and I've learned things from him that I'll never forget as long as I live.

Dear Mother,

There are so many sad things that happen to families here that I try to be prepared and strong without becoming hard or indifferent, so that I can possibly be of some help when needed. I found this week that you just can't be prepared for some things, and this one really got to me. Rodolph had carpenters out at camp to work on kitchen cabinets, tables, and chairs, and they had building materials scattered about. One of the workers who had been hired to help mix and pour cement arrived late and asked if we had any scrap lumber we might could give him. When asked what he needed it for, he replied that he wanted to make a little casket for his baby that had died during the night. Rodolph asked the carpenters to make it, and we lined it with a soft blue blanket I had here in our cabin. They set it on our front stoop for the worker to come and pick it up, and every time I looked at it tears blurred my vision.

Dear Mother,

One of our missionaries had a very upsetting experience this past week. He had been searching for property on which to build a mission house. He found what he wanted and in the process of trying to get the legal work done, he was confronted with the opposition of the neighbors and the refusal to sell it to him on the grounds that they didn't want Evangelicals in their community. It makes one understand a little more how it feels to be a minority group and an unwanted one at that! I think I will have quite a bit more concern and not just tolerance for ethnic minorities after this. I thought I had a good attitude toward them, but I have never been one of them before now. It gives a new perspective.

Dear Mother,

We have yet another new experience to add to our growing list, and this was a sad one. One of the young girls who comes to our house to visit Merry frequently (and I have the suspicion that she also comes to be near David and his friends) has a rather unusual household. They are a very prominent family because their father has been the chief executive officer of one of the major banks for all of the north of Peru. The mother died several years ago, and they recently moved to Trujillo. There are 4 boys and 2 girls and the oldest has just had his 21st birthday. This girl is 14 and is the next to the youngest; she has a younger brother. She was visiting us this past week while her father and sister were traveling to Lima by car, and we received word that they had a terrible accident on the way.

It was strange to see how Peruvians handle a tragedy like this. They first reported the accident and said it was serious. Then they said the sister was pretty badly broken up, but would be okay. Then they reported that the father was really badly hurt and the older boys had gone to see about him. They kept on reporting a little worse and a little worse, until even the young girl at our house knew they were not telling her the truth. She said, "My father is dead, isn't he?" Even so they would not tell her, but by then I had found out that he had died instantly in the wreck, and I told them it was cruel to prolong it like that and they shouldn't lie to her. Finally they told her he was dead.

She took it better than I thought she would, but the thing that surprised us so much was that she wanted to stay with us and wanted me to go with her to the viewing, etc. It was a touchy situation because there were no close family members to take charge, and there were many "friends" who wanted to take advantage of the situation. They were vying for favored positions with the family. I wanted to do what I could to help but stay in the background, and she wanted us to be with her and wanted to stay at our house as much as possible. It was hard to know the right thing to do to be a support for her, but not step over that thin line of interfering in the Peruvian ritual of having a Catholic funeral for a very prominent man. There was so much chaos during this time of people coming in and out of their house who were unknown to the children, that an unscrupulous woman, posing as a friend of the family, robbed them of many valuable possessions. This was not discovered until some time after the services were all over.

This young girl continues to come and stay here as much as they will let her, but it has become a problem for some of their friends to see her here, I think. We have just tried to be as supportive as we can, but my heart goes out to that group of children without mother or father now. The older ones are trying hard to get finances in order, etc. They have to move soon from that big house because it belongs to the bank. They have to make so many decisions for a family of 6 that it would daunt an experienced business man, and none of these have even finished their education yet.

All of this has really made an impression on Merry and David, too, and they have been great in the manner that they have given their support and comfort as friends. I pray our Christian witness during all of this has been positive and has spoken to them in some way.

Dear Mother,

We are so thrilled to get the notification that we will receive some relief money to help out in these crisis times. We can now go ahead with some of the plans we had for the area to let the churches be involved in a simple feeding program to help families that are literally starving to death. It is hard to see the circumstances in which we find many of our people who have been okay up until now. We, ourselves, have been inconvenienced by the shortages and prices, but there are many who have made a reasonable living up to this point who cannot provide enough food in these days to keep their family from feeling hunger. It made me feel sick to hear reports of people who were standing there in the market with tears running down their faces because the money they had wasn't enough to buy anything, much less what they needed. Money held from day to day devaluates to the point of being worthless. It can't go on and on like this; I wonder what will become of it all?

The wonderful thing that is happening, though, is the surge in attendance at church and even the rise in stewardship; that one is hard to explain. The most beautiful of all is the reaching out to one another in love and compassion that we see in all our churches. There is story after story of someone helping another in need, even when their own resources are very meager. This warms the heart.

(NOTE: A profusion of orchids seen during this time!)

Dear Mother,

We had another change of currency this week. The announcement came out that since the "sol" had changed to the "inti" at a rate of 1,000 to 1 (not so long ago), the money has devaluated so much that they are now going to come out with a "New Sol." This will have the value of a million intis to one new sol. My mind can't comprehend this kind of finance. When Rodolph changes a $100 check at the bank to intis, he can hardly stuff all those bills into his big briefcase. We have been buying simple things like vegetables and fruits for millions of intis, and I am grateful for anything that will simplify that. Gasoline is $4 a gallon and ground meat is $8 a kilo, to give you an idea of what we are up against. These are the prices that you pay if you can find it available. The merchants put things away and speculate on getting a better price than they paid for it, so many things are just not to be found. I am getting pretty good at anticipating and stocking up, too. Having a freezer has really helped out, but some of our people don't even have electricity, so their existence is from day to day. Learning how to use leftovers is one thing I have tried to teach here in nutrition classes at church, but it is an uphill thing. It is against what they have always known about things spoiling in this weather, so the custom is to just feed it to the animals if it is left after a meal. There are many things that could be recycled and good for the family, especially in these lean times, that don't get utilized just because they don't realize it can be done. One of our ladies at church has studied nutrition, and she is giving classes now on how to make the most of what can be found in the market and what foods have the most value for the money and the needed diet. Surely things will improve soon.

Dear Mother,

Well, chalk up another robbery for us! Rodolph and I were down in the main part of town and he said he needed to run in the bank for a minute. He parked the car on the main street right in front of the bank on the corner. It was rush hour (as much as Peruvians can rush) and there were people walking by everywhere. It was hot and so we had the windows of the car down. I knew that thieves had been known to grab a purse through a window, so I put mine on the floor and had my foot through the strap. I was admiring the many things one can see on a Peruvian street, when a man came up to my window on the passenger side of the car and asked me if the keys he was holding were mine. I knew he was suspicious and looked at him really carefully and told him, "No." I held my foot against my purse more tightly and told him to go away or I would call the police. He left, and I told Rodolph about it when he returned. We couldn't figure out what that guy was up to until the next day when Rodolph missed his good camera. I asked him where was the last place he remembered leaving it and he said, "On the seat of the car." I had not noticed it there right by my side, and apparently while one crook got my attention out of one window, his accomplice reached in the other window and robbed it. They are really slick!

Dear All,
   You know how upset we have all been about the missionary family who was in the terrible car accident on the 1st of the month. Well, we have more tragic news for the last day of the month. Lynn Davidson was on that plane that crashed two minutes from landing in Arequipa. She had been to a meeting in Lima and was returning home. There were no survivors. All bodies were so badly burned that they could only be recognized by dental records, and twenty people are just declared missing. I can't imagine the anguish of her husband and 3 young children. The whole mission is in shock, because we really are a family, as you know.
   When others are experiencing such horrible tragedy, it makes our everyday troubles seem mighty trivial. I had been complaining about not having water for 3 weeks and suddenly it didn't seem all that bad. We got that fixed and I began to relax, and then I saw a rat in the kitchen. We finally caught it in a trap, and it really was a rat not a mouse! It seemed to be an adolescent one, though, and not those cat-sized ones we sometimes see in the streets.
   When we were in Lima I did some shopping with Sylvia like usual. Her eyes are better but she still can't drive, so I was the driver and she was the navigator. What a combination! I think she could have driven, though, because I discovered the best way to drive in Lima is to just shut your eyes and GO!

Dear Mother,
   One of our older pastors visited us this week and he began to tell us tales of his life before he became a minister. He was a policeman and some of his stories had my hair standing on end. There was something he told, though, that I just can't get out of my mind. He said that he was sent to bring in a man who had escaped from prison where he had been serving time for stealing. He was

reported to be at his home, and our friend set out to find him. He approached the house very quietly and looked in the window. As he peeked in he saw that some of the children were sitting around the table ready to eat. A little boy who was sitting there was told by his mother to get up and leave because it was not his day to eat. He had eaten yesterday and hopefully could eat tomorrow, but not today. Our friend said he quietly backed away, tiptoed off, and reported to his superiors that he could not locate the escapee. The cake and coffee we had been sharing suddenly seemed like a scandalously sinful thing to be doing.

Dear Mother,

I was reminded of what that man in Costa Rica told us about Peru, and Trujillo in particular. We asked him what it was like, and he replied, "It is a lunar landscape." After arriving and especially during that first trip through the desert from Lima, I could readily see why he said that. I really thought God might have made his first mistake in thinking I could adjust to this place after the lush green of South Carolina. Would you believe that I can now see the beauty in those crescent sand dunes that travel across the desert floor and even across the highway. (They have men with brooms who sweep it regularly.) The bare rock mountains in one area are red and green and orange and blue, where minerals have tinted it with indelible color. Some days the ocean is an unbelievable shade of green or blue with huge waves rolling over onto the sandy beach or crashing into the cliffs. You can see forever, if a mountain is not in your way. I understand for the first time what some of the missionaries at orientation who were from Arizona meant when they said the mountains at Ridgecrest suffocated them, because they were used to open spaces like these. The Lord's power is amazing not only in the natural beauty of His creation, but the changes He brings about in individuals. I never thought I could learn to love this place like I do!

A funny thing happened traveling through that desert,

though; we were half way to Lima and needed a bathroom stop, and as you know, the better places for this kind of thing are not in a service station or store or restaurant, if you could find one. So, we were looking for a convenient sand dune that would serve for both boys and girls, and we finally stopped when we saw one that seemed to be a likely spot. I was walking across the desert floor and saw a piece of paper that the wind blew across my path. Would you believe that here in Peru, in this bleak spot, out in the middle of nowhere, there was a piece of sheet music that was entitled in English, "Take Time to Smell the Roses." It did not seem to even be dirty, but I was afraid to pick it up and take it back with me to prove I had seen such a thing.

(NOTE: Would this have been an Orchid?)

MEDICAL NEEDS

Dear Mother,

I am so embarrassed. Merry was sick the other night and we had to call the pediatrician that the other missionaries recommended, and he came right away. We were so glad to see him; he prescribed an antibiotic for her, his bedside manner was very pleasant, and he didn't seem to mind coming out to the house. Here we are in our first week in Trujillo and Merry gets sick just like she did in our first week in Costa Rica. At least we get to meet the doctors right away wherever we go.

The reason we have red faces, though, is this--we asked him about the fee for his services and he said, "3 libras." We knew the Peruvian currency is soles and we had never heard the term "libras," so we thought that was what he meant. (It took me the whole year to get the colones straight in Costa Rica, now we have another type of money to learn that is completely different in value and looks.) We exclaimed that we thought that was very economical and gave him 5 soles and told him to keep the change. Now it was his turn to have a red face, and he sputtered a little in trying to respond.

That was the first clue to make us realize we had done something wrong. It was then that we got our first lesson in local Peruvian language that is not quite slang, but not quite official either. A libra is worth 10 soles, so the doctor had just asked us for 30 soles and we had given him 5 and told him to keep the change. (He only asked us for $10 for a house call and we gave him $3.) Are we the last of the big spenders or not? The next time one of the kids get sick I think I will look for another pediatrician, because I am sure I will find it hard to face this one again any time soon.

Dear Mother,

I never thought I would have to do some of the things we have been called upon to do. Rodolph has encountered more than I, of course, but we both have found ourselves in situations where we were the nearest thing to a medical doctor in the vicinity. (Now that's being really bad off!) We fully expected to be asked to get a sick person to the doctor or to the hospital and help folks get medicine, but we have found that knowing how to clean and bandage a wound and give Tylenol for pain makes us modern medical experts in some areas. There are places where there is absolutely nothing for the patient except local herbs (many of which are very good) and possibly a witch doctor (which is not good at all). These witch doctors have done much damage to many of the poor people who come to them in desperation. Many of them try to cure the "evil eye" and other spells they think have been cast on their clients by dead people or who knows what all. There are a few herbalists who have a good reputation of just using folk remedies which have been known to help and actually cure some ailments. The majority of the poor folk, however, has a fatalistic attitude and says they will live or die "Si Dios quiere" (if God wills).

Did you know that the mortality rate for babies here is over 50%! That means they don't expect to raise half of their children beyond the first year of their lives. My mind and heart can't accept that. That is one reason they have so many children here if they can, so that maybe some will make it.

Dear Mother,

A few nights ago we received an urgent call from one of our pastors who serves in the next large town south of us. He had become ill there and had managed to get on a bus and arrive at the hospital in Trujillo. This had to be an excruciating trip bouncing through the desert for 3 to 4 hours. He entered the emergency room and was told to wait. He had been waiting for hours and could get no help. He was in agony, but managed to get to a phone and call us. Rodolph went out to see about him and stayed and stayed. I was getting worried about them both. He finally came home in the wee hours of the early morning telling us of the experience. It seems that Rodolph finally got some attention for him simply by being a North American and also because he knows some of the doctors there personally. They examined the pastor and said he had appendicitis and needed an operation immediately. Rodolph had to go out at that hour, find a pharmacy open, buy the things needed for the surgery, and carry them to the hospital before they could begin. When they finally did begin the operation, they found that peritonitis had already set in, and we are not sure if he will make it or not.

It is incredible to think how little value is placed on life here at times. That poor man started out in the early morning traveling to the hospital and then had to wait until the next morning before something could be done for him. He was standing a good bit of the time because there were no seats in the waiting room. There is some question that if Rodolph had not gone to help him, whether or not he would have ever been attended to. This has to be not only a frightening and dangerous reality, but a humiliating thing for our people who have limited or no resources. We get so angry when we see them treated like that.

NOTE: David went to see this pastor in the hospital several times, and I think this, plus other cases he has seen, helped to awaken in him the desire to be the medical doctor that he is today. He was just a teenager, but to this day, that pastor always asks about him and always mentions his visits during that tough fight he had in the hospital. Although no one really thought he had much of a chance, he did recover.

Dear Mother,

The pharmacist there in the States who has helped us so much is surely going to have a star in his crown and the eternal thanks from so many people that feel they owe their lives to him. In this one case, it appears the medicine he sent has really made the difference in life or death. The doctors here had pretty much given up on Hipolito and felt he would die soon from the malignant tumor in his stomach. They said the medicine he needed could not be found in the country, and when we obtained it for him through our friend they couldn't believe it. It has only been a few short months and they now say he is cured; that the tumor just solidified like a fried egg and they were able to peel it off and take it out. We don't understand it all; we just give thanks to God and to Christian friends who care enough to go that extra mile for someone that they don't even know.

The little 9-year-old boy I told you about, though, received the medicine, but never improved and recently passed away. It was so sad. It was even sadder to see the desperation of the parents who are some of our staunch older members of the church on the outskirts of town. They were so distraught that they even took him to a witch doctor after the medicine didn't seem to help. Rodolph was upset with them and felt they had lost their Christian witness by doing this, but I told him to not be so hard on them. It is difficult to know what you would do when you are in the process of seeing your little son fade away and be helpless to do anything about it.

Dear Mother,

One of our seminary students had appendicitis and couldn't get help at the hospital because they said he wasn't sick enough yet. The medical personnel are on strike and he was told they were only taking the very worst emergency cases and sent him home. He was in such pain that he returned again at 2 p.m., and again at 8 p.m. It was at midnight when they finally decided to operate. There were no medicines and no sterilized clothes nor bed clothes. They operated on a bare mattress, in street clothes, at midnight, and sent him home in the early morning. Actually, he was better off at home. At least he survived. (until now)

This is why we say our best doctor is the pharmacist down the street from our house. We go to him with most of our problems and he has helped us with a lot of our complaints. However, I went to him this past week to inquire about this pain that I have in my arm, and he said, "arthritis, bursitis, and old age." So much for him!☺

Dear Mother,

We had to take Amy to the doctor in Lima because she had a little growth on her eyelid that seemed to be getting larger, and the doctor said it had to come off. Now you know how Amy is about going to doctors! The whole family dreaded it and neither Rodolph nor I wanted to be the one to accompany her for the ordeal. I don't know how it was decided, but I was given the honor; so she and I went to the doctor after hours of preparing her. We talked and talked about how it shouldn't hurt much, and if it did hurt, it wouldn't hurt long, but most of all, that she had to do it and that was that. We would rather that she not get hysterical, but even if she did, we were going through with this and it would be better for everyone if she would just cooperate. We had gone through this kind of preparation before to no avail, so I really wasn't expecting a whole lot more than the usual dramatic display of temperament that went along with taking her to where she could see doctors and nurses that might be carrying a hypodermic needle.

We got to the doctors' office and he, also, tried to prepare her for what he had to do. It sounded so bad when he explained it that I thought I might be the one needing some calming down before it was over. I knew there was no way our terrified child could respond in the way he was requesting. She was to lie really still and not move anything, not even blink, and he would just snip that little growth off with the scalpel he was showing us. (This was to be done without the benefit of any kind of anesthesia at all.) I realized this could become a major war in just a few seconds and I was trying to steel myself for the first signs of the outbreak. Imagine my utter surprise when Amy lay down on that surgical cot, didn't cry, didn't say a word, and stayed rigid like a board without moving anything. She had her eyes wide open and tried not to blink. The surgeon came over and began to do his thing and then he exclaimed, "Oh my, look at that!" It scared me to hear him say something like that in the middle of a procedure! Then I saw what he was talking about. Amy still hadn't moved or made a sound, but a big tear had formed and was running down the side of her face! It nearly broke my heart and also that of the doctor, I think!

Needless to say, when we returned to report to the rest of the family, there was a huge celebration of this great triumph over fear in our daughter's life! (No one wanted to believe me at first, though!)

Dear Mother,

We are trying to help where we can with all the problems here; it is really depressing to hear all the suffering everywhere. A lady came to see me last night who said she and her husband work full time and make a total of $100 a month for a family of 6. They are people of what was the upper middle class before all this economic turmoil began. Now they can't make ends meet and the husband is sick. I have only been home from camp one day, and I have had 3 visitors with similar stories. What can we do? The group of volunteers brought a supply of vitamins and I have been so glad to at least offer something to help their physical state a little, but I feel so helpless in the face of such great need.

Dear Mother,

It was really a test of faith to leave Rodolph in the hospital in Lima while I settled the children here in Trujillo. It would have been ideal to be able to stay in the apartments, but they were full and I couldn't take a family our size in on another family there in Lima for that length of time. I was torn between staying with him and being with the children, and I couldn't decide who needed me most there for awhile.

I did get to be with him for 3 days. After I took the

children to Trujillo and set things up there, I flew back down to Lima and got in just after he came out of the operating room. Irving Northcutt stayed with him until I got there, bless his heart. It was a necessary hernia operation and shouldn't have been complicated, but one is always a little unnerved by the strangeness of hospitals in general, and Peruvian ones especially. The unknown sometimes brings on a lack of confidence that wouldn't occur in familiar surroundings.

Rodolph was so funny telling us about the doctor coming in just as he was given the anesthesia and saying, "Let me see now, this is a hernia on the right side." Knowing this to be wrong, Rodolph tried to say, "No, no, the left side!" He was too far gone to be able to get it out and went under thinking they were going to operate on the wrong side. He said the first thing he did upon waking fully, was to feel for the bandage and see which side it was on. He was so relieved to feel it on the correct side.

He has now been discharged from the hospital and is staying with one of the families in Lima until he is able to travel. They have been super nice to him. He has been with them for a week, but he says he is doing well and should get home soon. That is great news, all is well, God is good!

CAMPS

Dear Mother,

Every time I look about me at camp and see the beauty of it and see the children and young people so happy to be here, it just gives me chills. It is hard to believe that we could have this facility that is so useful and yet fits into the natural surroundings of these mountains as if it just grew here instead of being built. Our camp theme song is "I Will Lift Up My Eyes to the Hills," and it gives my heart a peculiar thrill every time I hear it sung (especially when the children sing it during camp time).

When we first bought the land I didn't give it much chance of ever being anything worthwhile, much less what we see now. I never dreamed it could become as special and cherished by us all as it has. It has truly become a place that seems set apart, where hearts are made more tender and God is able to speak to us in ways that are hard to hear in the hustle of the city. I know it affects us like that, but I have heard many Peruvians give the same testimony about going out there for a retreat. The wife of one of our pastors actually said, upon entering the gates one day, that she thought this must be what the Garden of Eden was like. Our records show that during summer camps, we have 60% or more of the campers who make life changing decisions and record it. We feel like that is a wonderful investment of our time and finances and physical labor.

NOTE: After we bought the camp property, the Peruvian government built a highway right through the middle of it, cutting it into two parts. I thought that was a tragedy until I realized it cut our traveling time in half also. We not only could arrive in less time, but on a paved road instead of the bumpy, one lane, dirt path we used before. This paved road opened up commerce for the farmers around here and they began a profitable production of pineapple, avocados, mangos, and other fruits. The camp is surrounded by this type of agricultural landscape now. It is beautiful because they have built many more watering canals, and that has made everything green where there was only bare desert before.

Before we bought it, the camp property was a place to raise coca bushes (used for cocaine) and avocado trees. The people could not understand our getting rid of a big money crop like coca. These bushes had to be cut down and dug up several times to finally be clear of them. Bit by bit, there were eucalyptus trees, palm trees, and pine trees as well as many shrubs and flowers planted, and the entire open space sprigged in grass. It is kept green by flooding the whole area when it is our time to have water from the canal. If we don't do this, it will return to desert. It is like an oasis, especially now that we have our own wells and water. I have seen many a child get off that bus and roll in the grass and just giggle at the pure pleasure of it.

We have dormitories, cabins, a dining hall, a chapel, and a conference room, all made of the native stone from these mountains. After we used all the stone left on our property from the road builders dynamiting the path for the highway, our workers followed the road on up the mountain and used the rock along the side until that source also gave out. Other people began gathering up the rock, too, when the idea registered with them that this was free building material. After that our workers had to dig it out of the mountainside. We finally finished the last building the very month before we left for retirement. We left behind a facility that requires little maintenance because it doesn't have to be painted. It is built strong to resist earthquakes, and its sleeping, meeting, and eating areas have a capacity for 250. We had volunteers from the USA who helped us plan and build and pay for it. One architect came who drew the plans for our dining hall in one week. He and his wife were a big influence on our son who is an architect now. I think Spencer got his love for his chosen profession as a teenager while helping his dad to design the camp.

When we were able to work with the camp full time, we experienced such a sense of satisfaction that Rodolph has said many times he hated to accept a salary for something he enjoyed so much. It was back-breaking physical labor for us both to get ready for each group, but once the programs were underway and we saw the results, it was pure joy! It was very hard to leave it. Rodolph would look at the finished buildings and beautiful landscaping and gaze at those majestic Andean peaks surrounding us, and say wistfully, "If I could just have another 20 years!"

Dear Family and Friends,

I am sitting on the patio of our little cabin at Shiran and watching the 6-8 year olds run around. It reminds me of an ant's nest just after you have disturbed it with your foot--constant motion! Part of our group each week this camping season will be the orphans from the children's "Village" that is located on the road out to camp. This is a first and something we have always wanted to do. I wish I could have had a picture of the group when the bus stopped for them. They were all waiting at the gate, dressed alike, carrying plastic sacks with their belongings, and wearing the biggest grins you ever saw. The director said they had not slept at all the night before because they were so excited! I told her that we in no way pressured the children with Baptist doctrines, but neither do we apologize for our beliefs. We do not alter our program for anyone who would choose to come, and we do study the Bible. She seemed to understand and accept what we said, and she expressed gratitude for our interest and invited us to visit there anytime with groups from our churches. This is a breakthrough for us because some of these places don't want evangelicals coming in at all. She even said, "We all need to learn all we can of God."

Rodolph is loving every minute--he grins and hugs the kids and keeps repeating, "Look at that face!" Then he gets tears in his eyes. (I guess maybe when I get that old I'll act like that too?☺)

We gave all the kids a toothbrush and the camp nurse taught them how to use it with a huge model of a set of teeth. It was touching to see the 10 kids from the orphanage all sharing one toothpaste tube in the mornings.

Please pray for us during these days--strength, wisdom and

all that, but most of all that these children and youth can be touched by a message that will be exactly what the Lord wants us to share and in exactly the manner He wants us to share it.

Dear Family,

We did survive 5 weeks of camp and feel like they were a real success in young people reached, response to the program, and decisions made. It was a thrill to connect with these kids and see our plans work out and even see results already. However, it was also a thrill to come home, get a warm bath, and not have to bathe in bug repellent (and only buy food for 8 instead of 100).

It was a real joy to see 4 young men between 21 and 24 years of age come down the aisle in Central Church this past Sunday to make a public profession of faith in Christ. They said that they had made a decision out at camp and it had made a real change in their lives. That makes all the headaches, bug bites, sore muscles, and lack of sleep, etc. fade into forgetfulness, and it lets us know without a doubt that it WAS worth all the effort. Its effect is like a shot of enthusiasm straight to the heart! It's wonderful to get to see the results, because we don't always have a response so soon or have it so clearly expressed. However, we also realize that there are some very important decisions made out on those hillsides between a camper and his Lord, of which we may never know. That is our hope and prayer and what keeps us going.

Dear Family and Friends,

We are in our 6th week of camp and we finish up tomorrow. We may make it after all! We have had to turn away almost as many people as have attended. We are happy that our camps are so well received, but it has truly been a big problem to not be able to accept all who wanted to go. We had to sleep 44 in tents this week and still had to turn away over a dozen who were very unhappy with us. Sleeping in tents was not all that bad, but the bathrooms and kitchen were badly overworked. We had to promise to have another camp soon for those who could not get in these camps. We think maybe the time is here for us to go into this work exclusively--on a full time basis. We see beautiful results not only in the joy expressed of being here, but in decisions made while here. We shall see what the Lord has in store for us.

Dear Mother,

We had 159 show up for camp this week and we have beds for only 112! You should have heard us extolling the wonderful adventure and unique experience that each group could have by spending at least one night of their stay in a tent! Some bought it and thought it was wonderful, but some didn't think so much of it-- and your granddaughter was one of these. Amy, along with some of the other girl counselors, were very resistant to the idea. As you know, even here in the mountains we only have a chance of rain on very rare occasions, and this week turned out to be one of those rare times. We managed for this week, but I am not sure we can pull that off for another year; we have to have more beds by then. Probably the tents are better than what many of our campers are used to at home, but they think of coming here like we think of going to a swanky resort in the USA, and we want to make it the best possible for them.

Dear Mother,

With the decisions made at camp this week we now have 6 of our staff who have made plans to study for the ministry. It is thrilling to think of having a part in the future work here long after we are gone.

NOTE: At the writing of this book, one of these is now not only a pastor in Trujillo, but the director of the camp. He keeps us updated on what is going on there and keeps inviting us back to help out. What joy!

Dear Mother,

I finally got to see Rodolph in an experience like those in which I find myself all the time. We had just arrived at camp for the beginning of a new season, and we always begin with the little folks, ages 6-8. The counselors were not doing their jobs like they had been instructed to do, and things were getting sort of chaotic. I could see that even Rodolph was getting a little frustrated and frazzled, and I wondered if I was going to see him lose it for the first time. Little Benjamin, the son of one of our pastors, walked up to Rodolph and gave a little tug on his pants leg. He was not much taller than his knee. Rodolph looked down at him and asked him a little gruffly what he wanted. Now Benjamin has the most angelic face; he has big gorgeous eyes and a dazzling smile, and he was looking up at Rodolph with all of this going full force. Rodolph asked him again what he wanted, and he motioned for Rodolph to stoop down there beside him. I could tell it was with an effort but Rodolph took the time to do as he asked, and Benjamin gave him a big bear hug and said, "I just wanted to tell you how much I love you." As he rose to his feet, I could see a vastly improved spirit in my husband.

Dear Family,

These alpacas that Larry and Joy gave us just may have to go, although they have been such wonderfully interesting pets. They attract so much attention and are beautiful. We named them "Ali" and "Paco." They have long eye lashes and are so tame that they will come up and "kiss" you right on the cheek. However, they also come right into the dining hall, and they are so friendly that they think everyone wants to run and play with them, and some of the folks are scared of them. They ARE rather big, and I imagine they do look gigantic to a little 6 year old! The thing that is really determining their fate here, though, is that they have eaten every flower and shrub that we have planted, and they have also eaten the leaves of the good trees (they especially like eucalyptus) for as high as they can reach. They don't touch the tall weeds that we don't want, they only eat the new tender grass that we have tried so hard to cultivate, and they are faster than any motorized lawn mower that I have seen! When we got back from our trip we saw they had eaten all the flowers I had just planted and even the roses around the chapel, so my suggestion to this problem is alpaca steaks!☺

(NOTE: We finally had to give them to one of our pastors who was delighted to take them off our hands. We missed them, but we could finally grow things again.)

Dear Mother,

The water fountain was installed at camp today and I had to apologize all over again to Rodolph. You remember how upset I was to use up that much space in our crates to bring it back? At that time we had to boil all our water, and it would have been quite a feat to boil enough water for 150 campers and then put it through a water fountain. Well, the missionary (Larry Johnson) and his crew have just finished up the well they were drilling, and we have enough pure water for the whole camp. I can't believe it; it is the first time in all these years in Peru that I have been able to drink water straight from the faucet! Every time we go to camp now I carry a jug of it back home on the return trip. I wish we had one of those wells at our house.

What I wanted to tell you, though, is about the reaction of our campers. I wish you could see those little children lined up for what would be a city block to get a drink of fresh, cold water. We had to make a little stool at the side for the smaller ones to reach it, and I admit that we both had tears in our eyes to see them enjoy it so much. I was glad to apologize to Rodolph again for my lack of vision and faith. Nothing we brought back in that crate could have been more important than this has become. The old hymn about "Just a cup of water" has taken on new meaning for us.

Dear Mother,

Well, we have another pet! As if dogs, rabbits, parrots, little birds, cuyes (guinea pigs), turtles, fish, cats, goats, and llamas have not been enough to qualify us as indulgent parents, we now have a monkey! I was rather upset about this one. A seminary student needed money to return to school and sold it to Rodolph for his tuition fee. (I actually think he would have paid us to take it!☺) I took one look at it and said, "That thing has to go out to camp!"

This was my salvation throughout the years when I could no longer stand things in and about the house--it was sent to camp. In fact, one of those times when we were offered someone's baby and were discussing it, Amy was overheard to say, "Well, if they did give it to us, Mom would just send it out to camp!" That gave me a little food for thought. Well, on to my story--this monkey's name was "Baki" and in his earlier life he had belonged to an organ grinder. When they first brought him to our house, he was in a crate on our porch. There was a bunch of bananas on our porch, also, but well out of his reach. When I looked at him a short while later he was contentedly eating bananas, but he was still in his crate. That was an omen and a forecast of things to come.

Baki quickly became the star attraction at camp. People came from miles around to enjoy his antics. He was particular about whom he chose to be his friends, though, and he took a particular dislike to some of our workers and actually inflicted some serious bites on a couple of them. He loved the little children and would show off for them with some really funny capers. One day he grabbed the little Bible of a camper and scampered up the tree and leafed through it like he was reading. I thought he was cute from a distance, but he even seemed to love me, and he adored Rodolph and Amy.

One of the funniest stories Rodolph has in his repertoire is about the day he was repairing the sink in our kitchen at camp. He was lying on his back under the counter trying to connect up the pipes when one of the camp dogs came running in and tried to get under there with him. That, within itself, was enough to cause some consternation, but the dog was covered with a swarm of bees! Rodolph managed to get out of there, but as he was escaping, he saw Baki covered with bees too. He grabbed a tool and cut Baki free and Baki wrapped himself around Rodolph's leg. Here he was with a dog who wouldn't leave him, a monkey who was fastened to his leg like a plaster cast, and a swarm of bees all over the three of them! Somehow, this is not the picture you usually get when we talk of "praying for our missionaries overseas," but believe me, he needed it then as much as almost any other occasion!

Dear Family,
     On Thursday morning we almost lost Shiran (the village and the camp) to a flood. We had really heavy rain continually for almost 24 hours. The river rose and broke through the main watering canal, and the water came down the highway above us. It came right up to the camp but detoured into the village. It flooded houses there--tearing down walls in some and leaving others with a foot of water inside. Rodolph took our workers, and as many others as could pile onto the truck, up to the site of the break, and the rest of the village ran up as fast as they could. With everyone working together frantically, they managed to repair the damage and re-route the water before the major crest of the flood arrived down from the mountains. It saved the village! Everyone was scared to death! Water did not get into camp, but it was close! It continues to rain, though, so we are afraid of what may yet come. It even rained hard in Trujillo; it came through our roof in the dining room. Imagine what it did to those poor folks who have straw and mud roofs, and even worse, those with only cardboard or open to the stars with no roof at all. They tell us they sleep under whatever plastic they can find to keep dry.

Dear Family,
     During this past week we have seen the realization of our

dream of many years-- we are using the new dining hall! It is so nice and it is such a joy to use the gas stoves and ovens--no more pumping up the old kerosene one and leaving it on all day long (because it is a major process to light it again). We don't have everything done, of course, and probably never will, but it is such an improvement over the old one. We now can seat 250 to eat a meal at one time. The dorm rooms and bathrooms upstairs are great, and we even have a water fountain that we can use because the water in this building comes from our well and reservoir. Not having to boil all the water we drink should be a wonderful help to our cooks. We are having the water tested, but since it is such a deep well it should be okay. Even so, we are treating it with chlorine so it will be safe.

Dear Family,

We are having good attendance at camp, and we feel like we are having a very special time this year due to the new program. Instead of a Bible Study where they must sit and read, we have a theme called "Living the Bible," and we are attempting to do just that. The first weeks the counselors do it for the little ones, and as they can, help them to take part. The older ones plan and do it themselves, and learn by doing. We take them to "Egypt" where they are the "Israelite slaves" and make adobe brick in a mud pit we have there. (Someone in the village had been making adobe for their house and allowed us to use it.) They are watched over by counselors who are the "Egyptian guards." Afterwards we cross the "Red Sea" (swinging bridge over the river), then we "wander" in the desert and eat "manna" provided by the camp kitchen and brought by car. Then "Moses" goes up the mountain and brings back the "Ten Commandments." Each week there are more embellishments as they study the scriptures and add to the scenes. We have been told that the land around the camp is very much like what is seen in the Holy Land, so all of this makes it even more realistic.

While I am sitting here writing this, "Joshua" is fighting the

"Battle of Jericho," and just before that I saw "Rahab" help the "spies" over the camp wall. We borrowed a donkey that takes "Maria" led by "Jose" up to a little village nearby, where they are told there is no room at each place they stop. (The villagers helped us out by taking part, too.) Finally, they are led to a stable--very authentic with real animals and all. Another day's studies are walking with "Jesus" to "Jacob's Well" (a spring of crystal water nearby) where he talks with the "Samaritan Woman." Later we go up the mountain and return along a road where the "Good Samaritan" is acted out. On the way back home we find "Zaccheus" in a tree. Another day we travel with "Paul and Silas" on a missionary journey and we get to see "Dorcas" down by the river. On the last day there is an enactment of the "Last Supper" and "Jesus' Arrest in Gethsemane" and on to "Calvary." It has been challenging and interesting and a lot of time, work, and energy, but worth it all to see young people respond. Merry has been a tremendous resource and even Amy has been able to help.

Dear Family,

     We had 18 of the little orphans attending camp this week. I was afraid Amy would try to bring some of them home with her--they are so cute! The camp nurse thought she had created a bunch of hypochondriacs with her talks on health because there were long lines of children waiting to see her every day. She finally realized they only wanted one of the "101 Dalmatians" band-aids the volunteers had left here. The imaginary complaints and the lines ceased when the colorful bandages were all gone. It seemed every camper was sporting one somewhere on his arms or legs, and I think I saw a couple of counselors with one, too. I asked Amy what she wanted to eat when we arrived home after camp and she said, "It doesn't matter, just as long as it is not rice!" At least we didn't have rice for breakfast! Actually, I love rice the way they fix it here, almost as much as they do.

Dear Mother,

We were out at camp this week and in the evening a couple, who live up the mountain in a small family settlement named San Antonio, came to see us. All the family members have farms round about and mostly raise pineapple, avocados, papayas, mangos, etc. To supplement their income, the young man helps out here at camp with the construction. Our caretaker had been witnessing to him and they came to ask more about what he had told them. The lady had the baby tied to her back in a "manta," (the shawl they use here for that). We sat and talked for a long time on the patio, and they invited us to come up to their village to start a Bible Study. We were thrilled to have someone come to us without our having had to initiate it. So after a prayer with them, we set the time for the next Sat. evening.

When we arrived on Sat. we discovered we could only drive the car a short distance up the mountain, and we had to get out and walk the rest of the way. There was just a narrow foot path going into the village. The mountain rose steeply on one side of it and the watering canal bordered it on the other. We had to hold tight to our equipment and watch our step. There were little streamlets of water from where they had been irrigating that we had to jump over or wade through. In spite of all of this, we arrived in good condition and felt like real live missionaries because this was what we pictured life "on the Field" would be like.

The young couple had prepared their little adobe home for us and we met under a brush arbor that served as their living room and dining room most of the time. There is a spectacular view of the valley and surrounding mountains from this area. They had invited the neighbors to come and a good group had already gathered. As I began to play my little keyboard and teach some "coritos," (little choruses) more began to come and join in. We had planned a flannel graph story for the children but the adults wanted to hear that, too, so we did everything for everybody. Some people came and stood at the edges to look and would not come all the way in. I hope they will feel confident enough to come in next time. Bryan and Doris went with us and were a tremendous help.

NOTE: Doris and Bryan Stone were in Trujillo for a school term to teach our children. We had no one assigned from the FMB to help us, and so these wonderful people from my home church volunteered to come several times at great sacrifice to themselves, to serve alongside the missionaries here. Bryan always had candy for the children and they called him "Tio Gringo" (Uncle Gringo). These great folks offered to go along with us each week and they were a tremendous help. Doris would have crayons and pages to color, and Bryan would help in anything he could, even willing to help us carry whatever was necessary in and out of there. They had not mastered the Spanish language, but their love was evident and contagious, and they were so very appreciated by missionaries and nationals alike. We were so blessed by their ministry here among us.

(They are a pair of special orchids in the bunch!) But back to the letter--

We had a wonderful evening with the people and it extended on after the sun set, so they lit a kerosene lantern that we needed both there and to see our way back to the car. As we started on that trip again along the side of the canal, our young guide told us that on this very day they had found and captured a huge boa in the stream right where we were walking. Now it would be a rare event to even see a snake of any kind in desert areas like this, but to have caught a huge jungle snake was a noteworthy topic, so we were listening intently. He continued on to say that they suspected the mate of this snake would be nearby. Can you imagine what went through my mind as we stepped along on that narrow path being able to see only a step or two in front by the light of the lantern? Remember I said it was straight up on one side and straight down on the other? Suffice it to say, from that point on I was the first person in line behind the lantern, almost stepping on the heels of that muscular mountain man who knew the ways of the countryside around here. I think I could truthfully report that my heels were stepped on by someone very close behind me too! We made it to the car and back home, which within itself was evidence of divine protection on that dangerous road at night. We feel like this group will grow into a vital witness for the people of the whole area around the camp. What joy!

Dear Mother,

Remember the little Bible study group we started up on the hill above the camp? Well, today they were organized into a church. They named it "Christ the Light of the World Baptist Church." We thought maybe a shorter name would be better, but this is what they wanted. They have built a little adobe building on a small piece of land that once belonged to the camp. This land was unusable in the master plan for building the camp because the road into the village cut it off. It is right at the entrance to the town, though, so it is perfect for this congregation. The church has one window and one door, and it has planks over cement blocks for pews. The ladies have crocheted or knitted little squares to put over some areas of the planks to help guard against splinters. This is a loving and beautiful group, who worship in a simple and genuine fashion. It is always a pleasure to visit with them. The music is something to behold, but it is theirs and they are learning. In fact, the whole thing is theirs--they have built it with their own hands, and it has been a labor of pure love and sacrifice. We are so proud of them.

Dear Family,

We went to another going away service today out at the little church at camp. They had the usual type of flowery speeches and tears and picture taking, but then at the end they presented us with a wrapped gift. I looked at it and thought, "Oh no! A huge breakable vase or something similar--I'll never be able to fit it into our suitcases!" They were so excited and insisted that we open it right there, which is unusual as you know. Normally they will never open a gift in front of a crowd. So we opened it and it was the sweetest thing you could ever imagine--a hand carved pineapple made from stained mahogany. They explained that they knew this represented the crop of the area and they had given us many pineapples through the years, so they wanted to give us one more that we could keep forever. It was life-size and inside each diamond shaped division on its surface was carved the name of a church member. They said they wanted us to take them with us and pray for each of them by name. They said to please not forget them, and my thought was, "How could we ever?" I feel like our kids now--are we going home or leaving home?

Dear Mother,

Your youngest granddaughter gave us a scare this week. We were out at camp with other missionaries and she and the MK teacher decided to hike up the mountain. It is a very strenuous hike, but we have all made it before and I knew that they knew the correct path to take, and I thought they were mature enough to not take chances. Well, they didn't get back about the time we thought they should and I was not too concerned, but I didn't like it too much. I liked it even less as it got later and signs appeared that the sun was getting ready to go down behind the mountain. We became concerned by then and got the car and drove over to where they started the big climb. We began to ask around if anyone had seen two young "gringas." (light skinned girls) Someone reported seeing them go up, but no one had seen them come down.

About that time the men were all making plans to try to find them and starting out in the direction they had taken. These are bare rock mountains that go straight up and there are only a few paths that you can follow. It can be dangerous in the day, but it is definitely dangerous in the night. By now concern had turned to near panic, and all kinds of scenarios flashed through my mind. Just as we had finished gathering together the flashlights, ropes, and whatever else they thought they might need, and the last light was fading from the sky, someone saw them coming down the mountain. We were so relieved and after I saw they were okay, I asked in that sweet motherly way I have, "What in the world happened to you? Couldn't you tell the time? Don't you know you scared us to death?"

Well, they related their adventure, and it seems they had gone up like usual but on the way back down, they decided to try another route that looked easier. There were a series of smooth dips that looked like they went all the way down on the other side of the mountain to the highway, and they began to slide down them. It was a sort of river bed eroded into the rock by the rains that had washed down. It was great fun. It was really smooth like a regular sliding board and much quicker to descend than the normal way. They slid down several of them, and when they got to what they thought was the last one, they were surprised to see there was a steep cliff there. It just dropped off straight down with no incline to it at all and much too high to consider jumping. There was nothing to do but go back up, so they started and discovered it had been a much easier thing to go down than they found it, now, to go up. It was too slick to climb and too high to reach the ledge without climbing. They were trapped.

They tried everything they could think of and finally decided on a plan that worked. The journeygirl had been a cheerleader in college and said she could put Amy on her shoulders and help her get to the next level. With much effort they managed to do this. However, once Amy was on the next level she couldn't reach far enough down to help her friend up, so she took off the black sweat pants she was wearing and lowered them down over the ledge and pulled her up like that. They continued on in this manner until they reached the top.

Amy said they had called for help and no one came, but then she was worried that someone would come when she was half dressed. When they got back to the regular path she redressed, and they found their way on down to the car where we were waiting. It was a funny thing to see the journeygirl tell about Amy without her pants on and to notice that while she was telling it, she was completely unaware that she had a huge hole scrubbed out in the seat of her own pants. We teased her about it of course. And just to show you what a profound effect it had on my child (and your grandchild), I told her that I hoped she had learned a lesson from this experience. She replied, "I sure did, Mom. Wal-Mart pants are really strong!" I give up!

Dear Mother,

A young pastor and his wife, who work on the weekends in a little church way up in the Andes, came to us and said that the children up there wanted to come to camp, but they were very poor and had no money to pay the very small fee that we ask for a week at camp. (We find that if we charge something the response is much better than if it is entirely free.) They live in the area where the big crop is potatoes, so we worked out a deal with them to pay their fee with potatoes. They worked in the fields and earned several bags of potatoes as a salary, and they managed to sell enough to pay for their bus trip down here. Then they came to camp and brought their bags of potatoes to us to help out with the food during the week. I wish you could have seen them coming in with their little red cheeks chapped by the cold, their huge straw hats, and their burlap bags of potatoes. They filed by and dumped them on the kitchen floor and we had more than enough; we are searching for other recipes in which we can use them. To be honest, we are getting a little tired of potatoes because we are eating them in some form every day. These kids were so proud of what they had done, though, and I thought it was great to do this instead of giving a handout.

Dear Mother,

I have told you about Elena, the sweet, talkative, little lady in our Sunday School class who has many family problems. Her main concern, however, has been the health of her husband, Walter, and the fact that he was not a Christian. We have prayed with her for a long time and finally after 47 years of marriage, he let her read from the Bible and pray with him there at home, but he would not come to church. This was progress because at first he would even prohibit her coming.

Remember that 3-D picture of Christ that Spencer gave us at Christmas? We had put it up on the wall of our dining hall out at camp, and Elena was fascinated by it. She had told Walter about it and he wanted to see it, too. So when we announced a couples' retreat out there, she asked if non-Christians could go. I said of course they could, and then she asked if old people could go, and I said that WE were going and by all means to plan to come. She asked for prayer that Walter would accept the invitation.

Well, he did accept the invitation and he went and he thoroughly enjoyed himself. Elena was very nervous the whole time, though, that he might say something inappropriate because he was known to be very outspoken, and earlier in his life he had said some very hard things against Evangelicals. Well, there we were in the middle of a discussion of marital problems arising from financial crisis. Everyone was listening to the guest speaker when Walter stood up. He said he had something to say and could not wait. Poor Elena looked like she wished the floor would open up and swallow her. We were shocked into silence, and Walter said, "I just can't wait any longer, I want to accept the Lord as my Savior right now!" We were stunned for a few seconds and then everyone just began to applaud. We stopped the discussion, of course, and had a prayer with Walter and we all congratulated him. Our little lady was hugging everybody and laughing and crying at the same time. (Actually I don't believe there was a dry eye in the place.) It was a priceless experience!

(NOTE: What an orchid that was!)

Dear Mother,

What a wonderful surprise! That church that promised to give us their church bus for camp, really did it! We will now have transportation for all those campers who otherwise would not be able to make the trip. The church is Hurricane Baptist Church in Clinton, SC, and so we have named the bus "El Huracan" (The Hurricane). It is an old school bus, but in good condition, and we pray it will serve for many years to come. There is a young man here who has volunteered to be our driver, and that leaves Rodolph free to drive the truck with luggage and me to drive the car with whatever is left over in the way of produce or people. God is good.

Dear Mother,

Well, we have our second camp bus now, isn't that wonderful? The "Hurricane" had been making two trips each camp time, and that made a long wait for many campers. When the Pendleton Street Baptist group was here they said they were going to see about getting us another school bus and they did! This one is a newer bus and more comfortable, and with the two buses going now we can take everyone at the same time. We have had over 150 kids at some camps, so we have had to use both buses, put the older campers on the truck with counselors to take care of them, and even I have had to stuff a few into the car with me. There are no Peruvian laws as to how many you can put into a vehicle, but we are being strict as to not exceed safety measures as we know them. The Lord has been so gracious to us all during these camping times with protection and health for these young people.

P.S. Have you ever seen a lavender rose? We have some blooming out here at camp.

Dear Mother,

We have discovered some very disturbing things about the lives of some of our campers in the youth group. One of them told us he had decided to leave camp and return to Trujillo, and he even went up to the road to get a ride without us knowing it. He was waiting for someone to pick him up and was thinking about what had been said in the services. He came to the conclusion that he was foolish to turn his back on good food and fellowship, and so he returned. He came forward on the last day to say he is having a terrible problem with drugs and alcohol, but wants to trust the Lord as his Savior and ask Him to help him overcome his addiction. The counselors and campers were all very supportive, and we are getting him some professional help as well through our clinic at church. We may never know of other cases like his. We pray something will be done in these camps to reach them and be of help to them.

Dear Mother,

One of the cooks at camp has an alcoholic husband; he is mean and abusive. He showed up at camp one afternoon this week after having walked most of the way from town, which is 25 miles. He was very drunk and loud and ugly. He told his wife that he had come to get her because their son had drowned. The lady was distraught and rushed around to get her things to leave with him right away. During the few minutes she was doing this, he changed his story to say that the son had been killed, but in another way, and we began to get suspicious. Sure enough, he was making up that awful lie to get her home because he didn't want her out at camp. She has told us that he has chased her around the house with a machete trying to kill her and related other terrible abuses that she has suffered, but she won't leave him. She has relatives in the jungle who would take her in and we have offered her the plane fare to get there, but she won't go, so we have to let the decisions be hers. However, we cannot let her come back to camp and have him coming out here and disturbing the routine and scaring everyone like that.

NOTE: After many more years of abuse, the husband was literally found dead in the gutter one morning after a night of carousing. They said he had been in a drunken stupor when he died there on the side of the street. Even though he came to church from time to time with his wife when he was in one of his rare sober intervals, he was one that I don't feel we ever really touched with God's message of love because his alcoholism kept him beyond reach. He came many times to get his wife out of church and to disturb the service. There were several men of our church who were designated to usher people like this out--those who only came to disturb. It happened so often that they became quite skilled at doing it. I felt better knowing they were alert to possible situations that could arise because many times a foreigner is an obvious target, and I stood out in a crowd!☺

Dear Mother,

We worked so hard getting everything ready for the opening of camp this year. It has been back-breaking and nerve-racking, and like each year at this time I begin to wonder if it is worth all this agony. At church this morning the pastor announced that camps begin tomorrow, and when he announced the age for the youngest group, a little 6 year old boy just threw up his arms and squealed out loud. His daddy grabbed him to hold him down and quiet him, but hugged him and grinned, too. That was my answer as to its being worthwhile.

Padrino (the camp dog) got hit by a car coming into camp. He yelped and ran away, and everyone looked and looked for him. After a long search, we finally found him lying under the desk at the nurse's first-aid station. Smart dog, huh?!

One of the pastors who was serving at camp this week told us that he asked Spencer what he was going to be when he grew up and got a priceless answer. Spencer told him that he didn't have to decide and that he didn't even have to worry about it. He would let God do the deciding and tell him, and he would do what God told him to do. We all thought that was a pretty good answer for a little boy, and the pastor said it would preach a good sermon.

The cooks provided us with a laugh this week. We had the course for the confidence and trust games all set up for the campers and there was one made of hanging ropes that they called the "nervous bridge" because it shook so much as you tried to cross it (and so did you). While the ladies in the kitchen did their work, they loved to watch those near enough for them to see. Well, they slipped out in the night to try these things out for themselves.

Now, get this picture, most of these ladies are at least middle aged and older, and all but two of them are quite a bit over-weight. The bridge was built for one person at a time but all 6 of them tried it out at once, and you can guess what happened. It broke with them, of course, and luckily the only thing they suffered was the embarrassment of having to confess what they did. It was so funny and revealed yet another side of Peruvian life I had not seen before. We, personally, were thrilled that they would do something silly like that; it was so out of character. It also confirmed the need for the things this camping program is providing; we just had not thought about ladies of their age enjoying it, too.

Dear Mother,

I told you last week that Rodolph was really suffering with a lot of swelling and pain in his foot. He went to the doctor and was given some medicine, but it didn't help. He also went to the pharmacist (who usually helps us the most) and what he prescribed didn't seem to do any good either.

We were out at camp for the entire week and the workers there saw his foot and decided it was time to do something about it. I was a little dubious, and I have to admit to being a little worried that they would do something to make it worse. They went about the camp looking for a certain herb, and when one of them found it they came back, made a poultice out of it, and put it on Rodolph's foot. They explained that they thought it was a spider bite and this was the proper treatment. Then they showed him how to repeat the process and told him what to look for to know when it should be repeated. Would you believe it began to feel better almost immediately? In only a day you could really see the difference, and by the end of the week he was back to normal. They came back to inspect it and said it definitely was a spider bite, because it had a black splotch around the small spot where the skin had been pierced.

I was amazed, and I want you to know I have gained a new respect for folk medicine and the ability of our people here to cope with what they have at their disposal! I remember one of the older missionaries telling us when we arrived that his mind told him some of the things they did for treating their sick couldn't work. However, when you see them use it and see the results, it certainly makes you not have a completely closed mind as to its possibility of merit.

Dear Mother,

How many times have I written you and said that this country always has surprises for us? I had another one this week as I noticed the stones lying about on the ground out at camp. Our workers had dug them out of the mountain and were ready to put them into the walls of the dining hall. The thing that caught my attention was the designs of ferns and leaves in the white and gray granite. I just assumed the rocks had been lying on top of some plants and had picked up a sort of tattoo that would wash off or wear off with time. As the walls went up inside the building, I saw these designs everywhere. As we were cleaning up before beginning the use of our new kitchen and eating area, we decided to wash the walls down and discovered that those "prints" of fern and leaves are not just a decal or even etched on; they are fossils that have been pressed into that stone millions of years ago. It is quite a lesson in natural science to walk through and look at these walls. Apparently our workers chipped into a vein of vegetation that had been covered over by the moving of the earth all those centuries ago, and we now have beautiful decorations in our walls for centuries to come. When your friends speak of their "permanent" arrangements of silk flowers, tell them about ours!

Dear Mother,

For the first time in my life I know what it is like to feel lost. We took the campers on a relatively short hike not far from the camp in well known terrain. Because the river is up and the bridge is out, we let them begin by going over the swinging bridge near the lower end of the camp. We decided to bring them back by letting them cross the river on the upper side by a cable car. It seemed safe enough and a great adventure, but only 3 kids could cross in the little car at a time, and it was taking quite a while to get them all over. The campers were waiting for their turn and we didn't want to get in front of them, but we realized if we waited much more we would be late for the evening activities back at camp. So--we decided to retrace our steps and return via the swinging bridge, and one of the girl counselors who didn't much want to cross over the river in that car, said she would accompany us.

We made pretty good time, but in the mountains when the sun goes down it gets dark all at once. We usually go out well equipped, but because this was an early afternoon hike, we had not taken a flashlight. We got to the area where we had to cut through the cane fields to get to the swinging bridge, and by this time it was pitch black dark. Being in cane that is higher than ones head and trying to find a narrow path in the darkness is no small feat, as we discovered. We walked in what we thought was the right direction, only to discover we had walked much longer than it should have taken to reach the bridge. We tried to retrace our steps and couldn't decide exactly where we had been. We were all three completely disoriented, and while not all that upset because the area is not that large and we knew we had to find our way eventually, it was a strange feeling to not find things where you thought they should be.

We were actually out in those cane fields about an hour before we saw the lights of a car on the road up on the mountain, which gave us a sense of direction and told us which way to walk. We had long ago given up trying to find the path and were just trying to find the river so we could follow it. It winds around and around, but would eventually show us something we could recognize. When we saw the lights we walked until we heard the river, and actually came out very near the swinging bridge. As we approached the bridge we saw a lantern bobbing on the other side, and it was our caretaker at camp who had come to look for us.

We got back to camp to find the activities going on without a hitch and everyone enjoying them. We thought we had to be there to initiate them--so much for our importance! Actually, it is wonderful to see how well our counselors have learned to carry on a program and take responsibility and be dependable! We are proud of them and feel that these young people are the future of the work here.

Dear Mother,

We are so fortunate that we have been able to get a wonderful nurse to help us for a whole month out at camp. We met her at the clinic in Lima; she is in charge of the emergency room at one of the main hospitals there. It is the one we all use when needed. She is a special friend of a missionary family in Lima, so we know her on a social basis as well as professionally. She is a tiny thing and looks Oriental; since her last name is Li, I imagine there is some reason for that. She is well educated and a fine Christian. She was delighted to come and spend her whole month of vacation with us to teach the kids and see about their health needs as well. She asked everyone to call her "Tia Meme," which we do, and she enters right in to all the activities with a cheerful spirit and boundless energy. We could only promise to pay her travel expenses, but I hope we can give her a little something at the end of the time. She only makes about $50 a month in a specialized and important position like hers.

She has a powerful testimony of her life as a nurse and being one of the only Evangelicals in the group. She said the other nurses used to clean the telephone mouthpiece with alcohol after she had used it, just to show her what they thought of her. They didn't want to catch what she had as an Evangelical. She said her father died when she was 8 months old and she related what a hard life she has had since then. She is very close to her mother and is still taking care of her now. She has one sibling who is married and helps too, but in these times it is hard for anyone to make a living wage. The Lord has surely provided some excellent care for our campers and lifted a burden of concern from our shoulders through the kindness of this dedicated Christian nurse.

Dear Mother,

We had a rather bad time of it this last week. Max came out to camp to help us take the campers back to town; he drove our car out and was to drive the bus back. The car was acting funny and running hot, so he and Rodolph looked at the radiator. They waited for what they thought was a reasonable length of time and they inspected it again. This time they opened the cap, and when they did, it blew scalding water up and all over Rodolph's hands! I had just left with Tia Meme to go into town and the other lady out there who is also a nurse, didn't know what to do. Somehow, Rodolph ended the camp, drove the cooks home, and came on home with his hands and forearms burned horribly.

Tia Meme took one look at him and went to work. It had all blistered up by then and was an awful looking sight! She cut away the burnt skin and blisters, applied ointment, and bandaged them up. She looked after them each day to see that there was no infection setting in. He has been in a lot of pain and can't use his hands much at all. He has some burns on his face, but his hands apparently caught the brunt of it. Where his watch had been was the worst burn of all. It seems the metal heating up had just branded his arm there at the wrist. It is going to take him a long time to heal, but thankfully, he has first class emergency room care right here in the house. One couldn't ask for better than that. See how the Lord provides?

Dear Family,

The economic situation is so bad here now that most of our people cannot even pay the small amount we ask for a week's stay at camp. They need that respite more than ever, but they don't have enough for the basic necessities, much less an extra like that. We asked for money from the FMB, but there was none available.

We decided to try to go ahead anyway, and we have been so surprised at the anonymous gifts we have received from here and there. Even our fellow missionaries have donated money because they believe in it and see the results. Many of our missionaries have given testimonies of what camp meant in their own lives as children, and also, they are seeing how many have joined our local churches here because of decisions made out at camp. We were touched by their support.

We economized everywhere we could. We cut our menu down to the bone. (Pardon the pun.) Actually, bones were part of what we used. We fed 100 people for a week on 10 chickens, 8-10 kilos of hamburger meat, 2 kilos of lunch meat (for fried rice), 6-9 cans of tuna, and 1 bag of bones. We use the feet, heads, and whatever of the chickens, too. You would be amazed at the tasty food and the amount of servings that come from that--adding lots of rice and pasta, of course! They are eating okay--not the really nutritional meals we would have liked for them in these hard times, but we are having camps and they (and we) are enjoying it.

At church yesterday, 3 precious little 9 and 10 year old boys came forward to say they had accepted Christ out at camp. What a thrill! These are ones who have grown up in the church, but one of their mothers said, "They are the fruits of the camps."

We pray for you each day and think of you and miss you. If I dwell on the "missing" part too much, I won't make it--I have to dwell on things like those 3 little boys yesterday, and all the others whom the counselors said accepted Christ during the week.

(NOTE: Wonder if those little boys would mind being called orchids?)

Dear Mother,

I hope you got what we sent by Sue Forrester. She was certainly a nice houseguest to have. She was with us 8 weeks and was never anything but helpful. Out at Shiran, she not only served as camp nurse, but when the villagers heard there was a medical person there, they came from everywhere asking for advice and help of all kinds. She cleaned wounds and gave Tylenol, as well as other over-the-counter medicines. She had one little boy in whom she took a special interest. He came with the worst infected ear you could imagine and he said the barber who trimmed his hair was drunk and made a mistake and nearly cut his ear off! It had been almost a year and it still had not healed up. By the time Sue left, his ear was looking good. She taught classes of first aid and hygiene, too.

When we were back at our house for the weekend, she sewed for us and patched things, and we had thoughts of hiding her tickets and passport and not letting her leave. The only thing that bothered me was that I thought she stayed out in our little guest room across the patio (the "Outhouse") all by herself too much and was just reticent to invade the family privacy, and so I asked her why she didn't come in more often to be with our family. We still laugh about her reply. She said she hoped I wouldn't be offended, but our house was like a three ring circus and she needed a little quiet sometimes. She had a pretty accurate description, but she should have seen it when ALL the children were here with all their friends of all ages!

(NOTE: Sue is so unassuming and quiet that she brings thoughts of a violet, but she is definitely an orchid in my book!)

Dear Mother,

We had a surprise on Rodolph's birthday! We were out at camp and in bed sound asleep when we were awakened by 3 policemen (and the wife of one of them) in an emergency squad car! They turned on the siren and nearly scared us to death! They came to the door and brought us a cake that the wife had made for Rodolph and wanted him to have that very day. I wish they could have found a gentler way of greeting him!☺

Dear Mother,

Well, Julio has taken on another project. Bill is an orphan,

15 years old, who showed up at Central Church and asked to leave his bag there while he slept in the street (because he was told it would be stolen while he slept). He said he had just come from up north, and he told Julio that his mother died when he was 8 and his father died the year after. He was living with his uncle and aunt in the mountains who carried him to the main plaza in Chiclayo and told him to wait there. They said they would be right back. He never saw them again. He supports himself by buying little candies and reselling them in the street. This is his story--it may be true and it may not--but he is living at Central Church right now. We took him to camp and he loved it and wanted to return another week. He accepted Christ and said he only lacked one thing now to be truly happy--a home.

Dear Family,

One of the helpers out at camp died last week, and Rodolph had to buy the casket and take it out to the family. The family members are not very nice and were drinking liquor at the funeral service, which did not improve their dispositions. It was hard to give a Christian witness in that atmosphere. We had to walk way up the mountain for the burial. It was steep and it was hot, and the men carrying the casket had to stop and pass it on to others at short intervals. The grave had been dug through rock. It was a deep pit and had a cave-like ledge chiseled out into one side. The men got down into the pit and put the casket onto that ledge. It was hollowed out to just the size of the casket. Then they filled in the pit. The idea is that so much rock on top of a casket would crush it, but putting it into a carved out space, it would be protected. This was a new experience for me.

Dear Mother,

I wish you could hear these kids sing out here at camp. This week we have 9-11 year olds and they are loud! But then, usually, to Peruvian children--"loud" is "good"! These hills are

REALLY alive with the sound of their music; I wouldn't be surprised if they couldn't hear it all the way back to Trujillo. I've enjoyed doing the music, though. I've written new words and translated some songs I used to sing as a child, and taught these "new" ones to them. They really seem to like them, or at least they sing like they do.

Dear Mother,

You know what a struggle we have had trying to get the children to come to camp in play clothes. Because our facilities are so much better than what most of their homes have, they want to come in their best clothes. Their best clothes usually are little frilly dresses for the girls and dress shirts for the boys. Another reason for this is that they usually have only a few clothes that they can wear out in public, and the rest are worn-out work clothes that they wear around the house. They don't have recreational clothes because they don't have much recreation. Through the years, though, most of them have found a way to come in something presentable that is also comfortable and suitable for play.

This week, however, we had two teenagers from way up in the mountains who came in their party dresses and high heels. A part of our weekly routine is to have a hike to the top of the mountain, and it is a really strenuous climb. Some of the faint-hearted always try to find some other activity or plead sick during that time, and we are forever trying to get them to extend themselves and dare to do something adventurous. Well, when we realized these girls did not have suitable clothes for climbing, we were worried and suggested that they find something to do here in camp for the afternoon of the hike. They wouldn't hear of it and said they were looking forward to it. We tried to get them to borrow clothes from one of the counselors who offered to loan them some. This, too, was rejected, and the afternoon of the hike they left with the group.

Rodolph and I were not going on this one. (After 20 years of climbing it, the mountain seems to have gotten steeper, and even with the most proper clothes we find it hard to do now.) We have very good, responsible counselors who know the hike very well, but even so, we were worried about these girls. I got out the binoculars and began to watch their progress when they got up to the highest peaks. The mountain girls were easy to spot because one of them had on a frilly, bright pink party dress and the other one's dress was bright blue. They stood out clearly against the stark tan of the bare rocks. At one point I lost sight of them and got worried. I saw the group and they seemed to be stopped. Some of them were sitting down, and I wondered what was happening. I could only imagine the worse. I then saw them frantically waving and finally realized they were waving at something up above them in the distance. I refocused the binoculars and looked on up the mountain, and there were the two spots of pink and blue--way on up ahead of all the group. I watched while they finally stopped and started back down and rejoined the group, who were sitting and waiting for them.

When the hikers returned to camp we questioned them about what happened up there. It seems that the two mountain girls in their high heels and party dresses had practically run up the mountain ahead of all of them, and the ones of our group with tennis shoes, hiking boots, and other professional type outfits were left in the dust. They could not keep up, and they went as far as they could. They had to stop and rest and call the girls to come back and return to camp with them. So much for proper clothes!

Dear Mother,

We had a horrible thing happen while we were out at camp this week. We had taken the campers on a hike to the puquio (springs). We had a pleasant walk and a good service sitting beside the clear water that was bubbling up and running down the valley in a crystal stream. The kids played there awhile, and just as we were leaving we heard a loud crash up on the roadside above us. The springs are at the base of a steep cliff that goes straight up some two hundred feet or more. The highway runs by on the top of it on a ledge chiseled out of the mountain which rises straight on up out of sight on the other side. There is a sharp curve at this particular point in the road that has been the site for numerous accidents in the past, so we had a pretty good idea of what must have happened.

We were not prepared for what we found, though. We sent some of the counselors and the nurse with the backpack of first aid equipment up to see what was going on. We could hear screaming and cries for help so we knew it must be bad. When we got a report of what had happened we chose as many responsible counselors, whom we thought might could be of some help, to stay with Rodolph, while I got the rest of the group back to camp. These were small campers who could not help and could possibly get in the way, and who were already traumatized by what we saw.

There was an old dilapidated truck that had been loaded down with people coming down from the high mountains. It did not make that sharp curve and turned over just before going over that steep cliff. It threw people out all along the road as it overturned and skidded along. There were quite a few, I am not sure how many, who were badly hurt and crying and bleeding and in shock. Rodolph managed to stop cars and ask them to take people into Trujillo. Some would and some wouldn't. Our nurse used up everything she had in her knapsack, and we sent up whatever else we had in the camp in the way of first aid supplies. Finally, there were only a few left who had not been taken in, and Rodolph took them to the hospital in our truck. One poor man, who was injured but not badly hurt, was completely distraught because he didn't know where his wife was. She had been taken in earlier with serious injuries and he had no idea where to find her. He didn't know anyone in Trujillo, and Rodolph managed to locate one of our pastors who came to help him, so he could leave this man in his care and get back to camp.

Of course, the wreck was the talk of the camp and we used it to teach many lessons during this week. We talked about safety, first aid, helping others in need, knowing where you're going and choosing the right way to get there, when to be helpful and take charge and when to back off and let others do their job, praying for the suffering of others, etc. It was quite an object lesson for us all. I pray we never have another like it, ever again.

Dear Mother,

I forgot how long these sermons here are! Our "Preaching" professor at the seminary spoke this morning and he had 4 sermons all rolled into one. He preached 1 hour and 10 minutes. He had texts from all four Gospels. Having to listen to so many long sermons has sharpened Rodolph's sense of compassion for the congregation and he has shortened his considerably. The other day he only preached 10 minutes and I couldn't believe it; I was so proud of him!

We have spent a lot of time out at camp recently (without lights most of the time and that doesn't make for me being a happy camper). When I have stayed in town, Rodolph leaves here by 6 a.m. which is a real sacrifice for him. He drives the workers up into the mountains to bring rock down for the new building. He has made 6 loads some days. They are trying hard to get what they need before the rains come. The rain makes the river rise, and this would prevent their crossing it to get to the site where they dig the rock out of the mountain. They talk of getting pretty rock for the walls and ugly rock for the foundation. It is not only hard work, but dangerous work, because they dig beneath overhanging cliffs which could (and do) fall quite easily. About 3 or 4 more days of this should finish up the rock collecting, and they will begin the actual construction on the building. I can see what this kind of physical work is doing to Rodolph but he denies it is bothering him. It is obvious to everyone that he loves his workers and what they do, and he enjoys being with them. I do what I can and I pray a lot!

Dear Mother,

People come from everywhere to look at the roofs of our

new cabins. The volunteers put stateside shingles on them and they have never seen that before. (They also threw rocks on them to see if they would break, and I didn't appreciate that!) The men also roofed our cabin with the left over shingles and I am so happy to think that I won't have to sleep under plastic if we have rain. It is wonderful!

Dear Mother,

We finally got all those dirty clothes washed that the USA volunteer construction team left to give away. The workers out at camp were really proud to receive them, but I can't wait to see some of our little guys in those size XXL clothes that most of the volunteers wore.

We are spending a lot of time out at camp, and everyone is working as hard as humanly possible, but the progress is much too slow for me! There is no way we can be ready for mission meeting. How I wish all of you could see what has been done, though; it is really beautiful. I am so proud of what Rodolph has been able to accomplish there. (Now, if he could just do it a little faster…!)

Rodolph woke up with "pink eye" on Monday morning and I thought it was sort of funny until I woke up with the same thing on Thursday. We think we have had a really strange case or have had something else along with it, because we have both felt really bad with fever, headache, etc. I think the main thing is turning 60! And now that I will soon be 62, I just can't even imagine what to expect!

Dear Mother,

I am sitting on the porch of our cabin at camp and I just heard all this cheerful singing and whistling. All the tunes were the little happy choruses the children sing at church. It didn't sound like a child's voice, and I wondered who else out here could be that happy. I finally discovered the source of the sound when I

276

saw Jose coming up the hill. He is a young man from the village who recently accepted Christ and is planning to go to the seminary as soon as he can pass the requirements. He has been helping out at camp here lately and has been a good worker.

I wondered what he was doing that could give him such pleasure, and I was astounded to see him struggling up the hill with the biggest garbage can you ever saw perched precariously on his shoulder. It was obviously full to the brim of something very unsavory, because the odor preceding him was just about suffocating. It was a lesson to me in the joy of service. He was happy; it didn't matter to him what the job was. He only knew this needed to be done, he could do it, and he did it cheerfully. He greeted me with a great big smile as he passed by, and as he went on his way I heard the words of the chorus trailing after him, "This is the day the Lord has made, I will rejoice and be glad in it." As he went on about his work I could still hear him whistling faintly in the distance, and I could make out the notes of "He Leadeth Me" and "Great is His Faithfulness."

(NOTE: That was definitely an orchid!)

CRISIS

Dear Mother,

This situation with the terrorists is really bad and it is affecting the entire country. It seems to get worse every day. There is rarely a day that goes by without our hearing of a bombing somewhere, and they are wiping out whole villages in the mountains. We are advised to stay at home as much as possible and be very alert. It is very unnerving to some of us who are not noted for our bravery, and I think the cowardly streak I have always had is broadening somewhat in these days.

NOTE: Trujillo, where we lived, was one of the quieter cities in the country during all this turmoil, and then we found out why--several of the main terrorist leaders were discovered hiding out there, right in our midst!

Dear Mother,

Well, "El Nino" has hit us again and we have our bags packed with a change of clothes and important documents like our passports in case we have to evacuate. They went through our neighborhood announcing to be ready. It is so strange to be threatened with floods in the desert! Rodolph came back from camp yesterday with water in the cab and headlights of the truck. This is the second time he has been caught in a flash flood with the water that high! The Lord just protected him; that is the only way I can explain it. This time he had a load of young people with him in the back of the truck and that really frightened him I think, but he always minimizes the danger. When he talks about it, he rarely mentions by how close a margin he averted a major tragedy, so I just thank the Lord for the safety that He provides and try not to let my imagination run wild. We have the Pacific Ocean on the west of us and we are cut off by flooding on the other three sides; even the airport is flooded, so we feel rather vulnerable, to say the least.

Dear Mother,

You are not going to believe what has been going on here during this time of flooding. You remember that dry river bed we showed you when you visited? It is on the east side of town and the ancient Indian residents of this area had built a huge sand dike across it centuries ago. Well, people have been using this dry river bed for the cemetery and they live all up and down the dike. When the rains came down from the mountains this year with that flooding I told you about, the dry river filled up and formed a huge lake about 30 feet deep. This began to worry the inhabitants of that area, so the engineers decided to try to drain off some of that water, and when they did, the dike broke and a wall of water 30 ft. high came through the community there! It washed away everything in front of it for blocks and spread out all over town, getting smaller as it went. It even reached our neighborhood and we're on the west side of town. It was only about a foot high or less by then, so we sandbagged our gates and did not get any at all in our house. It was a very frightening time there for awhile, though, not knowing exactly what to expect.

There are some terrible tales of some who lost their lives and also about the contents of the cemetery being distributed all about the city. Many eyewitnesses are relating gruesome stories of the things they saw floating by and left in the streets when the water subsided. There are chilling accounts of coffins, bodies, body parts, etc. and the detailed descriptions of all this seems to grow and become more elaborate with each telling. Even considering the possibility of some exaggeration in what we are told, the prospect of contamination in this heat presents a staggering reality. Rodolph went out as soon as he could to help and he actually saw several dead bodies in the streets, himself.

These adobe houses are just not made to resist water like that. Those that didn't just crumble or melt were filled with water, and the people had no place to go. When Rodolph managed to get to one of our little churches in that area he discovered the young pastor and his wife (who live in the church) had opened the doors and taken in 65 people. Now this church has a dirt floor and one very primitive bathroom, and they were cooking in a black pot over an open fire in the corner of the yard. The meeting area was filled with anything they had rescued from the wreckage. Sitting by the pulpit was a TV and there were mattresses, chairs, bedding, clothes, etc.--all stored anywhere they could find a space for it. They were cheerful and grateful for a place to stay, and we got busy and bought food to take to them. We also got a water truck to take water out and fill up the church baptistery so they could dip water out of that for their needs.

The pastor's wife was funny; she was like a little drill sergeant directing things, keeping the food under lock and key, and measuring it out as needed. She assured me they were being good stewards of what that had received. She said that one lady who had been put in charge of cooking the rice had let it burn on the bottom, and she told the lady that the burned part would be for her and her family that day. She said they had not had burnt rice again. It was amazing to see how it was working under impossible conditions, and it was giving a great Christian witness to the whole vicinity.

Dear Mother,

This cholera epidemic has been a terrible thing and a scary one! The hospitals are full and are having to turn away very sick people. We have been trying to help where we can, mainly by teaching how to prevent getting it and what to do to treat it. We heard it got started by a sailor on a ship from some Mid-Eastern country that was docked in the harbor at Chimbote and who was sent to the hospital there. It has now spread all over the country and people are dying by the thousands. We have to be careful of what we eat, where it comes from, and be sure it is sterilized. Raw foods like salads and fruits are out of the question. You don't realize how much you miss them until you can't have them. We were so glad to get the crates of medicine from the USA to treat it. We are told that if cholera can be caught in the early stages it is almost always curable with this medicine. I have been really worried about our children so that is a comfort to know. The medical clinic at our church has taken a big part in the treatment and also in the distribution of the medicine.

This happened on Fri. Sept. 23, 1988:

Dear Family,

I guess most of you have heard by now of our newest "adventure," but so you can have a first hand account, I will try to write it down for you. It was something I would certainly never want to repeat. Merry, Amy, and I were on the way to the camp at Shiran. Rodolph had gone on earlier and we were taking things to leave at the camp, plus all our recreational equipment for the weekend like camera, favorite relaxing clothes, sleeping bags, thermos jugs, games, food, writing materials (including my address book that I have had since college days), books, flashlights, embroidery work, etc., etc., etc. We were just a few miles out of town in the cane fields going about 60 miles per hour. It is a place where the cane is really tall and almost gives the impression of going through a tunnel. There were deep watering ditches on both sides of the road.

All at once I caught the sight of a car out of the corner of my eye and it was passing us very close. Merry screamed because she was sitting beside me in the front seat and was sort of facing that way, and she was the first to see them. Amy was in the back seat listening to her new Walkman cassette player that Merry had brought her from the USA and was oblivious to what was going on at first. I looked out the open window right into 3 guns that were aimed at me from about a foot away. There were 4 men in the car and they all had on stocking caps and scarves over their faces. All but the driver were leaning out of the windows pointing their guns at me!

The car was a new model, land rover type of vehicle. I jammed on the brakes and they scooted ahead and I moved to pass them, but they blocked the road and were at our car in seconds with their revolvers. The road is too narrow and our car too big to have turned around without backing up, and there was no place to run had I been able to pass them. We prayed to know what to do--how to act. They got in the car, one on each side of Amy and the third one pushed me over, hitting me a little on the head but not really hurting me. He took my place in the driver's seat, but couldn't drive the car because the indicator for "reverse and drive" is broken and you have to sort of know from experience where to put it. I asked very politely if I could help him, and he nodded yes and let me. He drove like a maniac and kept complaining that the car wouldn't go fast enough. He said he needed to change gears, and I told him it was automatic and he couldn't do that. It was then that I realized I had inadvertently put the indicator in "low drive." It was not an intentional mistake, but it kept us from traveling at even more excessive speeds over those dangerous roads.

They argued over where to take us and they drove a really long distance back toward town. We didn't pass any other cars during the entire experience. He entered the cane fields by way of some little dirt lanes and then stopped where we couldn't be seen from the main road. They kept the guns on us all the time and told us to not look at them and be quiet. The other car followed us.

During the trip they threw a quilt over Amy's head and I could hear her crying softly. Merry crouched down in the seat and ducked her head like they told us to do. They took everything we had except the clothes on our backs, my Bible, Merry's gold chain which was under her clothes, and my engagement ring. When one of them asked me for my rings I took the two off together and let the engagement ring fall into my lap and covered it with my leg. I asked him to please leave me my wedding band as it is only silver and not valuable (it is white gold), and with the gun pointed at my head, he said, "Everything!" I then decided life was more valuable than even a 31 year old wedding band.

Earlier I asked the driver if he was going to take the car, and if so, to just let us out and take it--he told me, "no." (The other missionaries teased Rodolph about this for a long time; they said

283

even the robbers didn't want our old car.☺) Merry told them at the very first to just take everything but leave us alive. Apparently she thought I was talking a little too much, also, because she told me to do as they say, not to resist, and not to make them mad. Everyone has said this is the best course of action because most of the time they are on drugs and the least little thing can anger them and cause them to react in a wild and violent way.

Even on that scary ride I kept thinking of what we might could do to save ourselves. It became very clear that we were in serious danger, but I wasn't sure of exactly how much or what kind. I couldn't judge if their intentions were solely the robbery or if they were planning more--and possibly worse. I was praying all the time, and after the initial fright wore off I had a strange kind of calmness and a clear mind. Amy said she wanted to hold my hand and one of them asked, "What for?" I told him, "She is just a child and she is scared." And with that I reached over the seat and told her to give me her hand, which she did keeping the cover over her head, and they permitted it. I took Merry's hand, too, and told them to pray, and I prayed aloud. I started off in English at first, but somehow I ended up praying in Spanish. I don't remember the exact words, but I do remember the gist of what I said and it was something like, "Lord we are Your children and we put our faith and trust in You. We know that You are in control of everything, even situations like this, and we know that we are all in Your hands--not only us, but these men here. We ask for Your protection and that You will help us do the right thing, but we pray for You to take charge. Above all we leave it to You, Lord, for Your will to be done." At that, one of them put the gun to my head and told me to shut up, which I did, but I continued to pray silently.

I was surprised at myself when I realized that my prayer and thoughts were not, "Save us, save us!" I was able to think calmly that this might mean we were to face death in a very few minutes. Several scenarios passed through my thinking. I did not know how I would handle pain, nor what I would or should do to protect my daughters. It was a release from numbing fear and

284

sense of complete helplessness to realize that our total dependence was on God, and that He was in total control. Whatever happened--it would be alright. If we died HE was certainly what we needed, and if we didn't that, too, would be according to His will. We could do nothing--we could (and must) leave it in His hands. It was a comforting realization at this moment that what we had been taught and were teaching all these years is true! It is REAL! Now this incident is not something I would ever want to repeat, but I am grateful for what I have learned through it. I have a new concept of death and what is needed to face it, as well as a sharp reminder of proper priorities and values in this life I have been given.

They finally parked way out in the cane fields. After they had taken everything from us personally and questioned me about how much money I had, etc., they unloaded our car and put it all in their car. The one driving couldn't get the keys out of the ignition and made me do it and give them to him. It was a key ring with the keys to our house and camp, as well as the car.

They came back and searched the front seat and floor, but didn't see my ring. They searched the glove compartment and even took our hot sandwiches that we had for the picnic lunch we had planned to have with Rodolph out at camp. They were in a little Styrofoam box which had fallen on the floor. They didn't touch my Bible, though, which was right beside it at the door. (Everything had been tossed around because the driver didn't know how to use power brakes.)

They finally left, but one came back to say, "See, Senora, we are not so bad, we didn't hurt you. Gracias, huh!" Then he told us to get down and stay down, which we did and they left. After a suitable time to make sure they were out of sight, we got up and I began to wonder how we could get out of the cane fields; that was when I saw the keys on the dashboard. Someone had also put a pair of my glasses in the seat. We went on out to Shiran and got Rodolph and then returned to Trujillo to the police station for the "fun" of reporting it!!! The next morning we saw in the newspaper a picture and a report that two of them had been captured in that same car which they had stolen the night before. It is the car that

Alan Garcia, the president of Peru, uses when visiting Trujillo. It is silver with a red racing stripe--easy to identify. We went to the precinct where it was being held and found two sleeping bags, one thermos, an ice box, 2 pillows, the spare tire, and a couple of Rodolph's oldest pants (which I wish they would have kept)--so we got something back. A few "Trivial Pursuit" cards were scattered around also.

We were asked to identify the two captured criminals face to face. I am sure they were the ones, but I couldn't have picked them out of a crowd. The owner of another car they had stolen was there. This man had stitches in his head and bandages everywhere for the injuries they inflicted, and he positively identified them. The driver of the stolen car they used to rob us was left in the cane fields without his clothes. We found out they are a very dangerous band and known to the police. One had just escaped from jail where he was serving a sentence for homicide. Two policemen in Central Church said they just couldn't believe that they had let us go without harming us--especially with two pretty young girls along! He said they never do that, and for one to come back and leave the keys and say they weren't so bad, was just incredible! It just had to be the Lord's doings. --So, there you have it.

The Lord is still in control and is with us when we need Him, and His grace is sufficient even for those moments that you think may be your very last on this earth.

I wondered if I would ever be able to ride out through those cane fields again without experiencing the terror of those first few moments and the possibility of a repeat performance. Two days after the robbery I was doing my morning devotional readings that had gone to press months before this event, and the Bible passage was from Joshua 1:9. It read as if it had been written especially for me. It said to not be dismayed, frightened, or discouraged for the Lord would be with you wherever you go. It was enough, and He has given me a peace about it.

Dear Mother,

I told you we could expect adventurous happenings when Merry arrived! We always happily anticipate the college vacation time in the hope that she might be able to visit, but we always know that her arrival brings the chance and challenge of never before seen or done activities in our lives! Yesterday, we realized this visit is turning out not to be an exception. We received a frantic call from Merry, and thankfully her daddy was here to answer this one. She reported that she had experienced a little accident in our truck (that she had borrowed to visit a friend). After determining that she was not hurt, Rodolph began to get the information. It seems that as she was turning onto the street where we live, the whole road gave way beneath her and the truck fell into it. The city had recently put new pipes underground there and apparently it was not a very good job.

As we arrived on the scene, along with many other onlookers, a small Volkswagen got too near the hole and it also fell in as the ground gave way beneath it. We called a wrecker to pull out our vehicle, and its front wheels also went in. With the help of yet another big truck they finally managed to pull them all out, and for once in my life I saw a Peruvian crowd that you didn't have to admonish to stand back. Everyone was afraid to get too near. The road continued to crack and crumble down its whole length and this morning we heard that several other cars had experienced the same fate. I know this was a most unusual happening and it was no one's fault (unless you would blame the company that did the faulty work), but what are the chances of it happening to the average person? Of course, we have never considered Merry to be average!

Dear Mother,

The cholera situation here is still frightening. Cases keep pouring in but there is medicine coming in, too, and they tell us the cases treated quickly are almost always successful. For awhile there was a shortage of medicine, though. There have been 6,000 cases in Trujillo and 24 deaths. Of course, even one death is too many, but we realize it could have been much worse and we are grateful. We are not eating any food that is not cooked. I plan to visit many, many salad bars on furlough! We are not sure that all the information we get is correct, but we are not taking chances. (One of the missionaries wanted us to ask if anyone was coming for a visit and could bring a suitcase full of lettuce?!☺)

Dear Family and Friends,

Crime and terrorism do get a little too close every now and then. Last week a missionary's 15 year old son came home for Christmas in an AeroPeru flight from Lima to Trujillo that had to turn back and land so they could take a time bomb off! His family ate Christmas dinner with us and they told us about it, because it did not make the newspaper. As I write this I wonder why I am telling you this--I think, more than anything, it is to let you know that even though we find the situation here disturbing and we do need your prayers, we want to reassure you that we feel protected and calm and at peace because we feel like the Lord is still in our decision to be here.

Good things are happening too! In times like these people respond, hearts are made tender, and doors are opened.

Dear Mother,

The political situation is pretty bad here; we are wondering where it will all end. What do the papers say about it there? If things continue we might be home sooner than we planned (if at all). (How's that for a cheerful note?) No kidding, those of us who have entered Peru in the last year have visas for a year only. If things get worse they might not renew them and we would have to leave. The personnel here with the US government are on standby to leave with a 48-hour notice if this thing isn't settled by April 9th, and that isn't too far off now. The papers are really building up this new relationship with Russia; everyone says that those political ties are stronger every day. I don't know what it is all about, really, but everybody is very concerned now about Peru, its people, and also the USA. It surely would be a horrible future for our Christian brothers here if communism should take over.

Dear Mother,

We are told inflation here in Peru is the 3rd highest in the world right now. It is 72.6%, and I believe it by what I see in the stores. We are actually getting some imports in, though, and that is a first. I saw a box of Fireside vanilla wafers that I used to pay $.59 for at home, and they were over $2 a box. (However, I guess there have been times I would have almost paid $2 for a single vanilla wafer!) The corn flakes were over $5 and a small can of corn for $2. I didn't buy anything, of course, but I had a good time looking. There is no peanut butter, so I bought some raw peanuts from the market. We toasted them, shelled them, and made some with that little machine we brought back. I had all the family working to help me get two small jars, but was it good! It is much better than what you can buy, and you can better believe I am not going to let them waste it!

Dear Mother,

Spencer asked if he could have a day off between 7th and 8th grades, so we gave him a one day holiday, and he is now in the 8th grade. How is that for making progress?

We had a flat tire on the way to Lima (as usual) and Spencer helped his dad change it. He is really becoming a help to Rodolph in things like that. He is getting strong as an ox. I remember the first time Rodolph asked David instead of me to help him lift something and then it was Merry before me and now he asks Spencer before Merry. So Amy is the only one weaker than I am it seems.

While we were in Lima we went out to see their camp, and it is a real disaster! The 14 mudslides that came down through the valley dumped tons of mud on all sides and right through part of it. The chapel was carried away and the lower area is now under 4 to 5 feet of dried mud. The dorms and dining room were saved but are now an island in a sea of mud and boulders. The deluge passed on either side of them. We rode up the mountain and looked back down. All the houses and landmarks, except our camp, are completely washed away or buried. You can see parts of roofs or debris in some places. It is incredible what the force of rainfall in a desert area can do! We once again realize what a close call we had in Shiran, as well as here, and we thank the Lord.

Dear Mother,

It was so good to talk with you; it tickled me when you said you didn't recognize Spencer's voice. It still startles me to hear it so low and loud (when he decides to say something, that is ☺). He is still a man of few words and still keeps his nose in a book. Someone asked us if he was happy here, and I told them I guess he could read a book anywhere! He just lives in another world sometimes.

Speaking of another world--we saw all of this happening in Trujillo, but I am not sure yet that I believe what I saw! Here in the desert where we always have a shortage of water, the quantity of water that was running in the streets just staggered your mind. The strange thing was the rate of the flow from the river as it flooded. It spread out all over the city maintaining a depth of about a foot. People built dikes to keep it from getting into their houses, and for the most part, it was contained to the streets and kept flowing all through the city until it got to the sea. There were practically no houses in the city proper that were flooded inside. Of course, there were a few, and the market was flooded as well as some other businesses, but it was Good Friday and most people were home and could sandbag their doors and other entrances. Because there are no hills and very few low places, the water just ran on to the ocean, but it left so much mud and dust that the city is now under a cloud all the time. You can hardly breathe, and the house is covered constantly in a thick film of red dust. The flood waters were all red-brown and heavy with dirt.

I think the worse happening that I heard of, though, affected some of the church families near us--someone opened the sewer to let the flood water pour into it, and the sewer waters all backed up into their homes through the bathroom fixtures. Some of the water was still running yesterday, but today all is under control they say (at least until it rains again in the mountains and we have a new break through the river wall). The road to Shiran is out again and they tell us it has 11 washouts and heaven knows how many avalanches. They just report where a road is gone altogether. Up north of us many of the little towns are isolated completely as they have only the Pan American Highway to connect them, and it is washed away in so many places. Lima is in danger of losing its water supply due to the mudslides between them and their source in the mountains, so water is being rationed there now. The whole country is in a terrible fix; I don't know when or how it can be brought under control.

Because of this emergency, there is a shortage of food, and the prices of what is available are soaring. We can travel now only by boat or airplane because by land is out of the question. In areas where there are only a few bridges out, the buses can drive up to one side of the river and another bus meets it on the other side. The passengers get out and wade across with their luggage, exchange buses, and continue with their trip. Some enterprising and strong young men were hiring out to carry people and their belongings across on their backs.

We took some things up to Shiran just before the last washout which has cut us off from there, too. We stood by the roadside up on the mountain and watched the river take away a chicken farm. The owners were there also, just watching like we were because there was nothing anyone could do. Two of the buildings had wedged behind big boulders and were still there and we could see chickens still inside. Three big buildings had disappeared and a fourth was broken open. Pieces of it kept breaking off and swirling away in the rush of water. There were poles and roofing going by, and we saw parts of two tractors that had been washed down from the mines way up in the mountains.

We are told they have planes that are patrolling to watch for mudslides heading toward cities. My question is, "What are our options once we hear it is coming our way?" This is some experience!

Dear Mother,

We have a lot of things to put up with in the aftermath of the earthquake, and now the government has taken over the dollar accounts here and we may have to get you to put our checking account solely in your name. If I write to you to "do what I told you" without actually saying what, in a letter or over the radio, this is what I mean. They are taking over all dollars and dollar accounts, and we can't cash checks like before. The mission declared a state of emergency and we are living off of mission money until things get straightened out. It is a mess! This happened a month ago and we are still waiting to know what to do. We'll keep you posted, but we may have to put EVERYTHING into your name. I am just glad someone could take this letter out to you so you could know what is happening; I can't write about it and send it through the post office because our mail is usually inspected. Please don't mention it in your letters, either. We have to be very careful during these times; this government is very suspicious of foreigners. It feels strange to be put in that category.

Dear Mother,

I am glad we talked to you last night after we got home to find out we had a tidal wave near here! We were out at camp and had not even heard about it! (There are no phones out at camp, nor TV, etc.) We checked the news after we talked and found it happened just south of us. The reports are that waves between 30 and 100 feet high came in at that site, twelve people are known dead, dozens missing, and homes washed away! At the beaches near us the little shacks were completely washed away, but even the sturdy homes had water inside and had doors and windows broken out. There was an earthquake out at sea that caused it. It sounded really bad, but we were completely oblivious of it up there in the Andes. Your phone call was the first information we had, and after you told us about it, we finally heard it on the news last night. I guess that we have had just about every natural disaster one can think of through this area since our arrival here-- earthquakes, floods, tidal waves, mud slides, avalanches, and dust storms. Did the Lord pick us a great place for our mission work or what? I can truthfully say it has never been boring in all these years!

Dear Mother,
       Another horrible incident occurred on Friday. Our missionary treasurer was shot in front of the mission office in Lima. He had just come from the bank with a briefcase full of money, and as he parked his car 4 armed men shot him, grabbed the briefcase, and fled. Thankfully, two of our men were in the office at the time and ran to help him. He was shot twice (a third bullet missed)--one in the elbow area and another in the thigh which severed the femoral artery, and he almost bled to death before they could get him to the hospital a block away! His blood pressure was 40 when they arrived! The Lima missionaries are really shaken up and we are all very upset, as you can imagine! It especially brings back some unpleasant memories for me. It was not terrorists, but a vicious gang of robbers, and apparently, they saw him receive that large sum of money ($5,000) at the bank and followed him. The missionaries who took him to the hospital relate a series of divine miracles that the Lord put in place to save his life--like having the proper doctor there when they arrived and even being able to get through the congested Lima traffic, etc. He was in surgery 6 hours but is doing fine now, considering what a close call he had.

Dear Mother,

We try to be careful all the time but especially during these times of military takeover. However, Rodolph and David got a scare while just driving downtown. They pulled up behind a truck full of soldiers at a traffic light. They were commenting on the fact that most of them seemed to be just young boys, when the soldiers began to point their machine guns at them and pretend to shoot. It was a frightening moment.

Dear Mother,

We were in Lima during this latest upheaval in the government and we tried to stay close to the apartments because things are happening in the streets all around. There is immediate police and military response to what they think might be a possible uprising or riot. They use tear gas and even shoot bullets into the crowds to disperse them. David and some of the other Mks went to the bowling alley nearby and promised to go straight there and come back without any detours. They bowled awhile, and when they started to leave to get a taxi and come home, they stepped out of the exit into the street and right into the midst of a riot in progress. They were astounded and stood there mesmerized for a minute or two just watching--until a canister of tear gas rolled right under their feet! With that they joined the crowd running for their lives in front of the tanks and rifles and machine guns. After that experience, we didn't have too much trouble getting David to stay home with us, too.

Dear Everybody,

The volunteer team leaves today so I am sending this with them. Our post office is not on strike, but they have no stamps and the stamping machine is broken. That is a new one!

The situation here now (politically and about every other way except climate-- which is story-book weather) is just worse and worse every day. Heavily armed terrorists have forced shutdowns of businesses. It happened in Lima in these days and there are rumors of it happening here. Businesses and banks have received letters from the terrorists to close, and one of our neighbors on the park here received a threat from the counter group. I saw that letter. One group says to close or we will shoot you, and the other says to stay open or we will shoot you! Everyone feels traumatized by the situation. It has been especially unnerving to have a big group of US citizens to take care of during this time. Please pray a little extra for all of us, we just don't know what is going to happen, especially in these next few days. I don't know what you are hearing but it is not making the newspapers or the other media here. What we learn about the situation is by word of mouth.

Dear Mother,

We are back home now after one of the scariest trips we have made yet. We certainly would not have traveled this time if it had not been absolutely necessary. We had to get Amy to the American Embassy in Lima to get her registered as a US citizen. We had to get those papers and, also, get her passport. In these times of so much uncertainty and unrest, we can't take a chance on being ordered out of the country and then not be able to take our child because she has only Peruvian papers. At first we could not travel at all because it was strictly prohibited, and even now it is very risky. There is an 8 p.m. curfew that is enforced by patrolling military police who have orders to shoot on sight.

We got to the mission apartments in Lima, and during the night we could hear gun shots and what sounded like bombs and machine guns, too. I couldn't imagine that anyone would be tempted to risk getting out during the curfew hours. We actually got to the Embassy and got done what we had to do and felt so much better about our child being legally inscribed as a citizen of the USA. The place was like a war zone, though, with guards checking everyone carefully. I don't blame them because the American Embassy has been the target of many attacks by different groups just in the short time we have been in the country.

We heard there was a very bad situation in a town north of Lima through which we had to pass to get back home. One of the missionaries gave us a report from there and said the steel mill workers were striking and there were riots all over town. They were stopping cars passing through, turning them over, and burning them; they were also robbing and assaulting the occupants. He warned us to not try to go through there for a few days at least. There is only one road in the whole country that goes from north to south and that is the Pan American Highway, so if one travels by car in Peru in either of those directions, that is your only choice.

As much as we wanted and needed to be home, we decided it would be foolish to try to leave Lima under those conditions. We kept trying to find out what the conditions were up north, and finally we got a report from a missionary colleague who said he had a friend who had gotten through the town in question with no problem. I had some reservations about getting out on the road with the whole family in uncertain conditions like this, but we really felt we needed to get home. We would feel safer and be safer if we just could get back to our own house and an environment we know and in which we are known.

We set out as early as the curfew would allow in the early morning and began our trip. Traveling along the Pan American highway was pretty much the same as all those journeys through the desert, until we came to the town about which we were so concerned. The whole area was still as death as we entered the city limits. The signs that a whole lot of destruction had taken place were all around us in the wreckage of cars and burnt debris strewn all along the road. There was no one on the streets, and this gave us a bad feeling.

When passing through this town we always take one route that is the most direct, but for some reason this day we chose to go another way around the town to get out instead of going straight through. There was no discussion or decision as to which road we should choose, we just went the other way which really is not considered the best. As we passed the route we normally take, we could see a group of people gathering in the center of town, but nothing like a riot was going on that we could see. We circled the town and were getting ready to give a big sigh of relief as we got out onto the open road again, when one of the children yelled, "Look!" We all turned to look behind us and saw that there was a crowd of men with guns and rocks and clubs and heaven knows what all. They had put up a barricade and were waiting for cars to come over the arched bridge that we have always taken on other occasions. They couldn't be seen from the entrance to the bridge, but were stopping cars and assaulting the passengers as they came over the hump and were surprised and trapped. The people in those cars had no place to turn aside and escape and were completely at their mercy.

None of us can explain why we went another way that day other than the fact we had prayed for God's protection, and we all believed that was exactly what it was. We have felt His hand guiding us through danger many times. Many other times, like this one, we can look back and see how He led and protected us when we didn't even know we were in danger.

SPECIAL ORCHIDS

Dear Mother,

Today is a typical warm Monday leading up to Christmas and last night our choir presented the cantata we have been working on so long. I had about 75 voices in this group and they have worked hard. Not only was it an inspiring worship service, but it turned out to be a significant evangelistic opportunity too. The pastor did not even have a meditation, but at the end of the program they sang an invitation and 6 people responded accepting the Lord as their Savior. That was really cause for celebration! By the way, do you remember those choir robes State Street Church gave us that they could not use any more because they were too worn out? Well, we are still using them. Every once in awhile some of them disappear, and we have seen some interesting outfits that were made from what looks suspiciously like that same material.

Dear Mother,

I asked an old man at church today how old he is and he replied, "I am nearly 80 years old, but I am 12 years old in the Lord and that is what really counts." What a thrill to hear that; it makes it all worthwhile to be here.

Dear Mother,

I remember wondering how missionaries do their work, and I have just had a lesson in how that comes about in what I believe is the best and most natural way. A new gardener came by to talk to us about cutting all of that out-of-control growth of bougainvillea vines on the roof and wall. It is gorgeous, but too heavy and full of thorns and bugs. He said he would come on Sunday and do it, and Rodolph told him that he could come on any day but Sunday because that is the Lord's Day and we don't do that kind of work on the day we set aside to worship Him. This seemed to anger the gardener and he went away in a huff and left us looking for someone else to do it.

About a week later, he showed up and asked for Rodolph (who is never home when I need him ☺). Since he was not here he wanted to talk to me, which was a little unusual. I came outside to see what he wanted and he said he had some questions about what Rodolph had told him. He wanted to know more about this "Lord" of whom we spoke. He spoke in gardener terms and said, "It seems that a little seed has been planted here."--and he pointed to his heart. I got my Spanish Bible and some simple helps that I had and we sat down on the little wall at the front step. I tried to explain God's love for him as best I could and used as many "gardener" terms from the Bible that I could think of like "I am the vine and ye are the branches," etc. He accepted the Lord as his Savior right there. I finally felt like a real live missionary. What a thrill!

(NOTE: I doubt if this gardener had ever seen an orchid before and certainly had not cultivated one in this desert--but he made a beautiful orchid for me that day.)

Dear Mother,

We had a young mother join Central Church today, and when we went up to welcome her she told us an interesting story. She said she had been watching us for years. She told us her father was the owner of the corner store where we bought things quite often, and when we moved into the neighborhood she was a young teenager. She said she saw us and our children come into the store and noticed that our manner was different. It was not just that we were "gringos" and had other customs, but Rodolph would always take time to greet her father and be kind to him. Now this man was not easy to love as he had a really abrasive way of treating people, and he had a bad reputation. He would shout at the kids, sell you something that had gone bad, give you the wrong change, and was a most unlikable person in general. The neighborhood kids had sort of made it a challenge to see who could torment him more or beat him at his own game. Well, this lady said that our kids never tried to steal from him or talk bad to him, and we were always polite and even friendly. She wondered what made the difference, and now that she had accepted Christ she knew why. We thought that was a wonderful compliment, but it nearly scared me to death to think that people are watching us like that. How many have seen me when my testimony has not been so Christ-like?

Dear Mother,

We are enjoying our short stay in Lima. We went to the big fair that is set up here once a year with vendors and displays from all over the country. There were some beautiful crafts and artisan works. While we were admiring those a young man came up to us and said, "Excuse me, but aren't you the Dixon family?" We were surprised, of course, but began a conversation with him and learned he was from Trujillo. He told us that his mother was one of the people that Rodolph had helped after the earthquake twenty years ago. He was just a little boy then, but he still remembers the food they received and bags of cement and other supplies that were brought in to help them rebuild their house. He had in his hand a beautiful eagle made of wood shavings. It was exquisite and about a foot high with outspread wings. We admired his handiwork, and he said he wanted us to have it. He said he understood that the eagle was a symbol of our country, and he just wanted to do something for us to express his appreciation for that time in his life so long ago, when something was done for his family in their time of need. We were dumbfounded that the "bread cast upon the waters" so many years earlier could "come home" in such an unexpected and sweet way.

Dear Family and Friends,

We find our work continuing to grow--Central Church has

around 325 in Sunday School every Sunday and more for the worship service. It is wonderful to see "standing room only" but we are hurting for space.

The answer to a long standing prayer was announced last week when our camp at Shiran received electricity. What a joy to plug in the refrigerator and snap on a light! We are starting construction on a new dining hall that will be able to seat 200-250 when completed. We are hoping for several work teams from the USA to help in construction of this. We had 6 weeks of really good camps this past Jan. and Feb. and the camp continues to be used all during the year by churches and related groups.

Both Amy and I will accompany Spencer to the USA in July to begin his studies in architecture at Clemson University. We are really proud of Spencer being a Merit Scholar finalist. He is the first Charlie Brown School graduate to achieve this!☺ Being the only student in your class, it is rather hard not to graduate as the top student (also the worst) but being in the top ½ of 1% of all students in the USA makes us think that this MK's education must not have been too bad!

Dear Family,

Yes, we are okay, but I just don't seem to spring back like I used to do, I notice. I'm sort of like an old tire that has lost some of its bounce and is not quite as lively, but if it doesn't lose all its air, it is still going to make the trip and the ride just might be smoother!☺

I have the honor of receiving what well may be the first and only honorarium from a church around here to a missionary for services rendered. When I finished up my 4th night of teaching out at Miguel Grau Church, the sweet little man who is the treasurer gave me a couple of bills wadded up and said the church wanted me to have that. When I refused, he said they wanted us to have that for gasoline. It must have been only around $10 total, but that has to be a unique experience. It really touched me. I didn't accept it, of course, and asked him to put it into something at the church, but I really appreciated that. It is a very rare thing to pay a visiting pastor, much less a missionary; it showed me that they are growing in their concepts of responsibility and it was a nice thing to see. The reason it was so touching is because they are so poor out there.

The work at camp continues, but it is at a pace that drives me nuts and doesn't seem to bother Rodolph at all!--The story of our life together! Now, as if camp is not enough, Central Church is planning a big building program and guess who is right in the middle of that? The only thing worse than Rodolph building something, is Rodolph building it with the help of Julio! They have been meeting now for two weeks, several nights a week, making plans--I get to serve tea and cookies!

I have had the "honor" of presenting the program for WMU for 6 weeks because the literature with program materials has not yet arrived. I have really had some fun with "off-the-wall" type of presentations that I wish I had time to tell you about--their response to it, I mean. They fixed me good, though, because they said they had planned a social for Mother's Day. I invited them to come to my house for it and they said, "Good, that's what we had planned to do." Even better, it lands on my birthday--what a way to celebrate, huh?

Dear Mother,

This past Sunday we attended Central Church because the pastor called me and said they needed me to play the piano. This was unusual because this is one church that now has enough folks with the talent to take over the keyboard for all their services. I thought it was because the young man who normally plays couldn't be there, but when we arrived, I saw him and asked why he was not playing. He said he had been accepted into the university, and I thought to myself, "What has this to do with playing the piano?" Then he took off his baseball cap and his head was so bald it was shiny--his normally beautiful wavy hair had been shaved off by his colleagues. This is an initiation custom for those young men lucky enough to make it into the university. He is a little vain and was embarrassed to be in front of the whole congregation like that. Thankfully they don't do that to the girls.

In the evening we went to an entirely different type of church. The young pastor there was one of those who made his decision to study for the ministry at camp. He finally found a wife, but they have had some rocky times and have come to our house for counseling several times. They seem to be doing a good job at a little church which is just a few blocks from where the ships dock at the port near here. The tiny building was as clean as a pin, he played the guitar reasonably well, and it was a good service. (Rodolph spoke too long, but other than that, it was good ☺). Then they told us that the church had raised enough money to put a new straw roof on the place. We were happy for them, but everyone realizes that this kind of roof won't be much good if we have a lot of rain this year. They showed us the little one room division off to the side of the meeting room where they live. They have made this out of straw matting. They said the group was going to be organized into an official church in December even though they could only pay him a salary that is practically nothing (and only manage that some of the time). He said with a smile, though, that he had bought some little baby ducks and he was going to raise them to sell by Christmas time. He felt sure he could get some extra money that way. It really touched me to see how hard he is trying.

Dear Mother,

We were told a really inspiring story by another missionary. It reminds us that no matter how unimportant and mundane the task seems, if it is done for the Lord and He is directing it, it can bring about great things. This colleague was giving out pamphlets on the street in his town and a visiting mountain man received one and took it home to read. He liked what he read and gathered a group around him up there in the high Andes to study it with him. He made the long trip back to the coast to ask questions and get more helps, and once again returned to share it with his friends. This he did several times, until he arrived one day to report that he had a whole group of people who wanted to be baptized, form a church, and join our convention. He asked the missionary to please come up and do the baptizing for him, and show them what else they needed to do. Now that's the way to do mission work, just hand out a pamphlet and sit back and let the results come to you! I call that beautiful!

Dear Mother,

We Dixons have left our name in Peru! On our last trip to Lima the family picked out the site, and coming back we stopped to carry out our plan. We had noticed the designs and advertisements on the sand dunes and sandy mountains along the highway about halfway between here and Lima. They are made from transplanting the little cactus-like grass sprigs that grow in this area into the desired pattern. So, we decided we could and should plant (another pun) our name up there for all the world to see. We parked the car and we hiked up the mountain, gathering plants as we went along. It was hot, back-breaking, dirty work, but everybody helped. It was a great family effort. They were not hard to pull up, but they were hard to hold because they were prickly and stuck into our hands. We managed to get enough to print DIXON right up there at the top of the mountain and far enough away from the advertisements for Inca Kola to be impressive. We expect to enjoy seeing it on every Lima trip we make now, but we wonder how long it will last.

(NOTE: We repaired it several times, but the last time we traveled by car to Lima, there it was--still clearly legible on that mountain at the side of the highway after 25 years. I guess there is more than one way to make a name for oneself!)

Dear Family,

It is so thrilling to be allowed to see some of the harvest.

Amid a sense of crisis times with so much unrest due to governmental instability, hunger, terrorism, earthquakes, floods, unemployment, etc. we can readily see the difference that Christ makes in the quality of life here. There is a peace and joy so evident that distinguishes the "evangelico" and is attracting many people who come asking, "How do I get what you have?" It has taken 19 years to get to this point, but in this past year we have had several who have come to us like that without our seeking them out--some completely unknown and some only casual acquaintances from the processes of daily life.

Dear Mother,

Gloria told us another story about her church. A little boy came to church and stood in the doorway and wouldn't come in. He said if he entered the church, the devil would get him. The next week the pastor's wife held her class outside and they sat around on the uncompleted adobe walls of the new church. He came and listened, and when his mother came to get him, she stayed too. They both watched the presentation of the Life of Christ on a flannel graph and listened until the teacher finished the whole story. We never thought unfinished walls could be an asset to reaching people.

Dear Mema and Amy,

Well, we have been back long enough now to not miss you all so much, but somehow my emotional makeup has not assimilated that fact just yet! We got our photos and there is a great one of Poppi and Nick fishing, and that brings it all back (especially to Poppi)! It is a cute picture with the two of them sitting there. Nick has the pole in one hand and the other resting on Poppi's knee. Just from the position of the two of them you can tell that this is serious business!

It is getting close to Fiestas Patrias (like our 4th of July), and all you hear everywhere you go is the distinct sound of

Peruvian high schools' trumpets and drums! Remember? No other sound like it. All the streets where you have to travel are blocked off with marching students. There is no escape from it; even when we went out to camp we found the Shiran band practicing. They were marching up and down that little lane right beside our cabin. It is really hard on the auditory and nervous system (and I know that Sousa is rolling in his grave☺)!

Dear Mother,

There is hardly a day goes by without someone coming to us with a sad tale and asking for help. Some stories are real and some are made up, and it is hard to tell the difference. It is impossible to meet all the needs. We had a man from the airline office who came by today and I wondered how much money he wanted. I was chagrined to think of my cynical attitude when we learned the reason for his visit. He said he came to see Rodolph because he wanted what he saw in him. The words he used were that he saw peace, sincerity and inner happiness that his other friends don't have, and he would like to know how he could have that, too. Can you imagine how that made us feel? He later accepted Christ and joined Central Church.

(NOTE: That was a whole handful of orchids!)

Dear Mother,

I surely am glad that you let me take piano lessons all those years and made me practice when I would have rather not. It is great to have a "Universal Language" when your Spanish is as poor as mine is. I have discovered another "Universal Language," too,--it's a smile. That really works better than the music, and you have it with you all the time!☺

Dear Mother,

I had a good lesson today about how to pray. Gloria came

for lunch after church service (as she does quite often at our invitation) and related this to us.   She said she had been so frustrated with the people at her church arriving late, that many times she was not in the proper spirit to worship by the time they finally got started.   It seemed that nothing she tried helped in getting them there at the proper hour.   So this morning she prayed that the Lord would either get them to church on time or that she would not get so upset over their tardiness.   She arrived at church and did a few chores and thought that surely it was time to begin, so she looked at her watch and found that it had stopped.   She did not know what time it was all morning and had a great service! She said it surely did teach her to be more careful about what she prayed.

Dear Mother,

We have enjoyed our volunteers this week.   One young man who doesn't know Spanish at all kept saying "blow my nose" for "vamonos" (let's go) and we all got a laugh out of that.   The blooper that really won the prize, though, is the statement by a lady who wanted to try her Spanish in greeting the congregation on Sunday.   She tried to say she might be able to speak better if she didn't have such a headache and pointed to her head.   She confused the two words "cabeza" (head) and "cerveza" (beer) and managed to convey the thought that she had a hangover.   Our Peruvian brothers are innately polite and there was not a roar of laughter as might be expected, but I did hear a snicker or two among the young people, and I saw a couple of the older ones with a sort of stunned look in their eyes.   Rodolph decided it was time for him to interpret for her at that point.

Even Chuckles nearly got us into trouble when one of the volunteers tried to talk to her.   You remember how she only speaks on her terms.   Even though I am convinced she can say anything she cares to in any language, she will not speak when you try to show her off.   He sat by her cage for ages saying "Hello, pretty bird, speak to me."   Chuckles turned her back and completely ignored him; she was mute. He kept on and on until I was getting a little tired of it, myself. Then she slowly turned around on her perch, looked him straight in the eye, and said very distinctly, "Hola, Feo" (Hello, Ugly). I nearly fell out of my chair and everyone else there who spoke Spanish were convulsed with laughter, but I don't think he ever knew that he had just been insulted by our parrot. I hope he never does.

NOTE: Chuckles was well named because she brought us many moments of amusement. She was one of the most clearly articulate birds I have ever heard. She could make any sound she heard and was always surprising us with new words and even phrases. The only drawback to this amazing display was that she would never perform on demand. If you wanted to show her off, inevitably she would be mute. If you needed silence to record something or have a solemn time of prayer, she would decide it was show time! We all loved her and hated to leave her, but we found her a good home where she is given a place of honor with one of our Peruvian families. We hear from them from time to time, and she is still making folks laugh.

Dear Mother,

I invited the WMU to our house today for a meeting and had 81 ladies show up. We had to meet outside in the yard, of course. We quickly made more lemonade and cut the sandwiches and cake into smaller parts. It was a thrill to see that many ladies respond and see them have a good time. What fun!

Dear Mother,

Guess what we have done now? We let the Acteens talk us into having a sleep-over at our house. We had 49 who attended, and we used the tents from our camp and put them up in the back yard. We have some older girls in the group now who are responsible, so I didn't have to stay out there with them all night. I just had to see they had food and other supplies. It was a completely new experience for most of them, and it was a thrill to see them enjoying themselves and learning at the same time. They were pretty loud at times, though, and I could only think it was "pay back" time for those neighbors who have the unbearably loud parties until the wee hours of the morning.

Dear Mother,

You'll never guess what I got for my birthday this year! Before I tell you let me give you a little history on the groundwork I laid for what I thought I might get. Every day as we passed a store on the main street, I looked at a beautiful hand carved room divider.   I had visions of it sitting just inside our front door entrance to shield our sitting area from the many callers that come each and every day. I couldn't justify just going down there and buying it myself (even though it was an unbelievably low price) so I dropped big hints about how useful it would be, how beautiful it was, what a wonderful art object, how much it would help out the Peruvian man who carved it, etc., etc. I would make a point of driving by to admire it and point it out to whomever I could. Then one day it wasn't there anymore. Since it was just a few days before my birthday and Mothers' Day, I had in my mind that I just might get it. I was planning how I would be properly surprised when the family presented it to me.

Well, sure enough, it was on my birthday that Rodolph drove up in the suburban and announced that he had my birthday present out in the car. I was thrilled and thinking about my response to this thoughtful and generous present. I ran outside to the back of the car, lowered the tailgate, and was greeted by a loud Baa-aaa! There lying on the floor was the most pitiful looking goat with his feet tied together and wanting out! Rodolph smiled and said, "Surprise!" I tell you now, it truly was a surprise! Our dear caretaker out at camp had sent me a present. If you would ever want a study in mixed emotions, I would have made a perfect model at that moment!

That was not the end of the story either! You remember

how Snoopy always protected her territory? Well, obviously she felt threatened with this invasion, and she began to bark without ceasing. The goat apparently didn't care for this and butted her up against the kitchen door. This brought on a new barrage of barks until Snoopy finally lost her voice. She was barking, but nothing came out. This was when Rodolph and Gladys decided to prepare this animal for cooking. (The goat I mean!) This they did to the consternation of everyone around. The caretaker at camp only asked one thing of us and that was to save the skin for him, so they hung that on the clothes line. The goat was gone and in the pot, but Snoopy kept barking at the skin, so we had to take it out to camp right away to get some peace and let the poor dog get her voice back. We invited Peruvian friends in and got rid of most of the goat in a surprisingly delicious meal served with rice, beans, and yuca. It was really good and there was enough left for another meal, so we froze it for a later time. Snoopy finally stopped barking and got her voice back, although it took several days.

The sequel to this story is that when we defrosted that other meal, poor Snoopy began the whole thing over again, and we had to eat fast! Getting a goat for one's birthday has many facets of interest of which one would not normally be aware!

Dear Mother,

We surely did miss you at Christmas. All four kids were in the church play here. David was Joseph, Merry was Mary, Spencer was a shepherd, and the greatest miscasting of all--Amy was an angel! We thought they looked good and did their parts well, but back at home we got the lowdown on what all really went on where the audience couldn't see. David got the worst evaluation because somehow it just didn't seem right for Joseph to be tickling Mary to get her to laugh during the pastor's sermon. The pastor should have known better than to have had such a long meditation with so many children on stage.

We had our lukewarm, greasy chocolate and dry paneton after the service as is the custom here, and everyone seemed so excited over it. I wonder if we will ever learn to love that particular custom as much as we have learned to love the people serving it? Then again I wonder if when we get home the things you have there will seem strange to us? It is amazing how fast one can adapt to things if you try (and get a whole lot of help from the Lord). You remember how we laughed at our Orientation when someone told us that one frequently used missionary prayer was, "Lord, I will put it down if you will keep it down?" Well, just let me say we have used that prayer quite a few times already.

Dear Mother,

Our Christmas this year was unique; it was very distinct, even for us! I am sure this is one we will never forget! On Christmas Day all the missionaries in the Trujillo area ate a mid-day dinner at our house which has sort of become the tradition for us now, as you know. It makes for a lot of extra work, but it is worth it. It means so much to be able to observe a few of our customs from the USA, albeit some of them are a little hard to recognize due to the necessary substitutions for the things not available here. We had a wonderful dinner--I provided the turkey and dressing and others brought a covered dish. There was only English or "Spanglish" spoken, and everyone was enjoying the occasion. It was good to see the Christmas excitement of the little children. There were several of them present who finished their meal rapidly and were running all over the place playing, while we adults lingered over dessert there in our dining room.

Then something happened that I am not sure you are going to believe--I almost don't believe it myself and I was there and saw it with my own eyes! We heard a loud commotion and everyone jumped up to see what was happening. Some of the men jerked off the covering to our fireplace to discover two little legs dangling there. Josh, the two year old MK of our colleagues, the Watts, had fallen down the chimney! Three of the Mks had gone up on the roof, and we have the suspicion that the older ones helped put him down--but there he was! The space at the bottom was too small to get him out that way, and nothing we tried could pull him back up either.

It took 45 minutes and a call to the Trujillo volunteer fire department to get him out. Here they came in the red fire truck with the siren screaming! There must have been more than a half dozen firemen all dressed in bright orange jump suits that came running in like the "Keystone Cops," but they managed to get him back up the chimney in about 10 minutes. They carried Josh off to the hospital to check him out, but he only had a small scratch on his elbow. However, I am not sure how long it took to clean him up, and our house looked liked coal miners had held their convention there.

Dear Mother,

A funny thing happened in church the other day. It made me think of back home at State Street and wonder what the congregation would do if something like that would happen there! A lady brought her two little chickens to church in her sweater and we could hear them cheeping during the service. She started to put them on the floor and Mrs. Davalos leaned over the pew and told her not to do that, so she gave one to her 10 year old daughter who put it inside her dress, and she returned the other one to her sweater. Now these chicks were not exactly biddies, but they weren't full grown either. I guess you could say they were adolescent age chickens and they were not very pretty. After all that, she sat there quietly during the sermon, but in a short while she dosed off and her head fell back on the pew. Right then the little chick popped up out of her sweater, roosted on her shoulder, put its little head right up against hers, and fell asleep just like she did. I could hear distinct snickers and see shoulders shaking all over the church. You should have seen Julio's face when he saw them from the pulpit and realized what it was. All he said was, "Well, I guess they are for Christmas." With that he went on with his sermon, but I must confess I don't remember much of his sermon for that day.

This same lady came to the WMU meeting the following Tuesday and brought her 2 daughters and the same two little chickens. Someone said that she has no one with whom to leave the chicks because she and her daughters live alone in a little shack in a bad section of town. If she were to leave the chickens unattended there for even a short length of time they would be stolen, so she carries them wherever she goes. Everyone has been very tolerant of the situation; I guess they figure that it only takes a short period of time for chickens to reach the edible stage.

And as if the chicken episode wasn't enough for one Sunday, that same day in the evening service, Rodolph put his foot up under the pew in front of him and his shoe got stuck on a wad of bubble gum someone had left there. We couldn't get it loose, and we wondered if he would have to leave his shoe or if it would have a hole in it when we finally pulled it free!

Dear Mother,

I think we need volunteers who are lifeguards to come and teach a course at our seminary. Rodolph was baptizing in the big river near Chimbote and he and the new believer stepped in a hole and had to swim out down stream. Actually it was pretty funny after I saw they made it okay, and I tried really hard not to laugh, but you know me.

There have been some memorable occasions at baptismal services, especially in the mountains. It is the joy of every missionary and pastor to get to baptize a new member into the church, but I have noticed that they are very generous in offering a colleague the honor when the location of the baptismal site is in the high Andes. The water in those mountain streams is so cold that if you are in it for more than a very few minutes, your whole body is numbed to the point of paralysis. Rodolph has many a story to tell of events occurring during what should be one of the most solemn and inspiring times of one's life. One tale I particularly love is about the man who borrowed Rodolph's underwear in which to be baptized. These people usually walk for miles to get to the site and they bring no other clothes into which they can change, so the ladies usually just pull off their outer garments and go down into the water in their slips. Well, this very little man, small even for a Peruvian, had no other clothes to wear and a long walk ahead of him after the service, so Rodolph gave him some of his own clean underwear. At that time Rodolph used an extra large size and his knit shirts had a vee neck. It was a very arresting sight to see the little man step down into the water with that huge shirt and the matching jockey shorts both on backwards!

Rodolph also has the distinction of baptizing a lady reputed to be over a hundred years old. He has baptized himself several times by being pulled down and under by the candidate who was scared or who stepped into a hole (or both). One time he baptized himself before the new member when he stepped back and off the rock on which they had been standing, and the candidate had to help him up.

NOTE: I find I miss the adventurous tone of our services there--here in the USA they seem rather tame most of the time.

Dear Family,

We are learning all kinds of things about ourselves at these going away parties. I never knew I was such a paragon of virtue. I keep looking over my shoulder to see if I have sprouted wings or above my head to see if a halo has appeared. Everyone feels like they should get up and say something nice about us. We realize how flowery our people are and accept it for what it is meant to be, but to tell the truth, I don't really remember many of the things they attribute to us having done here. For instance, one lady got up and said she wanted to thank us publicly for saving her little girl's life. We didn't remember that at all, and after the service, I asked her about it. She said her baby was very sick and we got her to a doctor and bought medicine for her that saved her life. I have no recollection of this particular case, but we did a lot of that like any missionary does in the course of daily life as the need arises. She could be right that it saved her child's life, because so many little children die just from a lack of medical attention for simple, curable diseases. The thing is, that we never know how our actions are interpreted. She saw in this something of which we were completely unaware, and it was certainly something that we would have never dreamed could have the far reaching implications on her life and our work here, as apparently it did. Her daughter is a healthy 16 year old now.

(NOTE: See what I mean about orchids?)

Dear Mother,

You remember how we brought back musical instruments for several of our people? Well, I am so happy to report that they are being used to the fullest. The young man who wanted the flute has taught himself to play wonderfully well. The young girl to whom I gave my flute has been studying at the conservatory of music in her town, and her mother reports that she has been giving classical recitals as well as playing religious specials in church. I think she plans to teach. The one who really got our attention, though, is Brother Miguel. He was so proud of his clarinet that he could only cry and cradle it like a baby in his arms. He had played with the symphony orchestra before his old clarinet gave out completely, and now he is ready to join this group again. The Sunday we gave it to him, he told me to please come and accompany him on the piano so he could play for the church. I did and we played and played and he just didn't want to stop. Even when I did, he just kept on playing without accompaniment, he was so happy and thanked us over and over. He really sounded good on it, too.

NOTE: Being the "jelly jar" for this kind of "orchid" makes one feel really good all over.

Dear Mother,

Two of our volunteers who were with us from the

Pendleton Street group were so concerned about sitting on planks at one of the little churches that they went back home and raised money to buy the wood for pews. The people here made them and we helped dedicate them today. Two years ago the volunteers were here and the money they sent arrived a year and a half ago. It has taken that long, but the pews are a work of art and love. Believe me, I personally appreciate them because sitting on a plank over two bricks at each end is not my idea of the way to sit through a long sermon! We are all so proud of this improvement and accomplishment by our hermanos, and we also see in this the evidence of love and concern by fellow Christians in the States. It makes you feel good.

Dear Mother,
      I know you are disappointed that Spencer can't be with you during the summer vacation from college, but we are so glad that he has this opportunity to work in the field that he is studying with a qualified architect. We just can't believe the Christian love of our friends like Jeanne and Bill Bailey who have done so much for us already, but who have gone beyond that second mile and invited Spencer to live with them all summer so he can be near his work. When they told us he could stay with them, we flatly refused to consider the offer unless they let us pay something. They didn't want to accept anything, but finally said we could pay them $20 per week and they would not hear to a penny more. Do you realize this includes room, board, and access to basically everything in their home and being treated like a son as well? (Hey, I just had a thought, maybe we could ALL go to live with them next furlough?☺) It is hard to know how to respond to generosity and love like theirs.
      (NOTE: They are a pair of orchids that stand out in the bouquet.)

Dear Mother,

     We have had such a wonderful week being the guests of the Pensacola Church. I have never felt so much like a celebrity in my life. It is very humbling to think of the love and concern of these people. It started with our arrival at the airport there. Just as we circled to land, the pilot announced first in Spanish and then in English, "The Dixon family is on board, welcome to Pensacola." Our mouths fell open in disbelief and shock. (The pilot was a friend of someone in the church who got him to do this.) These people have such a love to share and have done so much for our people and plan to continue a partnership with us by sending more volunteers. So far the work has been mainly with the medical clinic and attending to this type of need for our churches. People are ecstatic with what they have provided, and we are hoping they can expand to other areas as well. They have truly been an inspiration to know and work with and have surely provided us with a once in a lifetime experience in visiting with them at a time when we needed something personally. We weren't really aware of this until the Lord gave it to us through them. We were physically and emotionally wrung out, and this respite has restored our souls and given us what we needed to spur us on. We can't thank them enough for what they did for us, as well as all they continue to do here for our people.

Dear Mother,

     How wonderful it was to have Amy here for Christmas! The only bad thing about it was having to tell her goodbye again. Do you realize that she makes the 4th of our kids to have a trip back home thanks to our church family there? I have tried to thank them, but I don't think they could ever know what it means to have a visit from your child during their college years. I think sometimes just the reality of that visit has made it possible to stay here for all this years. Waiting four years to see a child is just about more than a parent can stand. I realize all over again what you meant when you made that statement to me in the airport when

I was leaving David and wondering if I could do it. Remember? There he stood, all 6 lanky feet of him with tears in his eyes. I said, "I just don't know if I can do this or not." And you said, "Now you know how I feel." And you know, I never really did until then.

We have done it three more times since then and lived through it, but the thought of a trip back within a year or so lessened the pain a little. I know, without a doubt, that the toughest thing a missionary has to do is send their 18 year olds back to the USA to college, or leave them there when you return to the field. Nothing that we have faced has compared to the test of faith that this is!

I do want you to know, though, that we appreciate all you do for them back there. I know what a nuisance they can be, but I also know they can be helpful. Sometimes it takes a reminder or two as to what they should be doing and when. If you find it too hard to tell them, just let us know, and we shall see that a word or two in the proper ear will be forthcoming very shortly. Okay? (Although, I don't remember you being shy about telling ME what I should be doing, so why them?☺)

Seriously, apart from missing all of them terribly, we realize how much they helped us in opening doors to new ministry. On the other hand, for the first time I am free to travel with Rodolph and spend as much time out at camp as needed, or even take the time to do some of the things I had planned personally but was never free to do before. It has its drawbacks, too, because I am asked to do more programs and other work and I have lost my excuse to turn them down. I would like to say, as painful as it is, the Lord helps one to get through the times of separation too. But then, I guess I am "preaching to the choir," huh?

NOTE: I would like it known how this wonderful blessing came about. Ruth Chiles is one of the most unique and precious ladies I have ever met (and one of my favorite orchids). She has been a friend of my mother and aunts since their girlhood days, and we have thought of her like family all through the years. Ruth was always loving and kind to us. She was visiting us in Peru when our children were little, and she met the teenager of another missionary who was home for the holidays. He told her that his trip was paid for by the WMU (Women's Missionary Union) of their home church. Ruth was very impressed with this and said she was going to start an MK fund at our church and send our children back when they got old enough to go away to college. We thought that was a nice thing to say, but we didn't think much more about it and really didn't think she would remember. Well, imagine our surprise, when she told us she had enough money to send David back and would have enough for the others when they came home from college, too.

I have never known how she managed to badger enough people into helping her raise that much money, but I want the world to know what those trips meant to us. I really don't think it is too much to say that it could very well be what made it possible to stay there during those hard years of separation. You see, if a lot is expected of you and a lot is done for you, you feel a sense of responsibility and an obligation to shape up! I just want all those who did this for us during those years to know that we are grateful. I wish I knew how to thank you. When the beggars thank you in Peru they usually say, "Dios le pagara." (God will repay you.) I believe that and I pray that He will.

PERU REVISITED

This event was not included in a letter to Mother because it happened on a volunteer trip to Peru after our retirement and after her death. We have told it on many occasions, though, and it still amazes us all over again each time we share it. We were invited back to help with some work in the Trujillo area and out at Camp Shiran, so we returned for a short visit in 2001. We visited with old friends, both Peruvian and North American. It was a wonderful time of reunion, nostalgia, bear hugs, and goat meat dinners. (I remarked to Rodolph that since we left Peru, we had apparently sprouted wings and a halo. ☺) It was a beautiful time for us, and I think Rodolph managed to do a little work. I mainly just enjoyed it.

On almost the last day we were there, one of the missionary couples said they would like to take us out into the desert to see a new village just being built there. Well now, we had seen new desert villages before and had driven miles through the desert on bone-jarring, practically non-existent roads, and frankly it didn't sound too inviting. After all, we thought we had seen most of what they could show us. They insisted, and so we accompanied them on an 11-mile trip off the highway over roads like those that I just described. The only thing different (and worse) on this trip was that our bones were a lot older and we felt it even more.

As we arrived in the village we saw it was like so many others we have seen--just straw-mat houses. There were four mats for the walls and one for the roof, and we could tell it was a new village because most of the mats were still new and clean. One lady particularly impressed me as we passed by because she had red geraniums growing all around her little house. She was outside then watering them with a tin tea cup. Now remember where we were--we were way out in the desert where there is no electricity, no running water, no river, nor even a little stream. We could not imagine where they got their water.

This was what the missionary wanted to show us and why he was trying to help them with a well drilling project. We saw the rig and greeted the men working on it; they were some of our good friends who have helped us with projects in years past. They had not completed their drilling and yet the village seemed to have water. They even had a reservoir into which water was flowing. Upon further investigation, we discovered what these villagers had done. They presented us the most beautiful picture of cooperation that we have ever seen to date. They first decided on the best area to build their houses, and then they searched for water which they found in pure, cold, clear springs 5 miles away. The problem then was how to get it to the village when they had no money for pipes. They solved that by collecting 2-liter plastic soft drink bottles of every kind. There were Pepsi, Coke, Inca Kola, Fanta, etc. and they cut both ends off of each one and stuck them together. They had no glue, but they were put together well because a pipeline of 54,000 plastic bottles could be seen there snaking across the desert for 5 miles and emptying pure water into their storage reservoir.

These people had so much faith in their projects that they had already built a little bath house and had a flush toilet in it (even though at that time it had to be flushed with a bucket of water carried out there for that purpose). They told us they were so very grateful for the well being drilled that the first real building they planned to construct would be a church. They were making cement blocks at that time and had quite a few out drying in the sun. I can't wait to go back and see how they have progressed in these last few years and what other surprises they can produce.

NEWSLETTERS

The following is a practice newsletter we were assigned to write while in Orientation:

October, 1967
Dear Family and Friends,

Here's hoping you'll be able to suffer through our first efforts to write a newsletter. This is just one of the many things we have yet to learn to do. We are discovering more each day that the skills our veteran missionaries have were not bestowed upon them during their appointment ceremony in Richmond. This Orientation Program was certainly planned with ones as green as we are in mind. We have classes from 8:15 a.m. to 3:45 p.m. each day plus extras in the afternoons and nights. I keep wondering if this heavy schedule was planned before or after they observed us! I get the feeling sometimes that our instructors are dolefully shaking their heads and wondering at the fate of Peru if we are all the Baptists have to offer to them. There is so much to learn and so much to do, please pray for all of us here that we will use this time of preparation well, so that the Lord will have abler hands and feet and hearts and minds to do His bidding. Please remember that your prayers will be our strength.

We are thoroughly enjoying our stay here. For a few days "October's bright blue weather" was a little out of focus. It was smeared by fog and splotched by rain, but now the chilling rustle of crisp leaves gives zip to our love of life! The awesome beauty of these color-splashed hills reminds us afresh each day that this is, indeed, our "Father's World." Such a vast display of His majestic handiwork makes us painfully aware of our smallness.

David and Merry manage to do a fair job of keeping us humble, too. They love it here and have adjusted well, but somehow they always seem to show their worst traits at the worst times. This has a rather disenchanting effect when we wish to present ourselves as a model family. Now that David can read about "Dick and Jane," he is sure that there is little else to know. Also, for the first time in his life, he has more than enough playmates. There are 114 assorted children here belonging to 48 couples. The two single girls have a hard time putting up with the rest of us.

While here we've encountered fresh faces, frustrating facts, filling food, family fun, and fine fellowship. We admit to feelings of fatigue, but know the time spent was not futile, and realize ourselves to be a fortunate few. As we face the future of foreign fields, we are especially grateful for you, our favorite folks, to whom we send our dearest love.--From friends in Christ

NOTE; You will notice excerpts from our newsletters scattered all through this book, but I thought that to reproduce a few in chronological order would give a sort of over-view of our life as missionaries as it progressed. For instance, this very first letter that you have just read was a class assignment in our Orientation sessions, and I am not sure if it was ever mailed out. It is full of such wide-eyed innocence, idealism, and optimism that it makes me smile. There was so much enthusiasm and zeal as well as determination to carry out all the instructions we received; one of which was to write letters of this type to our friends and family at least every 3 months if not more often. If you will take note of the dates, you will find that it was 4 years after our Orientation before our first real newsletter got mailed. Reading between the lines like that will tell you quite a bit about how our life developed as our time on the "Field" lengthened.

This letter was our first newsletter from the field:

Jan., 1971
Dear Family and Friends,
      Happy New Year! Here it is 1971, the year that we hope to see all of you again back home on our first furlough, and we are just getting out our first newsletter. Certainly we had hoped to

begin much sooner, but then we haven't had this much news to tell you before--the birth of Jonathan Spencer on April 14th, the big Peruvian earthquake on May 31st with our electricity finally restored on December 15th, and a visit from May's mother and niece (Dani) during the month of August--quite a year! We surely do hope your year was a good one and that you had a wonderful holiday season.

The children are really growing. David will be ten years old in April and is finishing up the 4th grade in the Calvert Correspondence Course taught here to the MK's by two journeymen (for which we are very grateful). Merry is now five and is enjoying the Peruvian kindergarten. She is completely bi-lingual to the point of playing with her dolls in Spanish and even talking in her sleep in Spanish. Spencer is the undisputed head of the household, keeping all of us jumping when he speaks. May tries to keep the house going and teaches a few piano lessons as well as the music and English courses at the Institute. I am sure that most of you know by now that our main work here is to teach in our theological Institute. Rodolph is professor of Old Testament, but he is also the area missionary and has really had his hands full trying to help out in the reconstruction of the houses and churches after the earthquake.

La Esperanza Baptist Church, where we are members, was completely destroyed by the earthquake and we are in the process of finishing the rebuilding of it now. We are so grateful to so many of you friends who have made this possible by your mission gifts. All of our people are anxiously watching the progress and are excited about our dedication service that we hope to have soon. There is never a service that goes by that they don't express their gratitude to God for our "Brothers in the North" who have helped them to have this wonderful new sanctuary. It might not show up too well beside your church, but it will be one of the finest buildings in the area as it is made of brick instead of adobe and will have cement floors instead of dirt ones.

We hope that it won't be four more years before we get out another letter. In fact, we hope to send one before we get home to let you know the date of our arrival. Thank you for being our friends (and family--though you didn't have a choice). We do thank God for each of you. Each of us sends his love, and we hope you will let us hear from you as you have a chance to write.

July 15, 1971

Dear Family and Friends,

This is just a note to let you all know that we will be home again in the good old USA the 2nd of Aug. 1971, if all our plans work out. We will be living with May's mother at our permanent address in the States.

We are all very excited about coming home. I'm afraid that "the States" and "Heaven" have been almost synonymous in the thinking of our children! However, now that the time has arrived for our first furlough, we approach it with mixed emotions. For the children, it will be a completely new way of life. Merry remembers nothing of the U.S. and Spencer, of course, was born here. David remembers much, but is a little fearful of not quite fitting in as this will be his first time to attend public school. He keeps checking up on things like, "How much did you say a quarter is? And how much is that in soles?" One of our recently returned missionaries assured us that he would need all of about three minutes to get this type of problem cleared up!

All of us look forward to fast foods, etc. and as I said, are really anxious to get home to see all of you, but we find that Peru has taken quite a hold on our hearts, too. The people we have worked with here have become dear friends and to leave them is "giving us pain" as the Peruvians express it. It also grieves us to leave so much undone. We have been busy, but not nearly as busy as we should have been. We have helped so little in the light of the great crying need here. Please don't forget to pray for this country and our people here; we believe that to be the source of any success we can hope to have for the future of our work in Peru.

July 8, 1976

Dear Family and Friends,

It seems we only get a letter out at furlough time or to announce the arrival of another little Dixon, so let me hasten to assure you it is furlough time again!

We now have 10 churches and 22 annexes in the Trujillo area. We are so grateful for this because it represents a 250% increase for us even though it may sound small to you. Rodolph has finished up this term's work on our regional camp up in the mountains near Trujillo, which we feel will be a real blessing to our area.

May continues to teach music at the seminary and has especially enjoyed directing the seminary choir and taking them on tour as a new activity.

David has reached a height of 5'11" at 15 years old which would make you believe he might be thinking basketball, but he's hoping to make the soccer team at B.C. High this coming year. (It's awfully hard to play soccer by correspondence course!☺)

Merry--well, she's still Merry--words fail me in describing her as always. She's 10 years old now and enjoys life wherever she is! (Those of you who know her, please don't warn the 5th grade teacher at Claude Taylor.)

Spencer is 6 now and is looking forward to starting "real" school for the first time. I just hope his teacher has a Spanish-English dictionary as he substitutes Spanish for anything he can't think of in English.

Amy is now one and a half and keeps us all running and laughing. She is very lively and speaks a rare mixture of Spanish, English, and some other language we haven't been able to decipher yet! The six of us plan to descend on Mema (May's mother) and live with her this coming year the same as last furlough--and that's the run-down on each of us. We thank God for each of you and for what you mean to us and for all you have done for us during this term. Thank you for your prayers in our behalf and please continue to pray that we can be useful in sharing the love of our Lord.

Jan., 1979

Dear Family and Friends,

We hope each of you enjoyed a most blessed Christmas season and are experiencing the beginning of a wonderful new year full of the good things our Lord provides for us each day. We enjoyed hearing from so many of you during the holidays and will probably hear from more yet. Our mail service, being what it is, we usually consider the Christmas mail all in by Easter, although we have received Christmas cards in May and June!

We can't help but wonder that as you read this, shivering by your fireside, if you might not be a little envious of us in this ideal weather we have at this time of the year. David and Merry are darker than some of their Peruvian friends from spending so much time in the sun. They love all sports, but surfing is a big favorite right now and since we live only a mile from the sea, they go to the beach every chance that time and parents will allow.

We find we don't have to look for things to do, we have to look for gentle ways of refusing pleas for help. There are not enough of us to go around, and yet the Lord has been able to work through the ones of us here, as few and as weak as we are. Sometimes I think He has to work in spite of us, we fumble so, but our Baptist work is growing in the Trujillo area. We now have 11 churches and 36 missions or preaching points. When we moved to Trujillo in 1969, there were only 3 organized churches, so it is a thrill to look back and see the numerical and spiritual growth. It is discouraging, though, that both increase so slowly.

As to family news--we usually send out a letter in each term at this time announcing the arrival of another Dixon. We have decided to do it differently this time and announce the departure of one. We plan to send David home in May to begin work and enter Furman University in the fall. It is hard for us to let him go, but we know you and the Lord will take care of him there. Merry is 13 and very active. She has grown about 6 inches this past year and passed her mother by a half inch in height. (Hope she won't get as tall as David for he is over 6 ft.) Spencer is almost 9 years old and while his blond hair and blue eyes still stand out in a crowd here, he is more Peruvian than North American. (I guess being born here has its effect.) Amy is 4 and a very noticeable influence around the house. We might just have to admit to the possibility that she is a wee bit indulged. (I believe "rotten" is the word you use back home?) We love her anyway, can you believe it? I think the problem is that she is smarter than we are.

Please continue to pray for our Peruvian brothers during these crisis times. I am sure you hear some of the happenings in your news, but to see the effect in the daily lives of friends here is a real heartache.

Here are excerpts from a typical newsletter (1991):

Dear Family and Friends,

I guess it is time for a newsletter since this term is almost over and we try to write once every 5 years whether you like it or not!☺ In May we finished up 24 years with the FMB and pray for health and strength to continue many more years here in Peru. This year our excitement over going home to the USA is challenged by our excitement over Merry's wedding plans for the 10th of August. She is marrying a fine young pastor and hospital chaplain named Keith DeBord from Greensboro, NC. David is still in Winston Salem, NC, and works with a rehabilitation center for drugs and alcohol. Merry has been teaching high school Spanish there. Spencer is a rising senior at Clemson where he is studying architecture. Amy will be a high school senior in Sept. May's mother, Mrs. Bailey (Mema) lives at our permanent address and celebrates her 86th birthday this year.

Please forgive us for not keeping in touch better during these years. They have been years of concern over the plight of the people here in Peru. The economic situation is just unbelievable and there have been earthquakes, terrorist activity, strikes, and now a cholera epidemic that has taken so many lives and changed the life-styles of everyone. We have seen more sickness, hunger, terror and misery than at any other time in our ministry here. Even during times such as this and (possibly because of times like this) we can see the Lord's hand at work and people coming to know Him and learning to depend upon Him. It has brought new insight into our own lives as to what depending upon the Lord really means.

We are truly looking forward to renewing the "ties that bind" during this furlough year. We love and appreciate each one of you.--Con Carino,

Aug., 1992
Dear Family and Friends,

Well, here we are back in the Land of the Incas and the City of Eternal Springtime (and eternal dust, earthquakes, terrorists, and no electricity)! Conditions have not improved here during the year that we were on furlough, and culture shock sneaks up on us in ways we are not expecting even after 25 years and many comings and goings. I guess probably the hardest thing to which we have to adjust is being here for the first time without children! Leaving our first grandbaby was not too easy either! However, the Lord does provide His miracles daily for those of us who are so weak that we need a major portion of miracles, and we have noticed each day the growing excitement of once again being here and the challenges of the evident needs on all sides.

If there was ever a time in Peruvian life when it needs all the help it can get, it is now! The economic chaos still reigns. There seems to be enough food available now but one has to find enough money to pay for it. The main shortage we suffer at the moment is a lack of electricity; it is rationed all over the country. Our lights are cut off at least 8 hours daily on a different schedule each day. It is amazing how adaptable one becomes. (You don't have to like it, but you adapt!☺) With the capture of the main terrorist leader here a couple of weeks ago which made the news there I am told, there seems to be a ray of hope that is giving a new light in the eyes of the people here. Thoughts of peace and a better life are springing up in print and conversations everywhere. We pray for this beginning, and even more especially, for that day to come in the near future for a people who have had just about all the misery that is humanly possible to endure.

The WMU groups of the whole Trujillo area gave us a reception and a beautiful plaque commemorating our 25 years as missionaries to Peru. This was really a touching thing for us, and also a surprise I might add. The real surprise, I suppose, is that we are the first Baptist missionaries to spend 25 years here--so we ARE first in something!☺ It just served to make us feel older, though, as most of the new couples here are about the age of our children.

Aug., 1993
Dear Family and Friends,

By the time you receive this we will have completed a year back on the field since furlough and it doesn't seem possible! (You know how it is when you are having fun!☺) When we arrived last August, the atmosphere here was one of frustration, depression, and despair on all sides, but now, even though the cause of it all (the "Crisis" as they call it) has not greatly changed, there is a feeling of hope that within itself is bringing about some changes for the better.

For instance, our electricity just goes off now unexpectedly and for unannounced spaces of time instead of the regularly scheduled 8 hours a day like before!☺

Central Church has called a fine young man as pastor and he is already doing a great job. He began his ministry on Aug. 1st with a big day of inauguration and dinner on the grounds (goat, rice, beans, yuca and the ever present purple corn drink). We served over 450 people; this would have been impossible a year ago.

We were able to survive our first year of "empty nest" because Amy was able to visit. How we loved it and thank the ones who made it possible! She helped at mission meeting "teaching" MKs and also helped us translate for a volunteer group in Cajamarca. So it wasn't all just sleeping late and seeing old friends. She is now back at USC--a college sophomore, no less!

Spencer will be finishing up his graduate studies at Clemson in May of '94 and will have his MA in Architecture. Hopefully he will be out of school, because David has decided to go back in! At the ripe old age of 32, David is finishing up some science courses to enter medical school. We were saying, "Three down and one to go," and now we have them start over again! He seems to be doing great and loving it, and we are proud of him.

Merry and Keith and Nicholas have announced that at the end of Feb. their family will increase, putting me right up there with the first class grannies who have more than one!

We are taking our first Christmas vacation back to the USA in 25 years and we are so excited! The entire family plans to be there for the occasion!

We had 7 really great, fruitful weeks at camp; we loved using the new dining hall. You would have to see it to believe how wonderful it is.

We were so blessed by the volunteers who completed 2 cabins and roofed a third and did finishing work in the dining hall. They were the "workingest" group I have ever seen; they not only didn't observe siesta time but they worked at night too! They were a real inspiration to have (if your old bones and heart can survive 'em ☺).

Dr. Margaret Hiers lived with us 6 months in the "outhouse" (our guest room out across the patio) and so many people were blessed by her care, dedication, and expertise in meeting their needs of a special type of education and therapy. She worked through our churches and gave a wonderful Christian witness along with the other hope and help she brought. She not only opened doors for us with her professional expertise, but impressed everyone with her sweet manner while doing it. She has also become a dear personal friend.

(NOTE: Another orchid that just keeps on blooming!)

Nov. 15, 1995

Dear Family and Friends,

What a joy to greet you at this wonderful season! I'm counting on the fact that hearts are made more tender at Christmas, and that will help you overlook the fact that our newsletters (besides being a literary disgrace) are rather far apart in arriving. Let me assure you it is NOT because we don't think of you, pray for you, and miss you very much. In fact we are counting on seeing as many of you as possible this time next year on furlough. It begins Oct. 1, 1996 and will be our last full furlough before retirement. We are halfway through our 29th year as Peruvian missionaries and we cannot believe it has been that long. We realize it sometimes, though, when we work with the children and grandchildren of the young people with whom we worked when we first arrived in the country.

Since giving up our teaching at the seminary, our major efforts have been in the area of camp work. One goal is to finish up the construction of the physical plant, and thanks to the mission offerings of all of you, the funds have been made available to do this. We are building the last 5 cabins now, and we expect to have a volunteer team to come in March and do the roofing and finishing up. We hope some of you will be a part of this. This will be the culmination of a 28 year old dream.

The camp is in use almost constantly for a variety of activities like retreats, conventions, conferences, mission meetings, and church programs. We, as directors, plan and carry out 6 to 8 weeks of summer camps for children and young people, and also plan retreats during the rest of the year for special emphasis groups like marriage enrichment, singles, pastors, etc. It has been a very satisfying and rewarding work, and we also feel that not only have many come to know the Lord through this ministry and others have strengthened their spiritual dedication, but it is also something that can be carried on easily by our hermanos here when the construction is completed. We have counselors and cooks who have helped us for 8-10 years on a purely voluntary basis. These seem to love and value what is being done now and can be done in this ministry for the future.

At our baptismal services in the churches the candidates give testimonies and we hear quite often, "I accepted Christ as my Savior at Camp Shiran." This is always a thrill! Our records show that over 60% of the youth attending summer camps (app. 800) make life changing decisions. We can't give statistics as to the follow-up by the churches, but many of these are expressed in the local church and show up in baptisms, church leadership, and seminary enrollment.

So, this is how we spend our time, plus working in our local churches. I continue to work in music, teaching piano and directing choir. Last year at Christmas our 60 voice area choir presented a cantata in several churches. We are working on Christmas music now, too.

Rodolph has not lost his title as "area missionary" because he is still invited to preach and counsel regularly. We now have 18 churches and many, many strong missions and preaching points in the area. We have been so privileged to see this growth from the 3 churches that were here when we arrived.

Most of our missionary colleagues are near the ages of our children but it is good to have the strength and enthusiasm of youth. Speaking of children--Our oldest son, David, is entering medical school at the ripe old age of 34. We are proud of this recent decision and his preparation, persistence, patience, and acceptance. Meredith is a Spanish teacher and she and her husband, Keith, a pastor, live in Maryland and have our two grandchildren, Nicholas (3) and Kaitlyn (20 mos.). Spencer is an architect and his wife, Ginny, is a school teacher and they live in Greenville, SC. Amy (the baby) who just turned 21 this month graduates Magna Cum Laude in Dec. and will come "home" for a visit and helping out at camp before continuing studies or a career. May's mother, Mrs. Bailey (90 years old now) lives at our permanent address where we can always be reached by someone if we can be of service to you.

Thank you for your continued love, interest and concern for us and our people here through all these years. We hope your holiday season and the coming year and years will be filled with blessings from our Lord.

1996
Dear Family and Friends,

So much has happened that we felt we must share with you. We truly believe that our joys are multiplied and our sorrows are lessened when shared with loved ones.

On the joy side--We had a wonderful visit from Amy and she had very mixed emotions about returning to the USA. She served as camp counselor and became very close to the young people here again. We had great summer camps. Most of these were pretty full and two of them had all 154 beds taken. We trust the many decisions made there will be carried on into the churches, and even more important in their lives.

In March a group of 32 volunteers came from SC, Texas, Georgia and Tennessee. They finished up the five cabins we had begun in September, renovated a sea container to make staff sleeping quarters, and made 40+ bunk beds. This was done in 2 weeks time! Yes, you read right! Two weeks! They were tired when they left (and so were we!☺), but we are so happy to now count sleeping space for 250. This is the capacity number of our master plan and dream. How can we ever thank this group for making our dream come true? I saw a little card that said, "I can never repay you for your kindness so I am asking God to." So many of you receiving this letter are certainly the focus of our prayers to our Lord for the many loving kindnesses shown to us through the years.

On the sorrow side--We as a mission family have suffered the loss of two families recently due to accidents. The Watts family here in Trujillo was in a head-on collision on a mountain road on Feb. 1. The mother and 8-year-old son are recovering from multiple cuts and fractures, but the father is still in a coma and the 10-year-old son, although now out of a coma, has paralysis, extensive head injuries, and loss of speech. It is a devastating situation, especially not knowing the prognosis. Then on Feb. 29, Lynn Davidson, a missionary from Arequipa, was killed in a plane crash as she was returning from a committee meeting in Lima. The plane hit the side of a mountain 2 minutes from the airport and there were no survivors. She leaves a husband and three children, ages 11, 8, and 4. These tragic happenings so close together have just left the mission family in shock. We really are a family, as you know, and we ask your prayers for all of us.

1998
Dear Family and Friends,

I suppose this will be our last newsletter as active career missionaries in Peru. After 31+ years here on the field, our plans are to leave Peru on Aug. 2, 1998, and have a short furlough with retirement going into effect on Oct. 1, 1998. Please call on us if we can be of any service to you, or just come by and let's have a visit. These things will be tops on our priority list.

We have found this past year to be a very difficult one due to the obvious things involved in bringing a conclusion to our ministry here like packing up and saying goodbyes. Recently, however, most of our time has been taken up in dealing with the devastating effects of the infamous "El Nino" in Peru. We have had to spend so much of our time in defense measures and repair work because the Trujillo area was hit very hard. It was a tense time from Dec. to mid April (besides having 98 degree heat and no air conditioning). We were on alert to evacuate our houses several times due to the river flooding its banks. Mud and rock slides, torrential rains, and flash floods hit the sections out toward our camp and the mountains and completely wiped out the highway and many little villages, leaving only rocks and mud where they had been. We were very fortunate in that the camp lost only the perimeter walls, a few trees, and suffered minor flooding. There is quite a bit of clean-up and repair still to be done, though. We were cut off from camp a month due to the roads being washed away. They finally put up cable cars in two places where bridges were out. These were connected to homemade tripods which the owners kept knocking back together with rocks as they came apart with use. Travelers rode to the first one, crossed over, walked about a mile to the next one, crossed over, and tried to find more transportation on the other side. The ½ hour trip was sometimes taking 8 hours to complete. Even now driving our car all the way, it takes 1½ hours because we have to ford the rivers and travel over non-existent roads.

Once again, we owe a great debt of appreciation to Bud Lovingood and his volunteers who worked in unbelievably terrible conditions to help us finish the last camp building. They sloshed about in deep mud and did incredibly dangerous feats and accomplished yet another miracle! As one of them said, "There's no amount of money in the world that could make me do what I'm doing here." I think that speaks volumes about the depth of their love and commitment to our Lord. We thank God for all of these and for all of you who have given so much for our people here and to us personally. This group left for home less than a week before we got cut off from camp.

On June 14th we are expecting a group from Pendleton St. Church in Greenville headed up by our son, Spencer and wife Ginny, and we are looking forward to that. Spencer is the architect who drew the plans for this last building, and we wonder if Dad will get a good grade on following instructions?☺

That brings up children--our oldest son, David and family are living in Winston Salem, NC and he is into his 3rd year of medical school and doing great we hear. We are proud of him, wife Nancy, Andrew and Joseph (youngest grandson) and also the fact that we can have medical attention in our old age!☺ Merry and her family are still in Maryland where she teaches Spanish and husband Keith is a minister. They both ride herd on Nicholas, Kaitlyn and Jonathan. Amy, the "baby", graduated from USC (Magna Cum Laude) and has made her wedding plans for this Aug. right after we arrive home. She is marrying Barry Sowers from Maryland and they plan to live in Columbia, SC, which pleases us, of course. This would leave us with an empty nest except for

"Mema", May's mother. She will be 93 on June 15th and we are looking forward to some quality time together with her now. She has faithfully supported us in our ministry all these years and we want to say a public thank you to her, too.

We can never express to each of you how much we appreciate your love, concern, and support over these 31 years and we ask that you continue to remember our people here in Peru. We sincerely hope we can visit in the near future and we pray God's richest blessings on each one. We love you.

ENDINGS

In the last few days before leaving Peru on that final trip to return home for retirement, there were no letters written because we would have arrived at our destination before they did. However, there were some memorable things that I didn't want to forget, so I tried to keep a journal. I have been reading my own notes to myself written during that time, and these I have used to refresh my memory of what it was like to leave, possibly forever, a place where one has spent over 30 years of her life.

This is hard. The house is bare and it is a strange feeling to realize that we no longer belong here. This is no longer our house and we are no longer a vital part of this place. At the same time that I feel this sadness and reluctance to leave loved ones here, I recognize a stirring excitement over the prospect of getting to serve in a different and more permanent way back in the USA and I try to keep my thoughts projected ahead to the vision of family, friends, and future there. I pray we can be useful there.

I don't think I can go through another "despedida" (goodbye party). There have been too many flowery speeches and too many tears (both theirs and ours) and too much food. I have always heard of being "killed by kindness" and I now think I fully understand the phrase. My emotions and my stomach have both taken all they can stand. We have worked past the point of exhaustion for weeks now just trying to finish up and leave things in good condition, and we are constantly interrupted by well-wishers from everywhere. I guess we would have felt bad if no one had even mentioned our leaving, but my only hope is that I can look back on this one day and appreciate it all as it was intended.

On Wednesday night before we left we went out to La Esperanza, the little church out on the side of the mountain, and this despedida was the most elaborate and sweetest of the whole bunch. This is where we began and where we ended up--very appropriate. By this time I was sort of running on left-over adrenaline and an overdose of despedida food.

July 26, 1998--The day we leave Trujillo. My Bible reading today was from Haggai, the part in the second chapter which is about being strong, and the little write-up accompanying it was about saying goodbye. Yesterday it was about "Consider the Years" from Deut. 32:7. Both of these seemed to speak to our needs and situation so much that it was down right uncanny! I don't know why it surprises me so much when the Lord speaks directly like this. It intrigued me so much that I looked ahead to next Sunday's devotionals and it is about the "Travelers' Arrival"! I could not believe it! That is the day we travel to the USA! I felt like God was saying to me to settle down and enjoy this, things are going to be okay.

We received some interesting things to take with us on the last day--a chunk of sausage, some buns, a long loaf of bread, some leather stuff, a carved bird, letters to deliver to other people, and many other things too numerous to mention.

Our next-to-the-last day in Trujillo was outstanding. It was beautiful; it was a joy; it was a highlight--and what made it so was the most wonderful parting gift ever from Gladys! She accepted the Lord as her Savior, and I had the privilege of leading her in this step of faith. She and I, along with her sister, Amelia, sat down for about one half hour together. (The only half hour of the day that was quiet). She had such a genuine sense of what she was doing and was so sweet and humble. Rodolph arrived just as we were ending and he had the prayer for us. It was just such a beautiful time. She said she didn't want to make this decision lightly and had been thinking about it for quite awhile, but she wished she hadn't taken so long. I thank the Lord for this privilege to be able to see this before leaving.

Gladys had worked for us and with us for so many years, and every time we tried to talk about spiritual things she would retreat behind a wall. That told us we could only witness to her by living a Christian life before her. The more we talked the farther she would retreat, and we didn't want to push her completely away. I think down deep inside I felt like a failure as a missionary if I could have someone work so closely with us for almost 15 years and not lead her to feel the love of our Lord. For me this was the icing on the cake! I could feel my exhaustion and tension easing away and I was ready to get the leaving over; I could go now. It was like another message from the Lord reassuring me that all is well, not to forget that it is He who is in control at all times, and everything will be done in His own time.

(NOTE: A late-bloomer, but a most beautiful orchid!)

We drove our little car out to the airport one last time and had to say goodbyes one more time to the friends gathered there. The airline personnel at the check-in counter also wished us well and told us they had put us in first class. This was a special surprise and a sweet gesture from them. We had to detour through another city before getting to Lima, but it was comfortable in first class and the food was good. When we arrived in Lima at the mission apartments, we found that our friends, the Fletchers, had stocked it with food and put a beautiful arrangement of flowers on the table. It made me feel so good. I called them "friends" but this is what I have spoken of all along when I talked about mission "family." It will be hard to tell them goodbye, too.

Rodolph got all his receipts turned in and money checked out and closed out all accounts. While he did this, I shopped for gifts to take home to friends and family. We collected our tickets and our passports and the day arrived. I was wired! We got up at 3:15 a.m. and began the complicated process of taking an international flight from the Lima airport. After the emotion of more goodbyes and the anxiety of getting to the airport and getting checked in, it was amazing how smoothly everything went, even the flights. There was a strange feeling as we lifted off Peruvian soil for what could possibly be the last time. The thought occurred that if we returned, it would be as tourists, but never again as residents. It was the usual long cramped flight, but we forgot all that when we found ourselves being met by a wonderful crowd of friends and relatives at home.

It is a strange feeling to think that this is our only home, now, but at least we can finally tell you if we are "going home or leaving home." However, a few years ago I embroidered a wall hanging for Mother that says, "Home is Where the Heart is." If this is so, I think I can speak for all our family and say we will always have a home in Peru-- because I know Peru and our wonderful friends there will always have a place in our hearts.

LAST LETTER

Dear Mother,

I guess this will be the very last letter I will write to you as an active missionary in Peru. We just had our 17th going away party or service--it seems our people are REALLY celebrating our departure!☺ I can't believe we are into our 32nd year here and I can't imagine what it will be like to actually live in the USA again. We are certainly looking forward to being with you and the family though, and I thank the Lord for letting us make it through and finishing the course. Looking back and looking ahead, I can truly say with Paul that I "count it all joy."

Recently someone quoted an old adage that I had never heard before, and it really spoke to me. It pretty much sums up the way I feel about our life on the mission field. I never expected to enjoy it. I had a peace about going and I felt the Lord would protect us and provide our needs, but I think I planned to be miserable--to be a martyr, maybe. What a shock to find we could have fun! How we were surprised by the sheer joy of it! Now, that is not to say that we did not experience difficulties, were never frightened, and were not pitiful failures at times, but through it all was the underlying, ever-present peace and joy that only our Lord can give. May that be the message I convey with my "orchids." I think that old adage makes a proper ending:

"I dreamed life was joy,
I awoke and found life was service,
I served and discovered service is joy."

Mother's 90th birthday celebration.